THE BOOK OF THE GODS

630 Gods from 20 Pantheons Explained

CHAS SAUNDERS
AND PETER J. ALLEN

The
History
Press

First published 2010

The History Press
The Mill, Brimscombe Port
Stroud, Gloucestershire, GL5 2QG
www.thehistorypress.co.uk

British Library Cataloguing in Publication Data.
A catalogue record for this book is available from the British Library.

ISBN 978 0 7524 5804 5

Typesetting and origination by The History Press
Manufacturing managed by Jellyfish Print Solutions Ltd
Printed in India

CONTENTS

CHASTRODUCTION

Mind the gap! Too late. A decade ago in my role of sagacious sage I was asked if I wished to contribute to a local magazine. Yes. So there came a meeting of minds ancient and modern and I fell through a generation gap into the world of Peter A, computer guru and classical geek expert.

In the Beginning was the Word – and the word was **GODCHECKER**. I had assembled some gods with a calendar in mind. Peter was intrigued and proposed a conjoining of cultures with a new revelation. A magic mirror called a website. I had only got as far as an electric typewriter and a printer but did not own a computer. I knew they were strange devices which usually involved going through the Gates of Bill while lots of windows opened and closed and sometimes crashed. But we went ahead anyway. Our excuse is that the gods nudged us. They were happy with our decidedly jocular approach. To this day not one single god has complained and we have maintained Mythology with a Twist ever since.

After a couple of weeks, kludge master Peter said 'We have ten hits'. 'Who is hitting us and why?' was my response, not knowing the garble of computerese.

With no hurry, pressure or deadlines it was fascinating. We grew at a very leisurely pace. Gods shrouded in mystery or misted in shroudery – or possibly lost in the shrubbery. Seers, Sages and Signs everywhere. At school at an early age I had been taught to chant 'Our Father Witch Art in Heaven' and much other hearsay chants. With a great interest in art there were certainly many Witchy and Heavenly images. Now the Chinese Peaches of Immortality take 3,000 years to ripen but in ten years we have moved a little faster than that. We swirl round the globe night and day and have clocked up millions of hits. And now the gods have found us a publisher. They will do anything to get noticed.

Chas Saunders
The Hub of the Universe
April 2010

PETRODUCTION

Creating a website devoted to the quirkier side of humankind's most profound beliefs has been tremendously educational and enlightening. More to the point it's been a lot of fun. Whether grappling with Aztec Scrabble letters, contemplating the spiritual nature of the boomerang or taking to the streets to measure the exact size of Noah's Ark in-situ, our research over the past decade has given us a wonderfully cheerful insight into human nature.

The wealth of gods that humanity has encountered, worshipped, invented, had sex with or generally irritated off the face of the planet is a testament to what you might call the 'Global Imagination'. We at Godchecker adore the rich colourful personalities, the complicated Heavenly soap operas and the practical problem-solving fables of a mythological passion which spans the globe. Every society gets the gods it deserves, and if we've learned nothing else from our eleven years delving into dusty tomes and hopping across the internet, it's that creativity, humour and a profound desire to connect and make sense of a bizarre universe lies at the core of every culture. If the gods didn't exist, it would be necessary to invent them.

Luckily, of course, they do exist. Our Holy Database is stocked with only genuine gods and goddesses. Some have even emailed us, which proves they are real. And logically, if you believe in one god, that can only open the door to the possibility of others. Richard Dawkins beware. There are thousands more deities still to be added to Godchecker.com. We are mere mortals trying to catch up with the infinite. So if you don't find your favourite god or goddess mentioned, rest assured that they are lined up for interview in the near future.

We are sorry that in this splendid but finite volume, we have been forced by space to omit many wonderful deities and cut short several intriguing tales. Fear not, you will find the full texts at **www.godchecker.com**. Modern Goddities such as the Invisible Pink Unicorn, the gods of Pratchett and the Flying Spaghetti Monster have also been ruthlessly omitted. Their time will come. In due course we hope to present a second volume of Godchecker incorporating many more extracts from our Holy Database.

Please enjoy this book. If you find any unholy mistakes or diabolical omissions, please let us know so we can update our Holy Database. Just drop an email to godchecker@gmail.com. Our amazing website visitors have helped us and encouraged us, so why not join them? You can follow the gods at twitter.com/Godchecker.

May the gods smile upon you.

Peter A.
Godchecker HQ
April 2010

GODKNOWLEGEMENTS

Thanks to Paul Clayton for the first nudge in the right direction. Thanks to Rowan Allen for inspiration, technicalities, pedantry and trouble-shooting. Thanks to Sonia Reis for support through earthquakes and eruptions. Thanks also to Tommy Martin, Jacqui Saunders, Mark Love, Google, Tera-Byte Inc, The History Press, Dave Woodfall and Peter Denton. And an extra-special thanks to our fantastic visitors at www.godchecker.com.

Most of all, thanks to all the Gods and Goddesses of every nation for taking the trouble to create the world and populate it with such wonderful things as mythology, websites and publishers.

THE GODS OF AFRICA

Traditional African belief is overwhelmingly monotheistic. Early missionaries made a complete pig's ear of their research in this respect and seem to have delighted in cataloguing as many 'heathen' gods as they could possibly get away with.

African creator gods seem to follow a distinctive pattern – they are all extremely dissatisfied with their creations. There is much shaking of heads, turning away in sorrow and avoidance of contact. The humans are left to fend for themselves. Attempts to regain contact with their god by building a Heavenly ladder are the subject of many an unhappy legend. On the whole, African gods don't like to be pestered, and humans have to learn to be content with their lot.

There is a remarkable innocence about the gods of Africa. They seem naive and unworldly, believing the best of everyone and optimistically giving the benefit of the doubt to all and sundry. No wonder they are rudely disappointed when it turns out their badly chosen favourites are up to no good.

Communication is full of problems. Vital messages of life and death are entrusted to whichever animal happens to be passing, and the resulting garble usually has disastrous consequences...

ABALUYIA TRIBE OF KENYA
WELE

Creator god known as The One On High, probably because his Heavenly abode perches on top of a magnificent set of pillars. He created everything in six days and on the seventh he rested. But he didn't register for copyright, and more worldlywise gods have since taken the credit.

WELE originally designed the sun and moon as twins. But he had to split them up and keep them apart because they wouldn't stop fighting. He then created Mwambu, the first man, so that the sun and moon would have someone to shine on. Mwambu and his wife Sela built themselves a house on stilts. This was probably in imitation of Wele's rather more expensive and upmarket Heaven. Houses on stilts are still popular in

Kenya today – if nothing else, stilts make it harder for critters and baddies to get in.

Wele's finishing touches included rainbows, weather and fairy lights. On the eighth day he rested again, and then again and again. He is still on holiday.

ASANTE PEOPLE OF GHANA
NYANKOPON

African sky god driven up the Heavenly ladder. The culprit was an old woman pounding yams with a long pole. The pole flew up out of control towards the holy anatomy. Thud! Ouch! **NYANKOPON** wasn't going to suffer indignities like that. So he ascended to Heaven in a huff.

The humans were terribly upset and tried to build a ladder to Heaven to find him. This was quite dangerous as the ladder was made of yam poles and quite rickety. But they persevered until they were just one yam pole short. 'Take one from the bottom', Nyankopon advised. They did. Crash!

When they hit the ground they became quite dead. Very peaceful and quiet. Silence. Bliss. Nyankopon found them quite tolerable in this state. That's why only the dead can get to Heaven – they're much quieter and don't disturb the peace.

BAMBARA OF MALI
FARO

Creator god who got himself pregnant by rocking the universe. (Don't try this at home chaps.) The resultant twins boosted the popular process of populating to explosive proportions.

FARO is now in semi-retirement and only pays a visit every 400 years to check that nobody else has rocked the universe. So far, nobody has.

BANTU OF THE CONGO
NZAME

The story so far…

After consultation with the animals, **NZAME** creates the first man, Fam, who is blessed with power, wealth and immortality. And he turns out to be an arrogant cocky wastrel. Nzame buries him in a hole and tries again.

Second man Sekume, being made mortal, is far more modest, and humbly makes himself a wife out of a tree. (Her name is Mbongwe, which may or may not be of any importance in the long run.) Original man Fam, playing the immortality card, comes back from the dead to create trouble. End of episode one.

Next week, Nzame falls in love with new girl Mboya, and they have a son called Bingo. Yes, Bingo.

There are many episodes of family quarrels, squabbles and feuds until Nzame, in a fit of rage, throws Bingo out of Heaven. (By now the soap was going on so long it needed a bit of fresh impetus.) Bingo is found by a wizard called Otoyom who secretly raises the Godly child.

Nzarne, now repentant, searches together with Mboya through many episodes to find their lost child, but Otoyom is always one magic step ahead of them. Bingo reaches adulthood and becomes a teacher to all mankind.

Will Nzame ever find him? Will he ever be reconciled to his parents? Will he ever confess to being **MEBEGHE** on his day off? What is Fam up to? Is Sekume still married to a tree? Meanwhile back in the East End of Coronation Street new neighbours have moved in…

BAULE TRIBE OF THE IVORY COAST
KAKA-GUIE

Bull-headed god of death. He turns up at funerals wearing the head of a bull, rather than the respectful dark suit you might expect. His mission is to protect nervous souls from all the annoying relatives who might cause distraction and distress, and provide safe passage from this world to the next. We feel this is a vital service. Funerals are no place for the dead.

BUSHONGO PEOPLE OF THE CONGO
BUMBA

African creator god of vomit. Yes, vomit.

In the beginning, all was dark. Then out of the darkness came **BUMBA**, a giant pale-skinned figure. He was not feeling well. In fact he had not been feeling well for millions of years. He was lonely, and the unbearable solitude was making him ill. Troubled by a ballooning bellyache, he staggered, moaned and vomited up the Sun. Light burst forth into the Universe – and he choked out the Moon. The stars came next and then, with a tremendous effort, he threw up the planet Earth. We do live in a very sick world.

This nauseating display was brought to a triumphant conclusion when, as an encore, he vomited forth nine animals, an assortment of humans, and a pile of diced carrots. Exhausted from his labours, he sat and watched as the nine creatures multiplied. After a while, they had evolved into every living thing on Earth. His loneliness abated and finally he was content.

Then Bumba's three sons appeared to add the finishing touches. Nyone-Ngana created the ants, Chonganda created the plants and Chedi-Bumba created the first eagle. Thus the world was made. Bumba spoke kindly to his human creations before ascending to Heaven, never to be seen again. So far as we know, his stomach has never troubled him since.

DOGON PEOPLE OF MALI

AMMA

His word created a primordial egg from the atom of a seed, which must have been some undertaking. This was actually a double-yolker which contained various godly goodies and not a little confusion. Then he made Mother Earth from clay and tried to mate with her. But a well-endowed termite hill caused painful obstructions in the most embarrassing place and he was forced to circumcise her to get the job done. Ouch. Sadly, the Dogons (and other tribes) still practise female circumcision, while termite hills escape scot free.

Meanwhile, the details of **AMMA**'s further career vary depending on the tribe, the weather, and the colour of your socks. We know that his offspring were Ogo, Yurugu, Yasigi and a host of Nommo godlets, but how, why and in what order remains a tangled mystery. We suspect the Dogon people are trying to confuse us. Unless, of course, they're just as confused as we are.

His daughter Yasigi is the goddess of dancing, beer and masks. Born from his cosmic Kinder Egg, she was taken into care at an early age to protect her from the incestuous attentions of her evil twin brother Yurugu, the rebel god of chaos. He escaped from Amma's cosmic egg and filched the whole yolk. Not because he was hungry, but because he thought his sister was hiding inside. She wasn't. The mysterious multiplying Nommo Twins were looking after her. These were also born from Amma's prodigious cosmic egg (second yolk on the right).

Frustrated Yurugu was left with egg on his face and a whopping big wobbly yolk to deal with. He decided to mate with it. But the yolk became hard-boiled and turned into a dry, dusty yellow Earth. Seeking the power of speech, he tried an incestuous union with moist Mother Earth which brought impurity and barrenness to the world. And also the two Underworld spirits Andumbulu and Yeban.

To save the world from Yurugu's incestuous behaviour, which was threatening the entire fabric of creation, Amma sacrificed one of the Nommos and scattered the bits all over the universe. Yurugu slinked away and might now be ruling the dry Dogon wastes disguised as a pale fox, known locally as the Jackal, a creature despised by all.

After that Yasigi appears to have become a celebrity figure. She presides over the Sigi ceremony, a ritual held every sixty years to commemorate the making of the Mask of the Dead. Statues depict her as an incredibly large-breasted female holding a beer ladle and dancing the night away. We never get invited to these Dogon parties.

Meanwhile the other Nommo, using the latest genetic modification techniques, multiplied into more twins and were sent down to Earth to become the descendants of the Dogon people. The Dogons' startling knowledge of esoteric astronomy has led some people to claim they were once visited by reptilian extra-terrestrials from Sirius. The Dog Star?

EFIK PEOPLE OF NIGERIA
ABASSI

On the suggestion of his wife Atai, **ABASSI** invented the first humans and somewhat nervously introduced them into the wild. As he feared, the first couple quickly discovered sex, and pretty soon were doing their own creating. This created a terrible over-population problem, and made Abassi feel rather insecure. So Atai gave humanity two gifts, Argument and Death, to keep the numbers under control.

FON AND YORUBA PEOPLE OF BENIN AND TOGO
MAWU-LISA

Two-in-one creator god. A divine duality, **MAWU** is the female moonly side and **LISA** is the male, sunny side up. Mawu created the world and

everything in it, for which we are very grateful. Her
creative energies were so abundant that she started to
worry about overloading the planet. So she asked
that nice World Serpent Da to curl around the
world and support it in case of accidents.

Their mother appears to be **MINONA**, and
between them they produced an impressive brood
of gods including Da, the Great Snake who coils
around the Universe and supports the Earth,
Age, the water god twins and a thunder god.

And where would we be without Gu,
the great god of tools, workshops
and smiths? The son of Mawu-Lisa,
he started off as a humble trowel
and was dispatched to Earth to
do little odd jobs around the place   –
filling unsightly craters, fixing leaky oceans, that kind
of thing. The humans were very grateful and he was soon
promoted to god of smiths, weapons and war. He has probably reached
Black & Decker status by now.

MINONA

Lives in the forest, is a good goddess for blessing crops and also looks after
women. She spent a lot of time teaching mankind how to read the omens
in palm cones and thus foretell the future. But that was a long time ago and
such knowledge appears to have dried up. Unless you count tea leaves.

She is also the mother of Fa, who became a far-reaching god of the
past, present and future. He uses windows – not the kind of windows that
you find in a computer but mystic apertures through which he gazes with
his sixteen all-seeing eyes. And to prevent his windows from crashing he
employs Eshu, another god, to open and shut the windows when they are
needed and prevent them from crashing. Perhaps this is an example of
early structured programming.

ESHU also directs traffic along the road of life from his abode at the
crossroads of fortune. If you have important choices or opportunities he
can act as a speedy go-between, and carry messages to the gods or any
living thing.

However, he does have a perverse sense of humour and will often throw
a spanner into the works to keep life interesting. This could explain why we

don't always get what we want. Just to make life even more complicated he also turns up all over the place as Legba, a shabby old man who is very clever and cunning, knowing all the languages of the world and is fluent in the cosmic tongue.

Then he will garble the messages using old age as an excuse. If this isn't enough, he also makes guest appearances in Voodoo ceremonies.

HERERO OF NAMIBIA
NJAMBI

Supreme creator god. He placed the primordial Omumborombonga tree upon the Earth, from which Mukuru, the first human, and his brothers emerged. No, they weren't growing from the branches. That would be ridiculous. They actually emerged from root holes underneath. We're not sure how they got there, but creator god **NJAMBI** probably put them there for safekeeping. The first herd of cattle also came from the tree's root holes, but according to Herero legend, the lesser animals (and rival tribes!) had to be content with ordinary holes in the ground to crawl out of.

Mukuru is believed to be buried under the very tree that gave birth to him. So what happened to the original Omumborombonga, which gave birth to humankind? You need to go to the veldt Windhoek, north of the river Ugab. It was said still to be standing in 1933, but we can guarantee nothing.

Like most of the African supreme gods, Njambi retreated to the safety of Heaven as soon as humans appeared on the scene. Now he's another aloof sky god that rules through spiritual wisdom alone. Although he occasionally rumbles and thunders, he tends to keep well out of the way. He's probably busy sending all that sun, rain, food, shelter and oxygen.

IGBO (FORMERLY IBO) PEOPLE OF NIGERIA
CHUKU

In the beginning **CHUKU** the creator was floating in the sky pondering on the Meaning of Life. In an inspired moment he created Ale. Stop. Before we go any further we must emphatically deny any association with the brewing industry. The Ale created by Chuku was Mother Earth. Perhaps it may be better to use her alternative name, Ala, to avoid confusion. She is the Earth Mother goddess of fertility and death. Thus she has a hand in the beginning of life and its end.

Life and creation were now off to a fine flourishing start. Chuku was particularly delighted with his humans, and thought immortality would be a nice prezzie for them. He decreed that any human dropping dead should be laid to rest on Mother Earth and covered with ashes. Restoration would then occur.

Sadly some woolly thinking marred things as Chuku chose a sheep to spread the news. The sheep muffed the message and put it about that dead humans should be burned to ashes and covered with Mother Earth. Result: the dead stay dead. We hope Sheep feels very sheepish about this.

IJAW PEOPLE OF NIGERIA
WOYENGI

Goddess who came down to Earth on a streak of lightning. All she found on arrival was a table and a chair and a flat stone standing on mud. However, she was very adept at creative art. She made lots and lots of little mud dolls and gave them the breath of life. They even had a choice of gender when it came to sticking on the extra wobbly bits.

Then came the job interviews. Each one was asked what it wanted to do, and sent off down different streams she had released from the mud. According to choice of occupation they were sent down clear, muddy or tempestuous waterways, some with rapids. Standing on the banks there were groups who now wanted to change their minds, but there was no going back even if you thought you had been sold down the river.

KAVANGO PEOPLE OF NAMIBIA
SHADIPINYI

Evil god of drunken behaviour and lager louts. He's credited with inventing beer, which he gave to mankind in an attempt to cause trouble. When the pubs and clubs are emptying on a Saturday night, it is **SHADIPINYI** you must blame for the resulting noise and mess.

KAVANGO PEOPLE OF NAMIBIA AND LOZI PEOPLE OF BAROTSELAND, UPPER ZAMBESI

NYAMBE

Supreme creator god with a very annoying neighbour.

It all started so well. **NYAMBE** created the forests, the plains, and all the animals. He created light and life through the Sun and Moon, and lived happily amongst his creations. He created his wife Nasilele and daughter Mwambwa and loved them even more. But then he created Kamunu, the first man. And it was just his luck to have created a real pest.

Kamunu worshipped the ground Nyambe walked on. He wanted to walk, talk and behave like his hero in every way. This didn't stop him from borrowing pots, pans, and garden tools every five minutes and peering over the garden fence to watch and copy everything Nyambe did.

One day he saw Nyambe forging iron to make ploughshares and scythes. So Kamunu had to have a go. Assuming that those sharp-looking iron objects were weapons, he produced spears and knives and things which killed. Then promptly went on a killing spree to test them out.

Nyambe and Nasilele were disgusted by this awful behaviour. But Nyambe, whose name means 'He Who Does Not Speak', didn't say a word. Instead, he and his wife sailed away to a remote island in a lake. Guess who stowed away on the boat? So they ran off at super-godly speed to the highest mountain on Earth – but two years later who do you think arrived on their doorstep?

The good-natured Nyambe was driven to distraction. It was all too much. He found Spider and forced her to spin a rope into the sky. He and his wife climbed up and then pulled the rope up after them. In cruel desperation, and totally out of character, they blinded Spider before they left to keep their new location a secret.

Spurred on by his wife, Nyambe even sent Death to finally rid them of Kamunu and his descendants. But it didn't work. They still spend much of their time gazing upwards worshipping the sun just in case it's him!

LOVEDU AND VHAVENDA PEOPLE OF TRANSVAAL

KHUZWANE

Creator god of the Transvaal. He's a very remote god, but he did at least leave some trace of himself behind. When the world was young and freshly made, all the rocks and stones were soft and squidgy. Just like clay. So **KHUZWANE** used this malleable muddy stuff to make the first humans, and the landscape around the Limpopo River bears the imprint of his bare feet as he walked about making model citizens. These godly footprints have given certain places a sacred aspect which persists to this day. Once a year, in a semi-secret ceremony, local beer is poured into them. We can barely guess the reasons for this practice, but we trust that good beer is not going to waste.

Meanwhile, Lake Fundudzi is a very special place to the VahVenda people. They believe it to be Khuzwane's private swimming pool; apparently he sometimes returns to Earth for a quick dip. Consequently, no-one is allowed to visit the lake without permission, and it might be advisable to take some beer as well. No wonder the lake is full of tribal taboos. No fishing! No swimming! And if you do get permission to visit, prepare to be humbled; first-time visitors have to bend down and peer at the waters from between their legs. We hope royalty gets to visit someday.

The Tshiavha clan of the VhaVenda are guardians of the lake, and their methods have managed to keep it pristine and pure for centuries. This has become increasingly difficult in modern times, but long may they continue. When they say no fishing, they mean it!

LUGBARA PEOPLE OF ZAIRE AND UGANDA
ADROA

A god of two halves. In fact he is a creator god, half good and half evil. Having created the Universe he decided on a final bit of DIY, and made Adro – the Earth. Being a half-hearted god, he was something of a split personality, so split himself straight down the middle. Literally. Each half had one eye, half a mouth, one arm, and one leg. But no naughty bits. No half measures for him.

The good half remained in Heaven, while the nasty side became the snaky **ADROA** and took charge of Earthly things. He swam the rivers of the world, producing evil Adroanzi offspring (from a slit in his side with no hanky panky involved). They tend to hide in rivers and behind rocks, lying in wait for innocent humans. If you walk past one at night, watch out! The creepy creature will follow you home, licking its lips. Whatever you do, don't turn around. If you so much as peep behind you, you've had it. Keep your eyes fixed ahead and pretend nothing is happening. That's the only way to stay safe.

LUMBA PEOPLE OF ZAIRE
KALUMBA

Creator god who built a road from Heaven to Earth. Being pretty busy with godly affairs, he got a guard dog and, for reasons best known to himself, a goat to watch this road, as Death and Life were both straining at the leash to try their powers on the newly formed Earth. 'Let Life through – turn Death back' were **KALUMBA**'s simple instructions.

Time passed. Dog got bored and wandered off. All was quiet. Then a group of servants came along carrying laundry. Bored out of his mind, Goat let these humble minions pass. What he didn't know was that Death had disguised himself as a pile of dirty washing and was now being ferried to Earth.

When Life strolled down the road, a now suspicious Goat jumped on her, and didn't realise his mistake until Dog returned. Kalumba was not pleased as he couldn't recall Death, so he took Life back into Heaven to be patched up, kicked both Dog and Goat up the arse, sent them off to Earth and promptly closed the road.

MAASAI PEOPLE OF KENYA AND TANZANIA
ENGAI

In the beginning, **ENGAI** lived on Earth in joyful communion with all the cattle in the world. Then one day a terrible catastrophe occurred which sent him – and the cattle – zooming off into the sky. We're not sure what kind of catastrophe, but there was a suspiciously active volcano nearby. Engai and the cattle tried to live in the clouds, but there wasn't a lot of grass up there to keep the cattle fed. So he called down to a human named Naiteru-Kop and told him to expect a special delivery.

Naiteru-Kop, who lived near the aforementioned volcano, must have been rather surprised to see a large herd of cattle sliding down to Earth on a vine. Cattle don't usually do that sort of thing. 'Look after them for me,' said Engai. 'They don't like it up here so I'm giving them all to you.'

Imagine Naiteru-Kop's amazement: he was rich! One of his neighbours was even more amazed – and spitefully cut the vine through sheer jealousy. Thus endeth the Great Cattle Bonanza. But with divinely granted sole ownership of the entire cattle population of the world, Naiteru-Kop wasn't complaining.

He immediately founded the Maasai, a tribe devoted to cattle. Looking after cattle was their *raison d'etre*; not just a means of survival, but a holy occupation expected of them by their god. The Maasai are still going strong today – and still believe that all the cattle in the world belong to them. This gives them the divine right to rustle cattle from neighbouring tribes, not as cattle thieves but as cattle rescuers.

As for Engai, he's still up there in the clouds, and can veer between two different manifestations. When he's in a good mood (Engai *Narok*), the clouds are black and full of nourishing rain. When he's annoyed (Engai *Na-nyokie*), the clouds are dry, red, and full of life-zapping lightning. When there aren't any clouds, he's probably taking a vacation at the holy volcano Oldonyo Le Ngai (Mountain of God).

MITSOGO-GABON AND FANG PEOPLE OF GABON AND CAMEROON

MEBEGHE

Drug-induced creator god of the Bwiti religion-cult. In the forest of Gabon grows a plant called Tabernanthe Iboga. It has twisted roots, polka-dot pink leaves and hallucinogenic properties to match. A few nibbles at the iboga root will send you soaring into a world of weirdness. You may even get religion – which is exactly how the Bwiti cult began. **MEBEGHE** seems to be a tripped-out take on the three-in-one creator god **NZAME**. An afternoon munching iboga must have given a completely new angle on everyone's favourite god.

Before you can make a cosmic omelette you have to make a cosmic egg. You will need underarm hair, a piece of brain, and a pebble from the sea. You can then blow on the ingredients and your egg will form. Hand it to a spider to hang between sky and sea and cook it in sunshine. There are more exciting recipes to create worms and termites. These in turn dish up a big ball of dung which becomes Earth Pudding. There may also be animals, birds, plants, and giant triangular zootfroodles, depending on how much iboga you are chewing.

When it is hot you must fertilise it, then when it cracks you have descendants. This is the exciting bit: In Mebeghe's case there burst forth Ninepone and her brother None. But there was also a cosmic placenta and umbilical cord. The leftover bits formed the body of Evus, a strangely twisted godlet with a co-joined twin by his side. This twin, named Ekurana, possessed the power of thunder. But he spent most of his time sleeping and turning a blind eye to Evus's goings-on. For Evus was often very naughty indeed.

Mebeghe's three new deities were placed upon the Earth and told to behave themselves which, needless to say, they didn't. It wasn't long before sex and drugs and dead warthogs had ruined all chance of a happy ending. Knowing Evus's nature, Mebeghe in his wisdom banished him to the jungle to prevent strife. So it was probably him that first discovered the hallucinatory properties of the iboga plant. Meanwhile Ninepone and None were treated to a nice village setting with all mod cons.

Evus prowled around the jungle growing increasingly bored and dissatisfied. He started to comfort-eat antelopes and warthogs, and make irritating noises in the dead of night. Finally Ninepone went out to see what was going on and found herself unexpectedly seduced. Entrusted with the guardianship of the night and the sanctity of the female spirit, she had remained a virgin right up until the first time she had sex. But Evus must have whispered sweet evil nothings in her ear, as she then made the leap from half-brother to full-brother and took None into her bed. It was a case of 'keeping it in the family' going a bit too far.

All these shenanigans made Mebeghe very cross – and as a punishment Ninepone now carries the world upon her head. There aren't many sexual positions you can attempt in that position. Meanwhile, None was faced with a multitude of screaming baby humans and no widwife. It was then that Evus proved he wasn't entirely evil – just misunderstood. He sat None down and explained to him the secret lore of ironwork, carpentry, bookbinding, textiles and painting. So a relieved and happy None set to work – and was able to keep the kids happy with toys, games, musical instruments, books and sports equipment.

The end came in a flash. Mebeghe gave Ekurana, Evus's conjoined twin, a prod which finally woke him up. He unleashed a thunderbolt which knocked his brother for six and sent him deep into the bowels of the Earth. We're not sure if the twins were separated in the process. Evus is stuck there to this day, but has anyone seen Ekurana lately?

The cult of Bwiti is still going strong in several parts of Gabon and Cameroon. There are many strenuous rituals to deal with and also a lot of complicated secret handshakes. Meanwhile, Mebeghe has found new fame in the West as Zame-Ye-Mebege, the discordian god of narcotics. It's a weird old world.

VARIOUS TRIBES INCLUDING KAONDE, BAILA AND TONGA, SOUTH AFRICA

LEZA

Tired weather god. A bit past it. In ages past he gave instructions to a certain Honeybird. 'Now look, I have an important task for you. I want you to take these three calabashes to Earth for me. These two contain seeds to distribute wherever you wish, but this third one must remain sealed until I come down and attend to it.'

You can guess what happened, can't you? Is a bird-brain not going to take a peek? It's **PANDORA** all over again isn't it? **LEZA** sighed. There was no way he was going down there to clear that mess up.

Now he spends all his time in Heaven spring-cleaning and rumbling around which causes thunder. When he gazes downwards with his rheumy old eyes it causes rainfall.

WEST AFRICA
WULBARI

Another pestered top god. An old woman was responsible for the final straw – in this case from a cooking fire sending smoke into his eyes. He was so annoyed that he upped and went, founding an entourage consisting only of animals and **ANANSI**, the god who was a spider anyway.

As well as being sneaky, tricky, sly and crafty, Anansi's also a creator god who made the sun and moon and hit upon the novel idea of day and night. Legends and tales abound. Anansi is very popular with the natives. In fact he's affectionately known as Aunt Nancy.

XHOSA PEOPLE OF SOUTH AFRICA
HAIURI

Half a god. He is only half-there, having one eye, one ear, one arm and one leg. You stand half a chance of being taken to the Underworld if you meet him as he has to hop after you and seize you with half a mouth. A bit half-hearted.

XHOSA PEOPLE OF SOUTH AFRICA AND KHOIKHOI PEOPLES, NAMA PEOPLE OF NAMIBIA

HEITSI-EIBIB

He had a strange birth. His mother, a cow, ate some magic grass which turned out to be full of maleness. She became pregnant and soon gave birth to this fully formed god. It's not everyone who can claim their father is a tuft of grass.

A great shape-changer himself, he became involved in animal evolution and did his bit for conservation by putting species in their right environment – taking fish out of the desert, stopping lions building nests in trees, that kind of thing. (He could teach David Attenborough a thing or two.)

He is also something of a folk hero, having sorted out Ga-Gorib, a nasty taunting demon who used a large pit to lure animals. 'I dare you to throw a stone at me', he would say. Naturally they would be unable to resist the temptation. But the stone would always rebound, knocking the thrower into the pit where Ga-Gorib would gobble him up. When **HEITSI-EIBIB** fell in the pit, he changed into we don't know what, but when he emerged he was licking his lips and the demon was never seen again.

Humans are his favourite animal, and he gave them lots of freedom to run wild and do their own thing. Which may have been a little over-indulgent. Now he lives in graves and caves, and can be approached when people need good luck in hunting.

DAMARA OF NAMIBIA

GAMAB

GAMAB lives in the sky and directs the fate of mankind. When it's time for someone to die, he gets out his bow and shoots them down with an arrow. He has his own village in the Heavens with a ritual fire. When a newcomer comes along, as a gesture of kindness he offers them a drink from a bowl of liquid fat.

Gamab's arch-enemy is Gaunab: The Evil One. Responsible for all misfortune, disease and death, with evil spirits and big snakes a speciality, Gaunab is unspeakably nasty – so we won't speak about him. However, he did unexpectedly create the rainbow, so he can't be all bad.

Luckily there's another goodie, in the form of Tsui-Goab, also known as Thixo (no connection with a brand of adhesive) who battled Gaunab, helped to create the world and got it into shape. Tsui-Goab's a real shape-changer. To populate the world, he transformed into all the plants and animals in turn, shedding his skin like a snake to become the next item. We're also reliably informed that he is the good god of rain and thunder, which is something of a hobby with creator gods.

YORUBA PEOPLE OF NIGERIA AND BENIN
ORISHAS

Guardian spirits under the collective patronage of top god **OLORUN**. At the last count there seem to be at least 1,700 of them. Many appear to be worshipped in their own right, and they include top names such as Babalu-Aye, Elegua, Obatala, Ochosi, Ogun, **OYA**, **SHANGO** and Yemaya.

There was a time when they conducted a power struggle against Olorun and tried to persuade him to abdicate for sixteen years. Unwilling to give up control of the Universe to lesser deities, he offered them a trial period of sixteen days. Within eight days the whole Universe had ground to a halt. They consulted the oracle Orunmila who could give no answer. So they had to eat humble pie and ask for pardon whilst Olorun, nice as pie about it, restored order. The **ORISHAS** are now highly thought of and are worshipped in places as far away as the Caribbean.

ESHU

Very popular trickster god. Particularly keen on opportunity, communication and instant messaging.

ESHU directs traffic along the road of life from his abode at the crossroads of fortune. If you're faced with an important choice or a powerful opportunity, Eshu can offer advice to help swing things your way. A super-speedy go-between, he can carry complaints to the gods, questions to the spirit world, and messages to any living thing.

With his connections, Eshu can be a powerful ally. But he's also a god with a sense of humour and will often throw a spanner in the works to keep life interesting. This could explain why we don't always get what we want. Be careful – this god of crossroads is also a master of cross-purposes.

OLORUN

Top sky god, but he's especially good at passing the buck. His wonderful blueprints for planet Earth were so amazingly ambitious that he prudently decided to delegate the construction to someone else. So he summoned Obatala, one of the **ORISHAS**, handed over blueprints, a handful of mud, a chain, a five-toed chicken – and detailed instructions.

Unfortunately, on his way to perform this important task, Obatala accidentally gatecrashed a godparty and spent the rest of the evening roaring drunk on palm wine. Seeing the chance for fame and glory, his younger brother Oduduwa pinched the holy building materials and attempted to jerry-build the Earth himself. Advised by a friendly chameleon, he lowered the chain over the edge of Heaven, climbed down, and tossed the lump of mud into the primeval sea. The chicken hopped onto the mud and began scratching it in all directions.

Pretty soon there was a decent-sized landmass and thus was the Earth born. Olorun was so pleased with Oduduwa that he promoted him to god of the Earth, while the disgraced and boozy Obatala was put to work making mankind as punishment. If you ever wondered why humans aren't quite as perfect as they should be, here's the answer: the creator was hungover at the time.

Obatala eventually learned the error of his ways and became the great white god of mankind, specialising in white wine, laundry and refrigerators. He's also god of the north, although in what capacity (Pole? Wind? Star?) we have yet to ascertain. As top god, Olorun's fame has spread as far afield as the Caribbean. But rumours persist that he's secretly married to Olokun. Some even claim that he leads a secret double life as windy Yansan. You can't trust everything you hear.

Perhaps we should ask his trusty messenger Elegua. He's the guardian of the crossroads of life. Whenever there are decisions to be made, he provides opportunities and second chances. On the other hand, as a trickster god, the childlike Elegua can sometimes make things even more complicated. At a whim he can turn a simple choice into a vast conundrum of paradox. He's partial to cigars and rum, but he is very good with children. His day is Monday – so you can start the week well under his ministrations, although he might well tell you his name is Eshu by then. And you can't believe everything he tells you.

OYA

One of the **ORISHAS**, **OYA** is one busy Yoruba goddess. She is involved in everything from wind, weather and marketing to undertaking and lung disease. She has a very colourful personality, favouring all the colours of the rainbow plus black and burgundy. She also likes a drop of red wine. Could this be burgundy to match her chosen colour? If so, where does she get it from?

She also likes Wednesday – maybe this is her day off. She deserves it, as one of her specialist duties is looking after mucous membranes and bronchial passages. You would never think it to look at her.

When things are quiet she sneaks off to become Yansan, a goddess of wind. We're not sure which way she blows. Not passing wind we hope. All this and she has found time to be the mother of nine and keep them away from the glare of publicity. They don't make goddesses like this any more.

SHANGO

God of thunder, drums and dance, having been elevated from being a famous warrior and the fourth king of the Yoruba. One of the **ORISHAS**, his special number is six. If you invite him to a feast you will need to stock up on bananas, apples, cornmeal, okra, red wine and rum. He has a relationship with **OYA** which can at times be very tempestuous; he is very much a ladies' man, and in great demand as a dancer, and for playing the drums.

He does not get on well with his brother Ogun, the god of metalwork, who is as inflexible as iron and not averse to a good punch-up. But he's a good god to have on your side as he can be very loyal and protective. Don't leave your drums or your tools out in the rain and they'll both be happy.

ZULU AND XHOSA PEOPLE OF SOUTH AFRICA

UNKULUNKULU

Top god. His parents were the creator gods Umvelinqangi, who was heavily involved in the thunder and earthquake industry, and swamp goddess Uhlanga. Together they created him out of reeds, gave him a good upbringing and made him aware of his responsibilities. Pretty early on in his career, he decided to bestow immortality upon mankind, and sent a chameleon down with the good news. 'Dear Mankind. Am giving you the gift of immortality. Hope this fits in with your needs. Best regards, Unkul. R.S.V.P.'

Unfortunately the bearer of this important message was delayed on the way and mankind didn't get to hear of it until far too late. Expecting a simple thank-you at the very least, Uncle Unkul was a bit narked and changed his mind. He sent a lizard with an entirely different message instead.

This lizard didn't waste any time and got there first. So mankind was presented with their fate. 'Dear Mankind. I don't like you any more. Drop dead. Best regards, Unkul.'

Apart from this unfortunate glitch, **UNKULUNKULU** was a wise and helpful god who did his best to produce a welfare state.

MBABA-MWANNA-WARESA

Goddess of beer. Now there's a deity we can all appreciate. She also produces beautiful rainbows when it's time to celebrate. So much nicer than other beer gods we could mention.

THE GODS OF ABORIGINAL OZ

Like most 'discovered' countries, Australia had already been discovered by its original inhabitants – the Aborigines. Small nomadic tribes with many languages and ideas roamed the vast plains.

Much of Oz mythology is to do with Dreaming and the **DREAMTIME**, a wonderful golden age in the remote past when gods were real gods and anything was possible.

Relying on memory and scratched images, Australian mythology is seemingly fragile, but in many instances in this very dry atmosphere it's amazingly durable. Many of the dreams were trampled on by European invasion, but fortunately there has always been a strong oral tradition, and the legends of the Outback have been making a comeback.

DREAMTIME

The original Aboriginal primordial timeless dream that existed before the world woke up. Known as Alchera, this was when the ancient spirits of all tribes walked the Earth in a state of profound dreaminess. Now they all sleep underground, but shamans and other interested parties can still communicate with the **DREAMTIME** past if they inhale the right substances.

Dreamtime was overseen by Altjira. He is depicted as having emu's feet, for no reason we can fathom. He created the Earth and supplied all the gear humans need, then retired without leaving instructions.

KARRAUR TRIBE

YHI

Asleep in **DREAMTIME**, a goddess awakes in a bare barren world. Her very presence brings light and radiance. She walks, and in her very footprints plants and flowers spring up. She peers into dark caves and butterflies and bees burst forth. She walks in deeper caves and can sense spirits yearning for existence. She bestows form upon them and myriads of creatures pour forth. Having spread light and joy, she departs.

All seems serene but nothing is ever quite perfect. **YHI** was not very good at anatomy. Most of her creations had no means of locomotion. No legs, no feet, no wings. They just couldn't get about.

Yhi had not planned a return trip, but Earthly pleas reached her ears, and what is such a darling goddess to do? Her best of course! So back she came and added legs and wings and fins and things.

But her anatomy is still far from brilliant which is why you have such weird and wonderful wildlife in Australia. Think duck-billed platypus and kangaroo. There was also a strange thing called man that wandered around on two spindly legs. He was shunned by all, so in her compassion she offered to make him a companion. Oh no, thought the man, what will she come up with this time?

But all that practice had paid off at last and, using the most beautiful flower stalk, Yhi created the first woman. This was much better than the wombat! Content at last, man wandered away in bliss and Yhi returned to **DREAMTIME** in triumph.

EINGANA

Rainbow snake mother goddess of primordial **DREAMTIME**. Initially she had a lot of trouble giving birth, not having the relevant aperture. This was rectified by another deity, who obliged with a spear in the appropriate place. Since then, creatures and humanity both great and small have issued forth. But **EINGANA** keeps hold of the mystical umbilical cord, attached to every living thing. If she cuts the cord, the creature dies. And if she herself should die, everything would cease to exist. This worries us. Who's holding her umbilical cord then?

GUNWINGGU FOLK OF NORTHERN TERRITORY
WARAMURUNGUNDJU

Fertility goddess. One day in **DREAMTIME** she walked out of the sea with her partner **WURAKA**. She was the one with the long name and he was the one with an even longer appendage. It was so impressive he had to keep it coiled around his neck. And then it was wham-bam fertility time. Finally their non-stop bouts of fulfilment and fertility culminated in multiple creation. **WARAMURUNGUNDJU** then taught her children to talk and gave them all a different language to play with. This magnificent piece of creative effort achieved, she and her partner calmly walked back into the sea again.

ULURU

Aborigine name for Ayers Rock, one of the world's largest, reddest, and most beautiful monoliths – and the ancestral site of primeval **DREAMTIME**. Legions of legends and multitudes of myths emanate from here. Unfortunately, most of these are top secret and can only be divulged to members of the appropriate tribe. However, we can reveal that **ULURU** is 318 metres high, 8 kilometres in circumference, and is host to a surprising amount of lizards.

The Lizard of Uluru is known as Adnoartina, but to be honest we're not sure which particular lizard he is. Tatji is the Red Lizard. His boomerang didn't come back. Out hunting one day, he threw the prototype hunting stick and it got stuck in the rock. Unable to scoop it out with his bare hands, he finally died in a cave of frustration and starvation. His remains are there to this day.

Lungkata and Mita are the dirty cheating Lizard Men of Ayers Rock. They have blue tongues and a sneaky stealing temperament. They lie in wait for hunters and steal their prey, being too lazy to go hunting themselves.

One day, the Bell-Bird Brothers were chasing an emu (which was something of a national sport at the time) and the two blue-tongued lizards diverted it into their lair. When the hunters turned up, out of breath and starving, Lungkata and Mita had scoffed the lot and could only offer emu leftovers. The Bell-Bird Brothers were outraged at this thievery and set fire to the lair. The lizards, not being used to exercise, were unable to escape and turned into burnt boulders which stand there to this day. Which just goes to show that you shouldn't trust anyone with a blue tongue.

NORTHERN TERRITORY
DJANGGAWUL & CO

There were two sisters and their brother **DJANGGAWUL**, who emerged from the Underworld to set the world to rights. First they did good by creating the landscape of Australia and filling it with goodly things. Then things went a little pear-shaped. The two sisters broke off pieces of their naughtiest bits to make sacred talismans. After that, legends based on hearsay abound and rebound and multiply.

One sister, Bunbulama, became a rain goddess who joined forces with Wuluwait, a rain god. Together they know the secret of making rain by tying strips of water grass together – extremely useful in drought situations. They appear together on a painting on wood from Yirrkala, where they seem to be waving sponges at the sky. Meanwhile, Djanggawul's daughters, the Wawalug sisters, became fertility goddesses and went to live in a whirlpool.

ARNHEM LAND
RAINBOW SNAKE

The **RAINBOW SNAKE** is a bit of a mish-mash, with a kangaroo's head, a crocodile's tail and a python's body, all decorated with water lilies and waving tendrils. Family portraits go back 8,000 years, which make the Rainbow Snake one of the oldest religious symbols, and one still going strong today.

The snake has many names across Australia and comes in male and female form. One female manifestation, Julunggul, oversees the initiation of boys into manhood. So if you're having awkward teen problems such as acne, bad hair, and social angst, slip her a note during break. Yingarna, another female, is the original Mother of Creation. Her son Ngalod is the Great Transformer of Land. Yrlunggur is the great Rainbow Snake of the Murngin people,

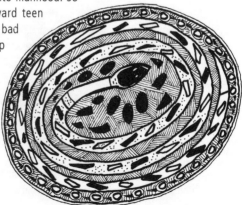

and not entirely nice. Roused to fury by the smell of menstrual blood, he swallowed the Wawalug sisters in one angry gulp. But later, at the Annual General Meeting of Snakes and Serpents, he was accused of eating his kin and throwing the good name of snakes into disrepute.

Not one to go against the status quo, Yrlunggur admitted his error and offered to make amends. The Wawalug sisters were promptly thrown up in a heap of vomit, as good as new and demanding compensation. We understand there was an out-of-court settlement.

TJINIMIN

Bat god of the Murinbata folk. Lust was **TJINIMIN**'s downfall. He just could not resist trying to get into the feathers of those Green Parrot Girls, consorts of the great **RAINBOW SNAKE**.

He was driven off with bees, and they tried to drown him by diverting a river. His biggest downfall came when he was thrown off a high cliff onto jagged rocks. But he had magic powers which were never available to Humpty Dumpty, and managed to put himself together again. Just to double check, he cut his nose off and stuck it back again. Yep – no problem.

Then he made a magic spear and went off to vent his rage on the great Rainbow Snake. He stabbed it in the side and watched as it writhed in agony creating an interesting new terrain. In its struggles the snake must have felt burning sensations because the next thing anyone knew it had dived to the bottom of the sea taking every last scrap of fire with it.

Tjinimin gazed apprehensively at one last charred stick. This is where Pilirin the kestrel god comes into the story. He was a bright spark and taught humans how to make fire using only two twigs. Just rub them together to wake up the spirits which live inside. Tjinimin went completely batty at this point and took to roosting upside down. Light and fire now scared him and he only wanted to look upwards at night. He decided he was never ever going to attempt sex again, and then his nose dropped off. This is why bats have snub noses.

BILDJIWUAROJU

Creator goddess among the Wulumba tribe. This is a somewhat complicated story of crudity and copulation. **BILDJIWUAROJU**, Miralalou and Djanggawul are the three Children of the Sun. Bildjiwuaroju and Miralalou had massive genitals, both male and female, but Djanggawul just had a willy. They came from Heaven in a canoe, landed on Earth and canoodled to such effect that they produced plants and animals at every coupling (or tripling).

One night Djanggawul went off to hunt, leaving the other two asleep by the fireside, but he crept back and hacked off their male appendages – leaving him the sole functioning male with two mates. After that he led the way and the others followed, creating the chauvinist myth that man always leads the way and women follow.

WESTERN AUSTRALIA
JULANA

Dirty old god. He tends to pop up in unexpected places, especially where women are concerned. He travels underground and in a flash pops up in front of them. And what also pops up is not a normal flasher's flash but a larger-than-life legend of phallic fantasy. If you happen to encounter him, it's probably best not to point and laugh. Shout for his **DREAMTIME** father Njarana.

BAGADJIMBIRI

Do you know the Kimberley Karadjeris? Out North West? Never mind, let us introduce you to their double deity. The 'Bag' were two **DREAMTIME** brothers who appeared from nowhere in wild dog form. In fact they were two dingos. They experimented with do-it-yourself creation and produced the world's first genetically modified body parts.

Up until this time, the human race was completely androgynous and terribly bored. So the **BAGADJIMBIRI** brothers mated a toadstool with a fungus and created sex organs for everybody. And bingo – or dingo – here we all are. There's more to mushrooms than you might imagine.

Very self-satisfied, the brothers laughed with delight and were suddenly murdered by a jealous cat spirit. But their mother, the fertility goddess Dilga, drowned the assailant in her own milk and brought the brothers back to life. Her milk was apparently very potent. They soared into the sky and become cloudy water snakes. Or watery cloud snakes.

KIMBERLEY REGION
WANDJINA

Intriguing creation gods. Wallungunder, the big boss **WANDJINA**, came down from the Milky Way during **DREAMTIME** and created the Earth and all its inhabitants. Then he took one look at those inhabitants and headed back home for reinforcements. This was going to be a tricky job.

With the aid of the **DREAMTIME SNAKE**, the Wandjina descended and spent their Dreamtime creating, teaching and being god-like to the natives. All was good, apart from the incident with Widjingara. He was the first human to die, allegedly killed by the Wandjina for reasons now lost in the mists of time.

His utterly shocked wife was at a bit of a loss, so she shaved her head and smeared herself with ashes. It seemed the right thing to do at the time, and she invented mourning quite by accident. But the process of death had not really been fixed or finalised back then – and three days later Widjingara came back. Unfortunately, he was so surprised and upset by his wife's mournful appearance that the shock killed him again. The human race has had death and mourning ever since.

Apart from that, they were definitely good guys, and are still worshipped and respected top gods to this day. These gods from the Milky Way were so powerful that they didn't need to speak. So they didn't bother to have mouths. Eyewitness reports are thin on the ground, but many ancient cave paintings still exist and show eerie creatures with large heads, huge black eyes and suspiciously spacesuit-like garments. In fact, they look just like grey aliens from modern UFO abduction scenarios.

Strangely enough, in 1838, a sea captain discovered an amazing treasure trove of Aboriginal artistry, filled with primitive and powerful Wandjina cave pictures. His name was Captain Grey. Coincidence? We can't tell you because the Kimberley tribes are very close-mouthed, just like their Wandjina.

VICTORIA
BUNJIL

The eaglehawk god. He had two wives, and a son who was a rainbow god called Binbeal. Busy with construction work and landscaping, he asked Bellin-Bellin, a crow deity, for some wind. Normally the wind was kept neatly in various sacks, but Crow opened his wind bag to such an extent he released a whirlwind which destroyed most of the trees and lifted **BUNJIL** and co. into the skyworld. We have since learnt that one of the four props that hold up the sky rotted away some time ago, and a portion of the sky fell in. Efforts to sue for faulty construction are still pending.

QUEENSLAND
MINAWARA & MULTULTU

Kangaroo creator gods. It's quite a handy form for getting about: hippety hoppety hither and thither, progressing in leaps and bounds. Just think, Skippy could be a descendant of theirs. There is an ancient legend surrounding their origins and adventures, but frankly it's so pointlessly unexciting that you would do better to invent your own. Skippy is far better value.

It's hard to take the idea of a kangaroo creator god seriously. However, no less a person than respected scientist Carl Sagan (in his book *The Dragons of Eden*) speculated upon Kangaroo Cosmology. And it turns out that the entire Universe may well be bouncing around inside the cosmic pouch.

DARANA

Creator god. He shared the Earth with humans in **DREAMTIME** and dreamt up the idea of witchetty grubs. He scooped up two large bagfuls and went off to invite other spirits to a feast. Two foraging mortals found the bags and raided them. Big mistake. The grubs glowed with an eerie light which alerted angry spirits who killed those two misfortunates.

DARANA, however, took pity and turned their bodies into destiny stones and gave them to the Dieri people to guard. They must not be scratched or famine will ensue – and if they get broken the Universe will end. They are kept carefully wrapped in feathers mixed with lard and we are not at liberty to tell you where.

THE GODS OF THE AZTECS

A host of interesting gods with completely unpronounceable names. By using Scrabble letters and adding the odd X you could probably make up your very own pantheon of Aztec deities.

The mighty Aztec Empire was happily established in Mexico before it was Mexico. Lots of colour, festivals, feathers and enough fighting and sacrifices to keep **HUITZILOPOCHTLI** happy and the sun shining. There was just one slight problem. Since that nice god **QUETZALCOATL** had zoomed off promising to come back one rainy day, Huitzilopochtli had risen to ascendancy – and he did like his heartburgers. In fact, the Aztecs believed that the gods needed constant supplies of fresh blood or they'd wither and die, which is why the entire culture was built around human sacrifice. It was practically a charity gore-a-thon on the gods' behalf. People queued up to donate their lives and even played charity football matches for the honour.

There came a day when it was time for the 52-year calendar calculations (no miserable 52-week wimpishness for the Aztecs). Now, where were all those tatty charts and ancient priests? Oh dear – what is this? It is the Day of Nine-Wind in the year of One-Reed, and it looks like Quetzalcoatl could return to overthrow Huitzilopochtli.

And return he did, or so it seemed, accompanied by strange pale men and many weapons. Ruler Moctezuma II chewed his nails and had another golden cup of hot chocolate. It was 1519 European Time and Cortez and the Spaniards had arrived…

TLALOC

Fertility god. Not nice. His favourite incense is the fuming stench of burning rubber. Worse, **TLALOC** is depicted in a mask with goggling frog eyes and outrageous buck teeth. His priests killed and ate babies to promote rain, which only appeared if the babies cried before death. What was necessary to make it *stop* raining we won't even try to imagine.

His first wife was Chalchiuhtlicue, who obviously didn't mind his buck teeth despite being the goddess of youth and beauty. Due to circumstances beyond our comprehension, she arose as a fruit-laden prickly pear tree standing in a river. Rivers are her thing, especially when she transforms into River Goddess Chalchiuhtlicue. Women in childbirth cry out to her for relief from their pains.

She prefers flowers to a human sacrifice, but that didn't stop her from flooding the entire world to drown the wicked. The entire Fourth Age of the world was destroyed. Perhaps her tempestuous husband talked her into it. After that he married again, to the so-called Lady of the Green Skirts Matlalcueitl, a goddess of singing in the rain.

His big sister is salt of the Earth Salt Goddess Huixtocihuatl. She's not to be taken with a pinch; she is a veritable saltmine of fertility. There was a yearly sacrifice for a full salt cellar. A youth had to impersonate night god Tezcatlipoca for a year, with four maidens chosen to be his wives. They must have died happy, because there was never a shortage of volunteers.

CHANTICO

Domestic goddess of the home and domestic hearth fires. Also has a neat sideline in volcanoes. She's in charge of precious things, and is very protective of her treasures. Look but don't touch, okay? Put your worldly goods in her care for the ultimate in home security. A very comforting goddess to have about the place.

But there's more to her than that. With her red serpent accessories and crown of poisoned cactus spikes, she symbolises the combination of pleasure and pain. What does that tell you about Aztec domestic life? One other thing: don't mention the paprika. There was a ban on eating the stuff during a fast put in place by Tonacatecuhtli, the god of food. Where would we be without him? Breakfast, lunch, dinner, supper: he supplies them all. And **CHANTICO** just couldn't help helping herself to a taste of the red stuff. As punishment the hearth goddess was turned into a dog. Perhaps that's why dogs like crouching beside the fire.

CHICOMECCATL

Wife of maize god Cinteotl. It must have been a staple worship. You wouldn't want to go against the grain. Not with blood sacrifices. A pretty young goddess of new corn, she sounds like a brand name for small coated crispy things. Fancy Chicoflakes for breakfast?

She can steal the hearts of eligible men. Meanwhile her priests stole not only the hearts, but every other organ. Young girls were sacrificed every September in a most unsavoury manner, to ensure the corn harvest was up to scratch. We always preferred toast for breakfast anyway. In her old age aspect she's known as Ilamatecuhtli. You should always be kind to old goddesses. Especially ones with large bared teeth. Now she likes to live in a darkened chamber where she keeps captured images of gods. Or she could just be a collector of antiques who doesn't like paying. She is also fond of fire festivals and likes burying bundles of reeds of enormous significance.

HUEHUETEOTL

The old Aztec god. He represents the Fire of Life, and therefore has a fire bowl balanced on his head. Every 52 years (an Aztec century), the gods' contract with mankind would come up for renewal, and this always caused much panic among the paranoid.

Negotiations were kept free of legal mumbo-jumbo as the Aztecs opted for chucking a bunch of victims on the bonfire. This always seemed to do the trick and **HUEHUETEOTL** was more than happy to sign up for another 52 years. Result: celebrations, feasts, gather round the hearth, keep the home fires burning etc. He also has an address: the Pole Star (post code unknown).

He may or may not have Chalchiuhtlicue for his wife. Perhaps a little bit of flooding on the side?

Huehueteotl is also connected with Xiuhcoatl, the Turquoise Fire Serpent and god of drought. Xiuhcoatl is very serpentine and is often portrayed as a jade figurine with a head at each end. This must be one of the world's most frequently used artifacts. There is hardly a book or article on Mexico that does not reproduce this image, from line drawings to full colour plates.

HUITZILOPOCHTLI

The mighty sun war god, born of Coatlicue after she was impregnated with a ball of feathers. He looks like a humming bird, but he could steal your heart. Up to 70,000 hearts could be sacrificed in one go. Team colours are blue and yellow.

After hearing nasty family gossip about his mother, he teamed up with a fire serpent and went on a murderous rampage. His brothers (who went under the catchy name of Centzonuitznaua) just happened to be the stars and were killed, and his stepsister **COYOLXAUHQUI** was given a head start in her new career as moon goddess, sans body.

Meanwhile, conflicting reports suggest that **HUITZILOPOCHTLI** was really the sun god son of Ometecuhtli and a nice friendly creator of life and vegetables. Bit of an identity crisis there. But one thing's for sure: under the name Mextli, he became the top god of war and sacrifice in Mexico.

MICTLAN

Lowest level of the Aztec Underworld, a vast veritable labyrinth of layers and levels which needed looking after by Mictlantecuhtli, the grinning god of death, and his wife Mictecacihuatl. He is very skeletal with big staring eyes, and guards the bones of those who've passed on.

Now here's a god that loves his work! He is a grinning maniac with his liver dangling from his chest. He almost looks like an over-the-top game show host. And ratings for Mictlantecuhtli's Supreme Sacrifice Show were unbeatable. He was never short of contestants — and with such a genial host it's no wonder that victims were queuing up to be sacrificed. Death was considered a much better prize than some boring old million-dollar cheque.

Gods of the Underworld were usually depicted in garish colour in two-dimensional form. Three-dimensional gods with those colours would be a bit over the top. But **MICTLAN** itself is a gloomy, dank and depressing place, full of worms and creepy-crawlies, and lots of bones. They loved their bones. **QUETZALCOATL** had a lot of trouble persuading Mictlantecuhtli to give them up for rebirth in the Fifth World.

PULQUE

Fiery Aztec alcohol which gave its name to a whole pantheon of drinking gods from Mexico. The Totonac goddess of alcohol Mayahuel invented Pulque, a potent tipple fit for the gods. She got the idea of distilling agave seeds after watching the exploits of a drunken mouse. At one point teetotallers tried to stamp her out. No chance – she is far mightier than Minnie Mouse.

Her husband **PATECATL**, the god of medicine, then pepped it up a few notches by adding certain roots to the maguey cactus mixture under the illusion that it was amazingly beneficial 'Pulque Physic'. This illusion was actually caused by the narcotic hallucinations on top of the alcohol. With many secret ingredients **PULQUE** had psychedelic properties in abundance. And no, we don't have a recipe.

Pulque proved so popular that it attracted a whole pack of drinking deities. These Pulque gods abandoned their agriculture, their farms and their mineral water in order to get royally drunk. Take, for example, the beer god Tezcatzontecatl. There is an unsubstantiated rumour that he owned a chain of taverns which once stretched across the Aztec Empire. Did they bear such names as The Pulque Pub, The Seven Rabbits, The Pulquinn, The Rabbit & Cactus, The Spinal Tap Room, Bunny's Bar and the Twitchery Brewhouse?

A particular group of them are called the Centzon-Totochtin, meaning 'Infinite Rabbits'. These drunken bunny deities represent the infinite ways that people can be affected by intoxication. Their leader is Ometotchtli – presumably he can drink all the other bunnies under the table.

XOCHIPILI

God of love and niceness. He's red and skinless but quite nice with it. Being something of an Aztec hippy, he goes for flowers, singing and dancing, as well as guarding the souls of dead warriors who turn into humming birds. Cute. He carries a pointy stick and likes to poke it around. If the tip penetrates your heart you'll fall in love. You get the point.

His sister is the love goddess Xochiquetzal, the flower feather goddess. She loves games and loves dance, but mostly just loves love. As goddess of love, she's surrounded by butterflies and creates a warm glow wherever she goes. Aren't they sweet?

His brother is Ixlilton, specialising in health and dancing. He's possibly the first god of aerobics.

TONATIUH

Sun god. Looks after warriors, particularly those who die in his service, and rules the present age of the world. He needs revitalising each morning with fresh hearts still pumping blood. Best stick to orange juice.

But he wasn't always so demanding. In fact, he started off as the lowly nonentity Nanautzin, and only got to his present position through good luck and fortitude. Known as The Scabby One, he was weak, diseased and cringy. But his modest courage led to the ultimate promotion as reward for his fortitude.

Nanautzin started out as the smallest and ugliest of the gods, but when the vacancy of sun god became available, he leapt at the chance to improve his lot. Dressed in humble reeds, he turned up at the interview to discover only

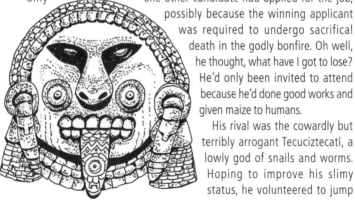

one other candidate had applied for the job, possibly because the winning applicant was required to undergo sacrifical death in the godly bonfire. Oh well, he thought, what have I got to lose? He'd only been invited to attend because he'd done good works and given maize to humans.

His rival was the cowardly but terribly arrogant Tecuciztecatl, a lowly god of snails and worms. Hoping to improve his slimy status, he volunteered to jump into the sacrificial flames to become the sun. But as soon as the fire was lit, Tecuciztecatl lost his nerve and chickened out. The courageous Nanautzin jumped into the flames and became **TONATIUH**, the glorious sun.

Ashamed, Tecuciztecatl leapt after his rival, but most of the fire had turned to ash. An eagle swooped down and carried them both to the sky. The sunny Nanautzin shone resplendent, but cowardly Tecuciztecatl made a very feeble moon. The gods jeered and threw a rabbit at him. Although he changed his name to Metzli to avoid embarrassment, he still bears the bruises to this day.

QUETZALCOATL

Famed Aztec feathered serpent and son of creator god biggie Ometecuhtli. **QUETZALCOATL**'s brother is Xolotl and his mother is top goddess Coatlicue. He helped create the cosmos and instigated the system of universal death and rebirth. Think wind rippling through grasses and foliage, green plumes, feathers, scales.

He also makes the odd appearance as Ehecatl, a wind and weather god. Archaeologists cannot make up their minds whether in this form he resembled a duck or a monkey. We've scrutinised many statues of him and still don't know the answer. All we know is that he always looks very pleased with himself.

Quetzalcoatl ruled the Fifth World cycle and created fifth-generation humans by sprinkling his blood over the bones of the previous tenants. Of course the bones first had to be rescued from **MICTLAN**, which was no easy task as Mictlantecuhtli was playing finders-keepers. Quetzalcoatl brought culture to mankind and also agriculture. But most importantly, he brought chocolate!

TLAZOLTEOTL

The eater of filth and dirt. Do you really want further details? Well, okay, if you insist. **TLAZOLTEOTL** is the goddess of confession, purification and rescue from spiritual uncleanliness, especially in the sexual line. If you have a filthy mind or you want to dig the dirt, just turn to her. She's ready to hear all your confessions and will delight in gobbling up your filthy thoughts. When she sucks up your sin this will hopefully leave you feeling pure and clean, but be careful -- you could run the risk of being flayed alive. Ironically she's often seen as a statuette in craft shops, sold as a love goddess giving birth.

Her son, Centeotl, is a transexual maize god. Yes, amazingly enough, he used to be a maize goddess. We don't know who performed the sex-change operation – possibly his mother.

YACATECUHTLI

Director of the chamber of commerce, **YACATECUHTLI** offers insider trading only and it's very difficult to obtain membership. The secret symbol is a bundle of twigs. Merchants (known as pochtecas) who travelled distant and dangerous lands would halt their caravans at night and build an effigy of him from their walking sticks. He would then guard their precious merchandise while they dreamt of wealth.

His symbol is the cross, which he appears to be carrying as though attempting to hawk it from door-to-door. Makes a change from double-glazing – although we don't know if he offers any kind of warranty. Some sources state that his name means 'Lord of the Nose'. He may have a nose for business but Lord of the Vanguard is a better translation. Or at least, a less silly one.

COYOLXAUHQUI

Daughter of Coatlicue, she is Miss Golden Bells the moon goddess. She caused a lot of domestic bother after disapproving of her mother's bedroom liaison with a ball of feathers. But from Coatlicue's pregnant womb sprang new brother **HUITZILOPOCHTLI**, who was somewhat over-protective of his mum and cut **COYOLXAUHQUI**'s head off. Still, the lad made the best of a bad job and flung her head into the sky, where it became the moon. We don't know who installed the bells.

ITZLI

God of sacrifice, in charge of the sacred stone knives used for ritual slaying. Like this entry, he's short and to the point. But we must point out that Aztec sacrificial knives were not the grim instruments of torture you might imagine. In fact, they were adorned with cute little faces with wide staring eyes. This must have been the Aztec equivalent of a dentist's drill covered in Mickey Mouse stickers. 'Open wide Johnny, this won't hurt a bit…'

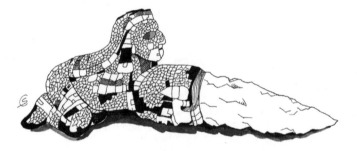

OPOCHTLI

God of all the tools for bird snaring, hunting and fishing. He was also left-handed, the only instance of a left-handed god we know of. So if you didn't catch anything, you could always fall back on the excuse of being forced to use a left-handed fish hook.

TEMAZCALTECI

She looks after saunas, baths, jacuzzis or whatever bathing methods the Aztecs used. We're not sure what manner of detergent is used, but she is very good at keeping demons away from naked people. Soap yourself in safety.

THE GODS OF THE CARIBBEAN

This covers the islands of the Caribbean including Cuba, the Dominican Republic, Haiti, Jamaica and Puerto Rico. Much of the slave trade was directed to these areas, especially Haiti, from the Dahomey, Ebo and Yoruba tribes in Africa. Unknown to their captors the enslaved took their gods with them.

Traditional beliefs were mixed and stirred with the prevailing Roman Catholic rituals and Voodou became a powerful influence, especially in Haiti where the slaves eventually launched a successful rebellion against their oppressors and have been independent ever since. Not always happily.

'Voo' means introspection; 'dou' means the unknown. Although possession is said to be nine-tenths of the law and the Catholic religion claims 85 per cent faith, this is not always what it seems – not even with syncretism. Voodou has spread and various brands have taken hold on other islands. Meanwhile, other deities have drifted in from the nearest parts of South America.

Principally the gods and spirits in this section will be Voodou, but not the Voodoo of Hollywood with zombies and pin-ridden dolls lurching all over the place. Voodou does have its unsavoury aspects, but the populist Hollywood version is a highly sensationalised fiction based on stereotype and brute ignorance. A myth based on myth, if you like.

LOA

Guiding god spirits. These are the lesser deities or spirits who act under **BONDYE**. They are comparable to angels and demons of Christianity, and to the saints of Catholicism. They guide you or ride you when prancing or trancing. In other words the **LOA** are spirits of possession. They include Grand-Bois, a Loa of the forest, and Loco, spirit of vegetation and herbs, and maybe Loco-weed.

BARON-SAMEDI

The great boss **LOA** spirit of the dead, and probably the most infamously famous character in Voodou. Stylish and sinister, he wears a black tailcoat, glossy top hat and dark eyeglasses. You guessed it – he's dressed like an undertaker. But unlike most mortal undertakers, he smokes cigars on duty, twirls a cane and goes in for trance dancing. When not on the graveyard shift he likes to party – particularly on Saturday nights which is why he's called **BARON SATURDAY**. He employs a bouncer called Bossu.

In his graveyard persona of Baron-Cimetiere, he watches over cemeteries. This isn't just a passive role, what with body-snatchers on the look-out for zombie material. As Baron-La-Croix, he stands at the metaphysical crossroads of life and death and may even be a manifestation of Ghede himself.

Of course he might just be a drinking buddy. There are those who claim to have seen them both together, but anything can happen when you drink vast quantities of rum and hot pepper and trance the night away. Not to mention the odd chicken sacrifice. His wife is Maman-Brigette who is so jolly and full of jokes that it's fun when she escorts you to the Underworld.

BONDYE

Very senior Voudou top god. He appears very aloof. Don't bother to knock – just go away. Being a mix of badly and vaguely taught Christianity and African mythology, Voodou is almost a monotheistic religion by the back door. Thus **BONDYE** is the Voodou monogod. But the polytheistic side comes with the **LOA**, giving plenty of lesser deity spirits to worship. Bondye does actually seem quite aloof (no doubt because of his African origins) while the Loa flit in and out of everyday life. Bondye is generally referred to as male although, like most monogods, it's really down to his own personal preference. Is he married to Mother Goddess Gran-Met or is he really her?

ERZULIE

The feminist **LOA** who displays every aspect of femininity that could or would be expected, with suitable titles so that you know what mood she is in. Her loving side is Erzulie-Freyda, and Erzulie-Ge-Rouge is the red-eyed version. Is it drink, weeping, badly taken photographs, or something more sinister? We don't like to ask. Her dark side is Erzulie-Dantor where she is all jealousy and vengeance in red and black. Her symbol is a heart pierced by a dagger.

Then there is Erzulie-Toho, the love goddess in a negative ugly mood. Love hurts – and it can cause sickness, depression, misery and heartache. We offer our profound sympathies and a comforting hug.

Not forgetting Erzulie-Mapiangueh, the justice version. We imagine that in this mode she rights the wrongs of painful love affairs and wreaks vengeance on judgemental jilters. But that's just a guess. And she also stands in for the Virgin Mary, although not, we imagine, in the meek and mild way.

JOYBOY

The Caribbean spirit of the drum. He is the beat-it-out bongo congo rhythm of contrapuntal conundrums. He is not averse to putting pizzazz into jazz. Rhythm is his business.

OGOUN

He is of course the African Ogun, god of metal of the Yoruba people, carrying on much as before in his new Voodou role. God of fire, war, iron, politics, blacksmiths and furnaces. If he shouts 'My balls are cold!' you must pour some rum on the ground and set fire to it. It's a rum business all round. If you see him wielding a machete, it is best to leave by the back door. He also has added extras and is Ogoun-Badagris who does phallic things, and Ogoun-Shango for fire and lightning. There's also Ogoun-Fer, fer all the other things. He is also on the Cuban Orichas List.

THE GODS OF THE CELTS

Refusing to acknowledge Roman rule, the Celts were formidable fighters under any circumstances. Exceedingly good at hit-and-run warfare, they were adept at scattering to isolated areas in small groups – taking their gods with them.

The famed Asterix comic strip gives an amusing indication of how the Gaulish contingent of Celts felt about the Romans. Ireland (never conquered by the Romans) became another stronghold, plus bits of Britain nobody else much wanted. Wales, for example. They also infiltrated the Orkneys, Balearic Islands, bits of Scandinavia and the Caucasus.

They were doing alright until Christianity came along. The church nicked some of their gods for promotional sainthood purposes and thus began the conversion process by building churches on already sacred sites.

Eventually Celtic gods got changed to trolls and fairies. It's all rather sad, but the power of the Druids is still contained in the yew trees – just check out all the yew trees growing in churchyards. And thanks to neo-pagan reconstructivism, the deity **MORRIGAN** in particular enjoys widespread worship in far-flung places. It's only a short flight to Celtsville as the crow flies.

TUATHA-DE-DANANN

The race of magical Irish gods born of the Mother Goddess **DANU**. They used to live in the Western Isles, until they travelled to Ireland on a big cloud and began beating up baddies. Their leader is **DAGDA**, and their number includes **MANANNAN-MACLIR**, Nuada and the **MORRIGAN**.

Milesius was a Spanish soldier and instigator of the 'Down With Gods' clean-up campaign. His nephew Ith had been killed by the **TUATHA-DE-DANANN** in a regrettable incident which called for retaliation, so Milesius invaded and drove them underground where they have been plotting as the Leprechaun Liberation Party for many centuries with no perceivable results. This also means the Irish are now actually Spanish.

LUGH

The Shining One. There was a race of gigantic warriors called the Fomorians who liked nothing better than to invade somewhere, pillage it and then gloat horribly. Balor, god of death and their evil king, had one huge leg and, with his one evil eye, could kill someone just by peering at them. But he usually kept it closed to avoid tripping over dead bodies all the time.

Hearing a prophecy that he would be killed by his grandson, Balor took the precaution of locking daughter Etheline in a transparent tower. (This was probably made of crystal as no Irish deity of double glazing has yet been discovered.) But he'd not reckoned on the craftiness of Cian, brother of **GOIBHNIU** the great smith, who disguised himself as an old crone with the help of the druidess Birog and wangled his way inside. The sneaky Cian had his wilful way under the duvet in the crystal bedroom. We just hope they drew the blinds first. No-one, particularly Balor, was the wiser until little baby **LUGH** popped out.

Balor was furious and tossed his baby grandson out to sea, but sea god **MANANNAN-MACLIR** was fed up with demons polluting his waters and came to the rescue.

Big Mac took the baby under his fin and raised Lugh as his child until he was old enough to stay with Uncle Goibhniu. His foster mother was earth goddess Tailtu, who died of overwork after clearing a forest on her own. Lugh decided there should be a festival in her honour on 1 August. This festival became known as Lughnasadh, and its symbol was the shamrock.

Under this parentage Lugh grew so strikingly handsome and amazingly skilled that he decided to apply for the post of apprentice god. Passing an interview at the god centre with flying colours (and flying stones), he zoomed up the career ladder to become top god. And the rest is history. Lugh waged triumphantly against baddies for many years and eventually slew his wicked grandad with a sling.

After fathering **CUCHULAINN**, the Irish hero, Lugh's Celtic powers dwindled as Christianity became ever more dominant. He slid slowly down the mythological ladder and ended up as the first leprechaun. How embarrassing.

CUCHULAINN

Known as the Hound of Ulster, **CUCHULAINN** was a champion tough guy. He was the son of the mighty **LUGH** and Dechtire.

Cuchulainn performed all manner of manly heroic deeds, armed with his trusty Gae-Bholg – a rather nasty spear. Whenever it penetrated a body, thirty barbs opened up, causing irreparable damage and a horrid mess. Cuchulainn's original name was Setanta – but he changed it after having destroyed the guard dog of Cullan the Smith. Regretting this action, the hero offered to stand in until a replacement beast could be found.

We're not sure if he actually crouched down on all fours and made barking noises, but he certainly kept the burglars away. From that day forth, he called himself Cuchulainn – 'The Hound of Cullan'. Our hero had many adventures, and in the end believed he was tough enough to beat death itself. Heroes like him didn't need wimpish immortality bestowed, so he turned it down. The **MORRIGAN** taught him a lesson about that…

MANANNAN-MACLIR

Mighty Irish sea god of many a heroic tale. His dad was the mighty Lir, possibly used by Shakespeare as the basis for King Lear. He can take the form of a heron or sneak around in his invisible cloak, and is fond of affairs with mortals. If you see any children with webbed fingers or toes it's down to him.

His son Mongan was the result of some hanky panky after a bit of shape-changing to impersonate a king whose wife he fancied. When the resultant baby was three days old, Big Mac sneaked him off to his 'Land of Promise'. Mongan grew up to inherit his father's shape-changing abilities. He put them to such good use that now no-one knows what sort of shape he is in.

His daughter Aine chose a life of landlocked love. She killed a king who tried to rape her, then branched out into Irish agriculture. She had her own Aine's Hill in County Kerry, where midsummer revels were held when she took on a new identity as a fairy queen.

A member of the **TUATHA-DE-DANANN** clan, Big Mac rules the sea, forecasts the weather and looks after Mag Mell, the seaside town of the dead. Realms of the deceased are usually pretty grim, but having kicked out the previous management he's transformed the place into a paradise. His official headquarters is the Isle of Man, but we're not sure how much of a paradise that is. Why not take a holiday there and send us a postcard?

DAGDA

Irish broth of a god. Leader of the **TUATHA-DE-DANANN**, he's the god of life and death, war, banquets and magic. He cornered the Irish fast food market with his huge cauldron full of everlasting food and a boar which never stops roasting.

His club is so large it has to be transported on wheels, and if he slaughters you with the business end, don't worry as the handle can bring you back to life. He's married to the **MORRIGAN** mob and his daughter is the fiery Saint Brigit, popular goddess in charge of poetry, healing, smithcraft ... and martial arts. He also got up to some extra-marital naughties with a water goddess named Boann. This liaison resulted in **AONGHUS**. Big-bellied, cheerful and raucous, **DAGDA** is known in Celtic circles as 'Da Good One'.

MIDIR

Son of **DAGDA**, he was involved with the **TUATHA-DE-DANANN** dynasty and tended to think of himself more as a politician than a god (a staggering role reversal in our experience). Naturally he wasn't too good at it; his policies weakened the party of gods, allowing the Milesian Party to win the next dictatorship.

His first wife Fuamnach was not at all pleased when he married a second, called Etain. With a little help from friends, she magically changed Etain into a pool of water.

MIDIR, very perplexed when his second wife went missing, started investigations on a godly scale. To keep ahead of the game, Fuamnach then changed Etain into a worm. And then a fly ... but whoosh, the fly flew down her throat, and – as happens surprisingly often in these cases – Fuamnach became pregnant. Eventually Etain was reborn – as a mortal. Growing from a baby into she knew not who, she married a king called Eochaidh. But she really fancied his brother Ailill, which probably caused a little ill-will.

To cut a long story short, one day she met Midir again, had a memory lapse in reverse and fancied him something rotten. To untangle the whole marriage confusion, he managed to win her at a game of chess, and although we're sure there's much more, we should stop whilst we have a relatively happy ending.

AONGHUS

The Celtic answer to **CUPID**. As a love child of **DAGDA** and Boann he carried on the tradition to become a love god, learning to play the harp and lulling the ladies with his smoochy lyrics.

To sustain his reputation as a romantic rascal he ran off with Etain, the wife of his stepbrother **MIDIR**. But eventually he plumped for Caer, the airy-fairy maiden. He dreamt about her, swooned and mooned … and finally passed the test of picking her out from amongst the huge flock of swans amongst which she mingled in her swan maiden outfit. **AONGHUS** was then granted permission by her father to feather his nest by marrying her.

Four lovebirds were often to be seen circling above the curly head of this holy heart-throb. These are the symbols used for kisses at the end of love letters: XXXX. More than four and they will go to waste.

FINTAN

The salmon of knowledge. Where did the salmon get its knowledge? From pootling around in Nechtan's holy well of all knowledge and inspiration. Where did the well get its info? From the hazelnuts of knowledge which overhung the well.

All was going swimmingly until **DAGDA**'s mistress Boann managed to upset the well. She upset it so much it chased her down the hill and boiled into the River Boyne. **FINTAN** went whooshing into the river as well and was caught by Finegas, an ancient druid. What bait he used is a piscatorial secret known only to those who go fishing for souls.

This was definitely catch of the day. Finegas was very pleased but also slightly druidcidal because he lacked an audience. But no – the legendary hero Finn-Maccool, cool young leader of the Fenians, had witnessed his triumph. After a bit of persuasion Finn was persuaded to try his hand at being a celebrity chef.

The poached salmon was soon sizzling knowledgeably on a makeshift spit over carefully selected kindling. But Finn-Maccool had culinary shortcomings and burnt his thumb on a hot fin. When he sucked the

resulting blister a great splurge of knowledge was released into his head. Finegas, who knew about these things, relinquished his portion saying: 'Go for it son – you need the wisdom. Eat all the half-burnt half-raw fish garnished with stinging nettles, I just enjoy the fishing. I'm not that hungry. Besides I'm already far wiser than I need to be.'

With a salmon that smart, it's more than likely that burning Finn with a fin was a ruse to put a cunning escape into effect. Meanwhile, Finn's digestive system couldn't cope and all the knowledge passed onto his son **OISIN**.

BELENUS

The famous sun god who shines through numerous names. Bel for short, Beli to the Welsh and Bile to the Irish. Billingsgate in London comes from Bile's Gate. The Romans liked him as well. On 1 May he has his very own festival called Beltaine where sun worshippers can turn out in force if they are hardy enough.

BODB-DEARG

Son of **DAGDA** and last of the Celtic top gods. When the gods thought it was time to call it a day and retire to luxury homes and palaces concealed in mounds and hills, he took over from Dagda, being his eldest son. **MIDIR** and Lir were not happy about this and went off in a huff to settle in distant districts.

CERNUNNUS

A very deer god. He has antlers and runs around a lot with wild animals. He is probably also the entity known as Herne the Hunter, worshipped in Great Britain and very popular with Morris Dancers.

CROM-CRUAICH

'Lord of the Mound'. A very primitive god of sacrifice, and the chief idol of Ireland. **CROM-CRUAICH** was a large Megalithic standing stone at Magh Slaecht, surrounded by twelve subservient stone pillars and an air of mystery. Each year children were sacrificed to him to ensure fertile crops and good harvests.

Eventually Christianity came along and put a stop to all that. St Patrick said it was made of gold, and that he destroyed it with a wave of his crosier. He also claimed that there was a demon inside which jumped out and ran off. Crom-Cruaich then bowed down to Patrick and went all droopy, remaining so forevermore. This was a great public relations exercise for Christianity. But we feel St Paddy was not one to let a little wild exaggeration stand in the way of one of his yarns.

DANU

Celtic goddess of wind, wisdom and fertility. More importantly, she's the Irish mother goddess who brought into being the **TUATHA-DE-DANANN**, her own chosen people who originally ruled Ireland. As a mother goddess, she's renowned for suckling godlets. There are two hills in County Kerry still known as the 'Paps of **DANU**'. You may have heard of Danny Boy, but she is the original Danu girl. She's also the mother and daughter of **DAGDA**, which is quite a neat trick.

EPONA

Horse goddess of mares, gallops and fertility. As a protector of horses, **EPONA** was held in high esteem by all Gauls, and even the visiting Romans thought it best to offer her lumps of sugar now and again. She rides side-saddle so is a bit behind in the equestrian department. In fact, there are those who believe Epona is actually the pony, and the woman rider is just someone to whom she is giving a lift.

FAND

Mrs **MANANNAN-MACLIR**. She caused a few difficulties when she left her husband and then had trouble when the **FOMORII** mob whistled at her and made improper suggestions. She sent for the hero **CUCHULAINN** to sort them out, but could not resist having the hots for him. He was already married to Emur, and this caused lots of soap opera hysteria with the two males and the two females pointing fingers and shouting agitatedly. Manannan-Maclir got into the best flap because he had a magic cloak. When he flapped it, **FAND** agreed to return to him, although she would never be capable of seeing Cuchulainn again however hard she looked. This was further reinforced by drinks of forgetfulness from the druid breweries.

FOMORII

The misbegotten, misshapen clan of creatures that crept out of the sea to try and take over Ireland. First were the Firbolg and last came the **TUATHA-DE-DANANN – DANU**'s mob who had **LUGH** to help kick arse. The top **FOMORII** of the time was Balor, who went down in an epic David & Goliath type duel with Lugh. Then it was goodbye to the Fomorii.

GOIBHNIU

The great smith, who loves tinkering about wid earthly tings. He's the sole supplier of weapons to the **TUATHA-DE-DANANN** and specialises in patent swords that never miss their target. He also has a good sideline in brewing beer of immortality. With an uncle like this, no wonder **LUGH** excelled at everything.

OGMA

God of eloquence and runes. His name seems to be short for Ogmious, who invented a sort of Celtic shorthand called the Ogham Runes. These are mostly symbols for various trees, and apart from engravings on funeral stones and the like, remain somewhat mysterious. It seems the Ogham Runes were used by druidic types for divination and possibly solving early crossword puzzles. So no-one in this day and age knows quite what he was trying to say. Probably blarney.

His ears are chained to his tongue, which seems rather masochistic, but we are told it is to signify in some bizarre way that he is the god of eloquence. Or maybe he is just tongue-tied. Or likes talking to himself. His son is Mac-Ceht. Does that seem eloquent to you? It looks like the sound someone makes when clearing a throat to expel a large blob of phlegm. Has he taken over as the tweeting god of blogs?

MORRIGAN

The megalithic mother goddess and the 'Phantom Queen'. Don't attempt to mix it with the **MORRIGAN**. You are very unwise to mess with her and her sisterly accomplices. She was one of the original members of the **TUATHA-DE-DANANN** (people of the goddess **DANU**) who chose Ireland as their headquarters. This was good preparation for battle and shenanigans as the Fir Bolgs had to be defeated first.

As a shape-changer she can turn from ravishing beauty to hag, from battle crow to **BEAN-NIGHE**, all in triple time. This has caused a great deal of confusion to careless mythologists and innocent Godcheckers. Some sources claim there are three of her. But as her sisters Badb and Nemain usually join in the fray, this is not surprising. There could have been more as Fea, Fotla and Nemain, other warrior goddess compatriots with shape-changing abilities, were hardly likely to sit on the sidelines when things got exciting. With crows wheeling and shrieking and startling transformations going on, who is going to stop to count? Especially when you are fleeing in terror, knowing they always picked the winning side.

When **MEDB**, the queen of Connaught, employed the Morrigan mob in her battle against Ulster and **CUCHULAINN**, more confusion was caused – as Medb is similar to Badb. Badb was not as bad as Medb, and the Morrigan forces used fear itself as a weapon rather than adding to the slaughter. Morrigan does have a loving side to her nature, and gave the Irish hero Cuchulainn every chance to make love not war. But would he listen? That's why he is now only commemorated as a statue of a dying warrior with a Morrigan crow on his shoulder. Who knows what she could be saying to him? Far from fading away, the Morrigan is still exceedingly popular and has many followers. There no longer seems to be a pecking order for battle crows; she is more into utilising Earth energy – which is very nice to know. A dark green goddess from the Emerald Isle.

MEDB

Bloodthirsty queen of Connaught with sex, death and drink thrown in. She liked her suitors to fight to the death, offering them a crown as a prize. Of course they had no idea how short their reign would be. Her name means 'Intoxication' – which in her case was invoked by more than just the drink.

Her boyfriend owned a famous white bull. She thought it would be fun to match it by sending some of her hooligans to snatch the famous brown bull of Ulster. It would also offer an opportunity to test the mettle of **CUCHULAINN**, son of **LUGH**. He was a real broth of a boy, who had taken the post of warrior and hero for the king of Ulster. This sort of cattle raiding leads to serious conflict and Cuchulainn was a serious conflictor.

Meanwhile the bulls were having their own conflict. They hated each other and, being seriously legendary bulls, rampaged and fought over the whole of Ireland. White Bull eventually won and Brown Bull thundered back to Ulster, mortally wounded and shedding enough entrails to start meat pie factories thoughout the realm.

Meanwhile the Ulster men, for a little light entertainment, had captured a female warrior called Macha and forced her to run a race whilst heavily pregnant. She won of course but cursed all Ulster men to suffer childbirth pangs whenever they engaged in conflict. They laughed, but Macha was related to **MORRIGAN**, a goddess not to be messed with. So when conflict started **MEDB** had the Morrigan and Macha's curse on her side.

Cuchulainn was impervious to such things and carried on regardless as his men writhed on the ground. But there was a weak spot. In his quest for fame and glory Cuchulainn had dismissed immortality as only fit for wimps. The Morrigan had tried to persuade him he was not going to win this fight, but he spurned her advances and was forced to lash himself to a rock. Mortally wounded, he fought to the last gasp, with Morrigan in crow form perched on his shoulder.

When Christianity arrived, Medb was taken down a few notches and faced relegation in the form of Mab, spiteful queen of the fairies. Think of her the next time you see Queen Mab in *A Midsummer Night's Dream*.

BEAN-NIGHE

The Washer at the Ford. She runs the **MORRIGAN** laundry service, coming soon to a battle near you. Think scare tactics. An unsuspecting soldier wakes up one morning, stumbles down to the stream and discovers that his smalls are in the clutches of a frightful hag. The creepy old washerwoman is scrubbing a blood-stained uniform in the stream. His uniform.

The garments drip red into the water and she glares at him with a 'you're next' look in her eye. Then she turns into a crow and flaps off. Result: the poor soldier returns to camp with the sinking feeling that today's battle won't be going his way. His clothes are sodden, his sword has gone rusty, and crows swirl around looking him straight in the eye. They lick their beaks as the enemy forces surge into the camp…

Gods are not much concerned with domestic duties. When you have incredible power you are not going to fiddle faddle around with the washing up. A swift thunderbolt or flood will get it out of the way. Gods that do take in washing tend to disguise themselves as hags or crones. It stops those awkward questions. A baleful look and a bucket of blood should be enough to prevent almost anybody from dumping a shopping trolley in the river.

OISIN

Son of the Fenian hero Finn-Maccool and a goddess called Sadb, daughter of **MEDB** and Ailill, the king of Connaught, whom Finn ran across when she was a deer. The circumstances become increasingly bizarre. Sadb was abducted by persons unknown whilst pregnant. Finn-Maccool ran across a small boy when out with his hounds one day, not realising it was his son **OISIN**. Finn was a great one for cross-country running into strange situations with dogged persistence.

It now turns out that Sadb had been the granddaughter of **DAGDA**, making **OGMA**, god of eloquence, an uncle of Oisin. What with Finn having eaten the **FINTAN**, the salmon of knowledge, without seemingly having digested it, all the eloquence and wisdom got passed to Oisin who became top poet, songwriter and sensational lyre-plucker.

Then Oisin met Niamh, a daughter of **MANANNAN-MACLIR** (how many daughters does this God have?) as she came trotting up on her steed

with the golden mane and silver hooves. To his delight she invited him for a ride to 'The Land of Promise'.

We don't know what went on there, but it went on for a long time, and Oisin not having been able to send a postcard home with 'having a lovely time – see you all soon' scrawled on it, due to there being no postal service at all, thought he should just nip home to let folks know. Niamh lent him her magic horse, but warned he must not get off it, as it would return without him and there would be no way back.

Back in Ireland, Oisin found he had done a Rip Van Winkle sort of thing; not so much sleeping, but you get the general picture. Everyone he had known was either dead or departed. Helping some men to clear a boulder from a track, he slipped off the horse. Then the thudding of hooves and the horse was gone. He tried to jump up and found that he himself was now incredibly old and frail. It is said he was found and taken to tell his tale to St Patrick, because by now the newfangled Christianity was claiming the land.

RUADAN

God of spying and espionage. The son of Bres and Brigit, he was sent by his sneaky father to spy for the **FOMORII**. He infiltrated **GOIBHNIU**'s weapon foundry and found him engaged in making the latest slim shaft, super-sharp, swivel action spears. Grabbing one, he stuck it into the great godsmith, but perhaps he had not had time to study the instructions as Goibhniu calmly pulled it out and showed him how it should be used – with deadly effect. Sklitch! When Brigit discovered that her son had been totally shafted, her wailing was such that it started the tradition of keening, used ever since at Irish wakes.

SHEELA-NA-GIG

Primitive goddess of fertility in the British Isles. She's lewd, rude, nude and very crude, displaying her most intimate parts to scare away death. She's highly respected – and something of a feminist icon due to her empowering delight in exhibiting her body without shame. Funny how things turn out. You may even find a representation of her on the outside of a British church, showing her wares to passers-by. Rubbings are strictly forbidden.

SUCELLOS

Very popular god of prosperity and good fortune – if you deserve it. He's known as the Good Striker. This has no connection with football – it refers to his hammer. If you're dying, he'll put you out of your misery. This is the origin of the phrase 'Three strikes and you're out'. On a more positive note, if he hits the ground, you'll get plenty of prosperity and luck. And also a dented lawn. Apart from the hammer, **SUCELLOS** is known for carrying around a large pot which is filled with goodies. In some regions he is known as a god of alcohol – so he might be on his way to a bring-a-bottle party.

THE GODS OF THE WELSH

ANNWN

The Welsh Otherworld. As permanent rest homes go, it has a five-star rating. Amenities include a magic cauldron presided over by nine maidens which has total restorative properties, a fountain of wine, splendid gardens and orchards, excellent bird-spotting facilities and unique weather settings which render central heating obsolete.

The place is ruled by the grey-cloaked Arawn. He is fond of taking his hounds of Hell for a run to track down lost souls. This causes people to stay away and shun the Otherworld, which helps to keep the riff-raff out. There is only one rule: do not attempt to touch or steal the cauldron. Any attempt is doomed to failure – with the emphasis on doom.

These days, the untrammelled wastes of Hell are always subject to the threat of golf courses and marketing conventions.

LLEU & BLODEUEDD

LLEU had a few issues thanks to his mother Arianrhod, the daughter of Don. She had given birth in circumstances she did not like to discuss.

As a consequence, she did a most unmotherly thing and cursed her son. He could not be called by any name until she said so, must not play with weapons and could never marry a mortal human wife.

Trying to fix the wife issue, Lleu's wizardy uncle and part-time child-minder Gwyddion got together with the equally wizard-like Math, whose major claim to weirdness is that he depended upon a rather extraordinary life support system. For some reason, his feet had to be held in the lap of a virgin or he would die. Which must have been rather inconvenient for all concerned.

Together they conjured up the beautiful Blodeuedd from blossoms. However, the blooming girl turned out to be flighty and not very nice with it. She found a lordly lover and together they plotted to kill Lleu.

This was no easy task as Lleu could only be killed with a spear that took a year to make, and then only if he was standing with one foot on a goat, or some other edible animal, and the other on the edge of a bath tub. This takes some serious planning. The would-be assassins almost pulled it off, but at the crucial moment Lleu managed to turn into an eagle and fly away. It took a while to track him down and restore him to human shape.

Math and Gwyddion were not pleased about all this and turned Blodeuedd into an owl, which in the circumstances they thought was rather a hoot. Since then Lleu has tended to stay out of the public eye and may only be seen at his own convenience. His half-brother Dylan is equally absent. In fact, he leapt from mum's arms straight into the sea. Sometime later his uncle, a smith god called Govannon, killed him. The waves sighed, as sometimes they still do. That's the end of that.

CERIDWEN

A Welsh goddess who was a bit on the witchy side. She had the ugliest son in the world, whom she named Afagddu, which is a pretty ugly name. She also had a cauldron, and set to work boiling up knowledge for a year and a day so she could give her son brains, if not beauty.

A young scullion called Gwion-Bach was given pot-watching duties, and just as the brew was due, a blob fell on his finger so he licked it off. It's first come, first served with knowledge and it was all concentrated in this blob. **CERIDWEN** was so furious she chased and ate him even though he had the knowledge to change into various animals first in an attempt to escape.

Later she relented and regurgitated him as her son, but he escaped into a river and was clever enough to get himself caught in a fish trap and thereby rescued. Delighted with his cleverness, he decided to rename himself Taliesin or 'Shining Brow'. He went on to become a wizard, bard and prophet – now there's clever. Poor old Afagddu stayed ugly ever after, and Ceridwen had another son called Morfan. He went on to be a warrior, but no-one would fight him because he was too ugly.

THE GODS OF CHINA

China – the Middle Kingdom – is an ancient country full of mystery and paradox. Although hard-working and down-to-Earth, the Chinese people have always had a streak of poetry in their souls. Only the Chinese could mix sublime philosophy and mindless paperwork and get away with it.

With a recorded history reaching back practically to the Big Bang, China has had plenty of time to perfect its pantheons. Over the aeons, primitive folk religion absorbed sophisticated ideas – the common sense of Confucious (Kongzi), the ritual and magic of Daoism, the sublime spirituality of Buddhism – to produce a stir-fry mix of gods for all occasions. You certainly get value for money with China.

One thing we love about Chinese mythology is its sense of humour. For every starched civil servant in Heaven there's a mocking fable or unexpected pun. Most Chinese gods and goddesses are deified humans – which makes them as prone to mistakes as we are. But rather than airbrush out the embarrassments, China revels in them. We suspect that even the **JADE EMPEROR**, the stern-faced ruler of Heaven, sometimes has trouble keeping a straight face.

BA-XIAN (THE EIGHT IMMORTALS)

Eight Chinese individuals who, by pure chance, achieved immortality:

ZHONG-LIQUAN – Explosive Revelations
LU-DONGBIN – Tactical Withdrawal
CAO-GUOJIU – Royal Outcast
HAN-XIANGZI – The Flying Philosopher
HE-XIANGU – Self-raising Flower
LAN-CAIHE – Drunk and Disorientated
LI-TIEGUAI – Body Snatcher
ZHANG-GUOLAO – Stubborn Old Mule

See their individual entries below for thrilling details of How to Become Immortal.

Each of them represents a different aspect of Daoist perfection. Over the centuries, these characters formed a team of kindred souls. Not having the usual godly pedigree, they couldn't just mix with the gods in Heaven, who are notoriously snobbish about such things. Instead they set up home at **PENGLAI-SHAN**, a mountainous island located in the mysterious east.

As told in many famous Daoist legends, they embarked on incredible adventures and quests – taking on dragons and demons, righting wrongs and putting things to rights. And every so often, a mortal would come along for the ride, hoping for a swig from the Bottle of Immortality.

We can't wait for the television mini-series.

#1 ZHONG-LIQUAN

Fat, bald and cheery with a long beard, he was fond of dabbling with alchemy, and became a bit of a hermit to pursue the esoteric. His peaceful dabbling came to an end when one particularly risky experiment caused an explosion in his dwelling. The walls shook and a large crack appeared, exposing to view a hidden container. This contained a goodly dosage of the elixir of life. Whether it was in tablet or liquid form we can't say, but it more than compensated for the damage because **ZHONG-LIQUAN** became immortal. Perhaps because of his explosive capabilities, he is also the god of military operations.

#2 LU-DONGBIN

He was of princely descent. In his privileged student days, he'd been given a magic sword by a passing dragon. But one day, after falling asleep in a pub, he dreamt of his future life. Things were going from bad to worse with him eventually being killed by bandits. To escape his fate, he decided to adopt the Dao way of faith, and became a buddy of **ZHONG-LIQUAN**. Not only did he escape the bandits, but he became immortal. Zhong-Liquan must have given him a nip of that immortality elixir. Moral: choose your drinking partners wisely.

#3 CAO-GUOJIU

Brother of a Song Dynasty empress, he hated all the corruption and left to meditate in the mountains, where his golden tablet of introduction ('I am the brother of Empress Cao and hereby command the utmost respect') was not a lot of use. But he did meet **LU-DONGBIN**, who coached him in finding the way and immortality. No doubt the elixir came in handy again. With his new-found status, **CAO-GUOJIU** was happy to become the patron godlet of actors and performance.

#4 HAN-XIANGZI

A highly educated philosopher who fell out of a peach tree. If he was testing gravity, it didn't work: he fell upwards. As luck would have it, the peach tree just happened to be sacred. Was it the blessed Peach Tree of Immortality, which bears fruit once every 3,000 years? If so, he was a very naughty boy for climbing it. Grabbing at a sacred branch bestowed immediate immortality. And now he hangs around with the other **EIGHT IMMORTALS**, playing his flute and making the most profound philosophical observations.

#5 HE-XIANGU

She is also a celebrity chef and goddess of housekeeping. One day, trying out new recipes, she ground up a shiny gem, which was more than likely a stone from a peach of immortality. She mixed the powder into a cordial and presto! 'Heshee Peachee, the flavour that stays with you forever.' After a sip or two she found that she could fly over mountains. At first she used this talent to fill her larder with new and exotic fruits from places far away. But it wasn't long before she spotted other immortals on her travels and threw her lot in with them.

#6 LAN-CAIHE

Originally a busker, beggar and herb seller, he was also very effeminate, and usually drunk. His fortunes changed dramatically after he came across a crippled beggar. For washing the beggar's boils and sores and nursing him back to health, **LAN-CAIHE** was rewarded with immortality. With bizarre dress sense, Lan-Caihe wears only one boot, and a belt made of wood. In the summer he wraps up warm with a thick coat, but this is discarded in the winter in preference for sleeping semi-naked in the snow.

#7 LI-TIEGUAI

This is an out-of-the-gutter experience. Ascetic and mystic, **LI-TIEGUAI** travelled far and wide. Not caring for the public transport of the time, he liked to float whither he wished minus body. One day, his spirit paid a visit to Great Sage Lao-Zi and learned the secrets of immortality. He arrived back to find his body had been cremated a little prematurely and was now a heap of ashes. In this situation you need to find a replacement body very rapidly indeed, or your chances of getting into Heaven are zilch. The best Li-Tieguai could find on the spur of the moment was a dead beggar in a ditch. Worse still, upon entry and activation, he discovered that the body was lame and needed support from an iron crutch. But beggars can't be choosers. He'd become immortal, after all, so he made the best of it.

#8 ZHANG-GUOLAO

This splendid old character did it his way. He simply refused to die. He did drop dead once, but just got up again and carried on as if nothing had happened. That's the kind of never-say-die spirit we approve of. Furthermore, he had an amazing magic donkey which could be folded up like a piece of paper when not in use. No parking fines for him.

#8a HUAI-NANZU

Profound sage and bonus immortal. The **EIGHT IMMORTALS** took a real shine to **HUAI-NANZU**, who was grandson of the Han Dynasty empress Gao. The spiritually inclined prince joined them on their travels, and after a while managed to wheedle some wishes out of them. Just simple things like ommortality, omniscience and omnipotence. As soon as he had partaken of the elixir of immortality, Huai-Nanzu's body shed its mortal nature. He became as light as a feather and found himself shooting up into the sky. This always happens when you drink the elixir of immortality.

Rapidly gaining control of his new-found flying abilities, Huai-Nanzu pointed himself in the direction of Heaven. He thought it only proper to introduce himself and pay his respects to the gods. But in his excitement he dropped the bottle of elixir, which went spinning back to Earth and landed in his very own courtyard.

Arriving in Heaven, Huai-Nanzu prepared to introduce himself to the great and majestic **JADE EMPEROR**, who any minute now would turn in his direction and address him. He composed himself with infinitely respectful sublimation, practised his kowtow and brushed his hair. He was terribly nervous. He was unaware that far below, his farmyard animals were licking up the dregs leaking from the broken bottle…

At last, His Imperial Heavenly Majesty turned towards the new recruit and opened his mouth to speak. Huai-Nanzu summoned up every ounce of his dignity – and was unexpectedly joined in Heaven by a motley collection of freshly immortalised pigs, dogs and chickens. Their immortal nature did nothing to stop them grunting, clucking and chasing each other around the imperial chamber. Huai-Nanzu was so embarrassed he almost wished he was mortal again.

FENG-DU

The Chinese Hells. Like so many other concepts in Chinese mythology, the Underworld is a tangled mix of Daoist, Buddhist and traditional folk legend. It's not actually underground but housed in an enormous mountain on the other side of the astral plane. But all legends agree that it's a dark and sinister place something like a prison complex – with ample torture facilities.

We don't want to worry you, but Hell is open to everyone and the invitation is not negotiable. When you die, officers place your soul under arrest and march you to the office of Yen-Lo-Wang, the king of Hell. He originally ruled the place, but the **JADE EMPEROR** gave the post to Qin-Guang-Wang instead when it turned out the god of death was a bit of a softie.

The righteous take the Golden Bridge straight to eternal happiness in Western Paradise. The rest of us have to repent and suffer punishment – And **FENG-DU** is well-equipped in the punishment department. Depravity and perversion are punished by slow drowning in a putrid stinking cesspit of yukkiness, full of unspeakable stench and horrid floating things. Escaped prisoners, drug addicts, blasphemers and murderers are hung upside down. That might not sound too bad, until you discover that knee crushing, skinning and eyeball torture are part of the bargain. Then there's the black pool department. Nothing to do with the seaside resort, black in this case means the dark red of freshly congealed blood – of forgers, counterfeiters and people who write warranties for electrical goods. Atheists are flung into the Burning Wok of Oblivion. There's the Place of Screaming Torture where sexual sins are dealt with by rats who gnaw at the bodily parts concerned.

And if you have bad personal hygiene, don't think you will escape justice. For your entire life, people have been too polite to mention that you smell like an orang-utan's laundry basket – but when you're thrown into the Pool of Reeking Filth even you will get the message.

Then along comes Meng-Po, the Buddhist goddess who dishes out the Bittersweet Broth of Oblivion. Thankfully, you completely forget all the punishments you've just been suffering. You also forget your previous life, which means you are free to make the same mistakes all over again in the next one. Then you are strapped to the Wheel of Life and sent rolling into your next incarnation. And the very best of luck.

CHUANG-KONG & CHUANG-MU

Husband and wife bedroom gods. They are in charge of the bed and its associated physical activities (changing the linen, folding sheets, etc).

Together they control every aspect of our bedly behaviour, specifically sleep, sex, love, and birth. Very popular. You should leave offerings of tea, wine or After Eight mints for a good night's rest. Their festival is at the time of the Lantern Festival. This is probably a propitious time for success in the bedroom. Sleep well!

SAN-XING

The three gods of good fortune, happiness and wealth. Their name means 'Three Stars', and they are the starry-eyed stellar gods who bring luck and wealth. They are **FU-XING** (god of luck and happiness), **LU-XING** (god of wealth), and **SHOU-XING** (god of long life). If you want to find them, it's easy. Just look for the three stars of **ORION**'s Belt.

Lu-Xing is the star of honour, offering unlimited employment and promotion prospects, but first you must prove yourself worthy and industrious. The gods help those who help themselves, you know. Work hard and apply yourself with dedication, and this god will smile upon you.

Lu-Xing's special symbol is the stag; not very industrious but a runaway success when it comes to leaping up the mountain of life.

Fu-Xing is bright and cheery and full of boundless optimism. The legend tells that Emperor Wu Ti (AD 502–550) was obsessed with midgets. He ordered that all midgets be brought to the imperial court to be forced to serve as his clowns. The mothers of the midgets were heartbroken. But Yang Cheng was a kind-hearted soul and, risking his very life, wrote a forceful petition to the emperor asking him to please leave off. Instead of the instant death such impudence had earned him, Yang Cheng was granted his request. The midgets and their mothers were so grateful, they worshipped him ... and lo! he became Fu-Xing, the god of happiness and disasters averted.

The most venerable of the **SAN-XING** is Shou-Xing, the 'Star of Long Life'. He is old and bald, and carries a golden peach of immortality from Xi-Wangmu's Holy Peach Garden. These are found only in Heaven and ripen once every 3,000 years. Once he was a young and sickly lad named Zhao-Yen, who was destined to die when he reached 19. Told by a fortune-teller to enter a certain field armed with a packed lunch, he found two men playing checkers.

Having been warned to keep his mouth shut, he silently offered them spring rolls and wine, which were gratefully accepted. So gratefully, in fact, that the men, revealing themselves to be the gods of birth and death, offered him longevity. That must have been a very impressive packed lunch.

The San-Xing are symbolically attended by stags, bats and cranes, which denote their respective qualities. You'll find these on many a calendar at your local Chinese restaurant.

MONKEY

The infamous, irrepressible monkey king, trickster god, and great sage equal of Heaven. Star of stage, screen and scroll, **MONKEY** is the true hero of *Journey to the West* (*Xiyou Ji*) – the amazing novel of frivolity and profundity written by Wu Cheng'en in the sixteenth century. The lord of the apes, he was high-spirited, egotistical and full of mischievous pranks. But a niggling worry began to gnaw at him: the monkey king feared death.

To find immortality, Monkey became the disciple of Father Subodhi, a rather dour Daoist sage. After much haggling, Monkey learned about illumination, cloud-flying and the secret of the seventy-two transformations, which, thought Monkey, was extremely good value for money. It wasn't long before reports of Monkey's tricks started to reach the austere ears of the **JADE EMPEROR**. First the Dragon-Kings complained of rudeness and theft. Then Yen-Lo-Wang, the god of death, lodged a formal protest. 'That intolerable ape has just vandalised my filing system and made monkeys immortal. What are you going to do about it?'

But by his very nature Monkey was irrepressibly naughty. He just couldn't help it. He gobbled up **LAO-ZI**'s longevity pills, stuffed his face with the precious peaches of immortality, gatecrashed official parties and made insulting gestures. There was nothing for it – the ruler of Heaven called for **BUDDHA**. After a Monkey vs Buddha pissing contest, Monkey found himself lying on the ground with a mountain on top of him.

And there he stayed for 500 long years, until **GUAN-YIN** enlisted Monkey as chief disciple of the young Buddhist monk Tripitaka. Together with Sandy and Pigsy, he protected the boy on his quest to India, battling demons and righting wrongs along the way. His natural monkey trickery now had a holy purpose which he unleashed with much enthusiasm – and his uncontrollable ego was kept firmly in place by a little device of Guan-Yin's devising: a head-band made of gold which gave him terrible headaches.

After adventures beyond count, the travellers fulfilled their quest. Monkey was rewarded for all his efforts with the title 'Buddha Victorious Against Disaster' and finally made his peace with Heaven. We don't know what the great sage gets up to nowadays, but presumably he keeps himself occupied.

JADE EMPEROR

Starting at the bottom by creating the Universe, he helped **YUAN-SHI-TIAN-ZONG** bring order to the cosmos. Working his way to the top, he spent a billion aeons contemplating his holy navel before finally achieving a state of the most amazingly perfect godliness.

Having achieved illumination and omnipotence, he went on to become supreme Heavenly ruler and emperor of the universe. The human imperial ruler of China was merely a manifestation and vassal of the **JADE EMPEROR**. Earthly emperors were given leave to rule by the Mandate of Heaven, provided they checked in every so often via a Jade Pi-Disc.

The Jade Emperor's word is law and he rules all Heaven and Earth with a vast company of civil servants and bureaucrats at his beck and call. The Cheng-Huang and Tu-Di look after Earthly paperwork, and every year the **ZAO-JUN** file a report on your conduct for him to assess.

If all that's not impressive enough, the Jade Emperor found further fame when Daoism and Buddhism came into play and engulfed him in the utmost holiness, not to mention the most amazingly complicated symbolism. His list of official titles expanded in all directions: 'Most Venerable Jade Emperor of the Heavenly Golden Palace'; 'Supremely High

Emperor of the Heavens, Holder of Talismans, Container of Perfection and Embodiment of Dao' and finally, 'Most Venerable and Highest Jade Emperor of All-Embracing Sublime Spontaneous Existence of the Heavenly Golden Palace'. We think that just about covers everything.

In fact, the Jade Emperor is a master of winning without really doing anything. He knows all aspects of the Way (Dao) and its principle of least action (Wu Wei), making Heaven's regime the ultimate example of a do-nothing policy. He can become almost flustered if anything actually happens.

LONG-WANG (THE DRAGON KINGS)

Chinese dragons. Everyone knows what a Chinese dragon looks like, or do they? Actually they can have a camel's head with stag antlers, a snake neck, clam body, carp scales, eagle talons and tiger legs.

Being in charge of water and rain, the dragons can dribble themselves into dewdrops or come in floods. There are several groups of them, including celestial dragons and, most important of all, the four **DRAGON KINGS** who rule the oceans. These are the guardians of wetness in every form – rain, river, and sea. They each control one of the oceans that surround the world, and have connections with the **JADE EMPEROR**, who tells them where rain is needed.

Dragons absolutely love a party. If you're suffering from drought, get all the neighbours involved and hold the biggest street party you can manage. Buy fireworks, make elaborate dragon costumes, hire multitudes of musicians, and get ready for a good time. And then it will start raining.

They've had their ups and downs, particularly their king Ao-Kuang, who suffered humiliation at the hands of practically

everybody. Regarded as the highest and mightiest of the four ocean dragons, Ao-Kuang is majestic, utterly regal and aloof. Despite that, he's always being pestered by people after a favour. Probably the cheekiest request came from architect Lu-Ban, who wanted to borrow his entire palace for a blueprint. The king was highly flattered. 'Very well,' he said, 'I'll have it delivered first thing in the morning. But I'll need it back in three days; I'm expecting company.' As promised, the palace was flown over by a team of dragons and Lu-Ban set to work on his own version. Unfortunately, the palace was so impressively built that after three days he'd only managed to lay a few foundations and order the timber. He wanted more time.

Along came the dragons to collect the palace. Funny, it wouldn't budge. They heaved and strained but it was stuck fast. Lu-Ban had nailed it to the ground. It was a very hot day, the sun dried them out, and they all collapsed from heat exhaustion. To Lu-Ban's amazed delight, their dried-out bodies curled around the palace and around each other, and presented an awesomely impressive spectacle. He immediately tore up his blueprints and began plans for a range of templates with curled dragon motifs. These were highly successful and are still seen in China today.

Other dragons include Lei-Gong, the thunder god. But he doesn't create thunder by roaring or growling. Not him. His ear-splitting bangs are made with a hammer and chisel. We hope that doesn't spoil the magic for you.

SAN-HUANG

The legendary three sovereigns who ruled the dawn of China. They taught mankind essential survival tips and how to make a living. If you look closely, you may notice that the **SAN-HUANG** are actually snake-like reptiles with human heads. Please don't stare. Dragons are very beneficial in China.

First was Fu-Xi, a civilised god of creativity, arts and crafts. An all-round goodie, he lent a vital hand in the invention of fishing, farming and domesticating animals, and invented writing, music and do-it-yourself. Fu-Xi is very strong on home improvement, and also spiritual improvements. He's often seen with a carpenter's square — which symbolises both as he created the eight trigrams for divination.

Talking of numbers, he also invented the mathematical Magic Square after noticing cosmic numbers on the shell of the Celestial Tortoise:

```
4 9 2
3 5 7
8 1 6
```

Each line adds up to 15, however you try it.

In charge of cosmic harmony and contemplation, Fu-Xi is very popular in Daoist temples. His wife is Nu-Gua, who invented humans to give her husband something to do. The early Universe was extremely dull so she decided to liven things up by creating an exciting new species. There was plenty of raw material available, even if most of it consisted of brown mud, black mud and yellow mud. Using her own body as a guide, she fashioned new beings from the Earth. She then invented sex and marriage, for which everyone was very grateful. It certainly saved her from spending the rest of her existence playing with mud.

With her husband Fu-Xi as first ruler and teacher of mankind, all was going well for Nu-Gua until monstrous rivals Gong-Gong and **ZHU-RONG** got into a fight and caused the first great flood. Water poured from the Heavens and her human creations were devastated. To restore cosmic harmony, Nu-Gua took some brightly coloured stones from a river bank, melted them down and used them to repair the hole in the sky. She then propped up the Heavens as best she could using the legs of a turtle.

Next was Shen-Nong, a mortal in the very earliest days of China (2800 BC). His slash-and-burn policy of clearing scrublands left the ground rich in potash ready for ploughing and planting. He then taught his fellow mortals how to farm. But he's best known for his knowledge of herbs, drugs and medicine. He single-handedly tasted each and every plant in China to see what was yummy and what would kill you. Legend tells that during his research he was once poisoned no less than seventy-two times in a single day. Amazingly, he suffered no long-term ill effects. Perhaps the medicinal plants and poisonous plants cancelled each other out. He also had a transparent stomach, which did come in very handy for seeing what all those plants were doing to his insides.

Last of the three kings was Sui-Ren, god of roasting, boiling, baking, frying and toasting, who built upon the work of his predecessors. They taught mankind how to grow plants and farm animals – he taught mankind how to transform these raw materials into tasty dishes. His invention of the campfire, which led to the cooking stove, the oven and finally the computer-controlled dual-grill self-cleaning microwave appliance, lifted ancient China from a wild feudal domain to the lofty heights of civilisation. After that the humans took over with the Five Kings (**WU-DI**).

WU-DI

The legendary five kings who ruled China after the **SAN-HUANG**. The first was Huang-Di, popularly known as the Yellow Emperor. He was a skilled tactician and ingenious inventor who created many useful things, including the wheel, bricks, and astronomy. He also discovered magnets. Some tales suggest that he invented tea after a leaf fell into his mug of hot water. His wife Lei-Zu invented silk but we don't think a silkworm fell into hers.

Their sons and grandsons were not nearly as clever but ended up on the throne anyway. Although tall tales and unlikely legends make China's earliest history seem like a fairytale, the **WU-DI** are genuine historical figures who lived around 4,500 years ago. Scholars have waged many paper wars over their exact historical names and dates, but we will remain aloof and let them fight it out.

LAVATORY LADIES

Goddesses of toilets, latrines, lavatories, outhouses, closets and washrooms. Don't mock — it's the sign of a closed mind. Few outside the country know that China had toilet paper and flushing while the rest of us were still wiping ourselves with leaves. Of course, only the richest emperors could afford such luxury; common peasants had to make do with communal holes in the ground.

Anyway, to make lavatorial life a little easier to bear, the Chinese have female toilet deities, protecting, blessing and disinfecting all who use the smallest room in the house. At least two are known by name: **ZI-GU** and **QI-GU**.

The story goes that Qi-Gu was the mistress of Liu-Bang, first emperor of the Han Dynasty. It was one big unhappy family. Empress Lu hated her so much that when the emperor died, she stripped away Qi-Gu's official title — and several of her body parts. Unsatisfied, she threw the poor girl into the dirtiest, smelliest, ugliest, foulest latrine in the whole of China. She then invited the new emperor and all his ministers of state to come and look. It must have been a very carefully worded invitation, but come he did, and fainted dead away at the sight. Qi-Gu's torment became infamous, and soon she was elevated to the rank of goddess.

Zi-Gu was the beautiful wife of an actor during the Tang Dynasty. All was good until a high-ranking minister named Li-Jing fell in love with her, killed her husband, and took the unfortunate Zi-Gu as his mistress. His wife was insanely jealous. One day, while Zi-Gu was taking what can only be described as a delicate pee, Li-Jing's wife leapt out from behind a pile of toilet paper and murdered her in cold blood.

From that moment, Li-Jing's lavatory was haunted by the ghost of his ex-mistress. Strange spooky noises emanated from the closet at all hours, and even the most stout-hearted visitor would cross his legs and wait till he got home. When the news got out, Empress Wu, concerned for the kidneys of her top minister, blessed the ghost of Zi-Gu and elevated her to godly status. The haunting of the lavatory immediately ceased. A Royal

Flush. The grateful spirit of Zi-Gu ascended to Heaven and the toilet was safe to use once more.

As goddess of toilets, Zi-Gu appears in the form of a beautiful contemplative woman, her lower body wrapped discreetly in clouds. This soothing image is a far cry from the typical Chinese hole in the ground, but that's mythology for you. Perhaps due to the thoughtful navel-gazing which takes place in the bathroom, Zi-Gu is also known as the goddess of spirit writing. She inspires mediums with messages from the Astral Plane. That's why mediums never take a newspaper into the bathroom.

There may well be another toilet goddess. Any reported sightings gratefully received.

THREE BROTHERS OF THE PEACH ORCHARD

As told in *Romance of the Three Kingdoms*, the Three Brothers were **ZHANG-FEI**, **GUAN-YU** and **LIU-BEI**: a sort of Dynamic Duo plus one – or a Fantastic Four with one on holiday, or less than half of a Magnificent Seven. Pledging to save the empire from rebels and war, they plunged into the fray and performed many mighty deeds.

Zhang-Fei is the god of butchers and he's very butch, being 8 feet tall with a pantherish face, a roaring voice and mad staring eyes. He was a meat distributor by trade. He started out with animals and ended up with humans, but the principle is the same. A large, bellowing butcher of a general, he charged in regardless of danger, lost his temper every sixteen minutes and was liable to explode with fury whenever an underling dared to speak. Little wonder that Zhang-Fei was eventually killed by his own men. Steer well clear of sausages from now on.

Although a shoemaker and weaver by trade, Liu-Bei was actually a distant relative of Han Dynasty emperor Liu. In that troubled time of rebellion and civil war, friends in high places were of no avail. Still, he thought, at least everyone needs shoes. As all hell broke out across the country, with rebels and war all over the place, Liu-Bei swore a mighty oath to defend his emperor. He joined forces with Zhang-Fei and Guan-Yu and became one of the Three Peach Orchard Brothers – and an instant hero. Liu-Bei was tall, extremely good-looking, and, thanks to the fortuitous positioning of his eyeballs, blessed with amazing eyesight. Not only X-ray vision, but Y- and Z-vision too.

Guan-Yu started life as a mortal vendor of soya bean curd. But after a heroic incident, he got the taste for battle and embarked on a famous military career with Liu-Bei and Zhang-Fei. Unusually for a god of war, he uses his skill to avoid confrontations if at all possible. A peace-loving deity, he tries to minimise every battle he's in (surely you've heard of Kung Few?) But his bravery is legendary. In one famous tale, his arm was damaged in battle and needed surgery. To the incredulity of onlookers, he calmly sat playing solitaire while field surgeons did excruciating things to his tendons (just as well Solitaire is a one-handed game). When he was finally captured, Guan-Yu was told

by Wu, the evil new emperor, to change sides or face death. Guan-Yu not only refused, he uttered a terrible insult which made even the soldiers blush. For his bravery, and because he died defending legal issues, he also became the patron god of police officers. He is also worshipped as a god of literature because he managed to read a whole page of Confucius without going cross-eyed.

WEN-CHANG

The Daoist god of literature, books and writing – but only in Chinese. He started out as Zhang Ya Zi, a Zhou Dynasty sage who could predict the future and perform great transformations. With his superior knowledge of The Way (Dao), he was elevated to Heaven and now sits enthroned in the Big Dipper (Plough). He is also a god of education and learning, helping students and blessing schools. It's easy to get on his good side: all you need to do is love books.

His attendants, Kui-Xing and Zhu-Yi, stand beside him in the Heavenly hot seat. Kui-Xing was once a mortal in the academic world – a highly talented but extremely ugly student. In fact he was a typical nerd. But after having fallen off a cliff, he was rescued from certain death by a dragon and given the job of literary affairs minister. Now he oversees official paperwork, publications and post-it notes. No memo or email is small enough to escape his scrutiny.

Clad in the red robes of Heaven, Zhu-Yi is the god of school tests and examination panic. A nod from him can turn crosses into ticks and fail into top marks. A kindly god who rewards scholastic effort, Zhu-Yi comforts and supports students and test candidates who've forgotten their calculators, their pens, their crib sheets and their own names.

XI-HE & DI-JUN

XI-HE, goddess of light, and **DI-JUN**, god of the east, were parents of the Ten Suns. During the old Chinese ten-day week, every sun would take it in turn to appear in the sky each day. At the end of the week they all gathered together at the Valley of Light in the east. Being a doting mother, Xi-He would wash them, brush their teeth with Sunny Smiles Toothpaste and put them to bed in the branches of a giant mulberry tree.

After a while, the Ten Suns became bored with this routine, ran riot and all leapt into the sky at once. This caused global scorching of an apocalyptic nature, and the Emperor Yao was very cross. Di-Jun was told in no uncertain terms to take his delinquent children in hand. But they were having far too much fun to take any notice of dad. So Di-Jun decided on the short sharp shock approach and went off to have a word with Yi, the great archer, to frighten them into behaving themselves. But instead of scaring the Suns into submission, the over-enthusiastic Yi shot nine of them out of the sky. He would have shot them all, but his last arrow had been pinched by the emperor. That's why we only have one sun in the sky.

Di-Jun was so upset at the blatant murder of his nine children that he banished Yi to Earth and stripped him of all godly status. However, the western goddess Xi-Wangmu took pity on him and offered an elixir of immortality. This was promptly guzzled by his wife Chang-O, leaving him no better off.

She may have heard the elixir was great for losing weight – but when she became truly weightless and started floating up to Heaven, she began to regret her impulsiveness. Fearing Heavenly reprisals, she took refuge in the Moon and was transformed into a toad, where she remains to this day. There are many things beyond the comprehension of us mere mortals.

As lady of the moon, Chang-O glows with a brilliant eerie light and offers good fortune to those that remember her, particularly during her festival on the fifteenth day of the eighth moon, when prayers and offerings are most welcome. Being separated from her husband Yi, she's sympathetic to all lovers.

Incidentally, her brother is He-Bo, god of the Yellow River. The Yellow River (*Huang He*) is China's second longest river and probably the muddiest in the world. Over a billion tons of silt and sediment flow through it each year, giving the Yellow River its distinctive yellow colour and making it a poor choice for washing your socks in. After the Great Flood, the Yellow River was still prone to flooding. So an enthusiastic mortal named He-Bo tied heavy rocks to his back and jumped into the water as a supreme sacrifice. For his pains he was granted immortality and promoted to god of the Yellow River. Following his example, it became the custom to throw a young virgin into the river on the anniversary of his death. This practice appears to have died out, along with the virgins.

BA-JA

This dear old Mongolian general with a splendid record was rewarded in extreme old age with the job of celestial scarecrow – or Scarelocust, in this case. His new uniform included an eagle's beak, talons and a blue skin, but he was allowed to keep his general's cloak. **BA-JA**'s image was put on poles and was not always very effective as he was inclined to doze off, but as a Worzel Gummidge sort of god he is regarded with great affection.

CAN-NU

Goddess of silkworms. She was carried up to Heaven after walking past a magic horse skin, which rose up and whisked her off. She returned as a silkworm and lives in a mulberry tree. Silky but not sulky we hope.

FEI-LIAN

God of the wind. We will breeze through his most notable features: bull's horns, sparrow's head, stag's body and snake's tail. He also appears in human form and may have been that blustering gentleman you bumped into in the street last week. Something of a trouble-maker, at some stage his arch-enemy Yi shot a hole in his windbag and now he has almost run out of puff.

GUAN-YIN

Goddess of compassion and caring, and one of the four supreme **BODHISATTVAs** of Chinese Buddhism. **GUAN-YIN**'s mission is victim support. She succours the distressed and hungry, rescues the unfortunate from peril, and gives comfort and aid wherever it is needed. Guan-Yin's work would put many a charity to shame – and she doesn't ask for donations.

Known as **AVALOKITESVARA** in India, she had finally attained enlightenment after much non-struggling with non-things. She was just about to enter Heaven to join the other **BUDDHAs** when she heard the cries of the poor unsaved souls back on Earth. Her heart touched by pity, she vowed never to rest until every single soul was brought to Buddhahood. The magnitude of contemplating this task made her head explode into a thousand pieces, but she was perfectly fine after Buddha gave her a few Aspirin sutras.

Turning aside from Heaven, Guan-Yin went to the sacred island of Potuoshan and embarked on her new career. This selfless sacrifice brought her much credit, and reverence which persists to this day. As a deity often called upon to appear in the most unusual and difficult situations, Guan-Yin has the ability to transform into any living thing; in fact, she's better known in India as a male. But she often appears in female form to avoid gossip – and because she likes it. Like her Japanese equivalent **KANNON**, Guan-Yin is known as a female deity, and has taken on a modest amount of fertility work. Childless women pray to her for offspring. In this respect she is also a goddess of rice, filling it with her own milk to give nourishing titbits.

The Bodhisattva who saves us from the Three Calamities and the Eight Disasters, Guan-Yin is always on call. His – or her – peaceful benevolence has soothed many a worried brow.

HUN-DUN

Ancient god of chaos and creation. This is a whodunnit – or rather a hundunnit. Ruling the centre of the universe must have been a little tricky without eyes, nose, mouth, or indeed any orifice at all. Was he an egg (cosmic of course)?

The pre-emptive emperor before there were any empires, he was an implosion of orifices without substance, a faceless bird-like entity, and a representation of chaos. His fellow rulers from across the sea felt sorry for him and decided to give him a few useful apertures. Much time was spent boring experimental holes and drilling features into his face. Finally their work was done, and very good it was too. Unfortunately, the strain of this primitive cosmetic surgery without anaesthetic was too much for **HUN-DUN** and he keeled over, dead.

LI-JING & LI-NEZHA

Gatekeeper of Heaven and an immortal of the Han Dynasty and his son. Even if you are well-versed in godly ways, it's just possible his story could stretch your credulity. Formerly a monstrous immortal with three heads, eight arms and nine eyes, **LI-NEZHA** was sent down to Earth by the **JADE EMPEROR** to subdue a plague of demons. Smuggled in by a fellow immortal, he turned up in the womb of Emperor **LI-JING**'s wife and would have been killed at birth if he hadn't made certain auspicious signs and flashed a magic bracelet at them.

They called him Third Prince. Soon he was a strapping six-year-old lad, 6 feet tall and with pants of fire – literally. One day, while he was paddling in the sea, he set it alight. Puzzled by the mysterious flames, Ao-Kuang, the **DRAGON KING** of the Eastern Sea, sent his princely son Ao-Ping to investigate. But in a playful mood of boyish high spirits, Li-Nezha killed him.

The enraged king zoomed from his underwater palace seeking revenge, but was defeated himself in a most humiliating manner. The other Dragon Kings, pausing only to squabble over the empty throne, got their own back by bursting into the emperor's home and kidnapping both **LI-JING** and his wife. This was a delicate situation requiring the utmost diplomacy and tact. So an abashed Li-Nezha sulkily committed suicide and his parents were released.

But the next morning a rolling ball of flesh turned up at the palace. Li-Jing sliced it open and *zoom!* there was Li-Nezha again. His dad was very angry at all these goings-on, and tried to cut him down to size. Father and son battled furiously, and it looked like the end for Li-Jing. The **JADE EMPEROR**, who couldn't help feeling that his original plan had gone somewhat awry, intervened and made peace between them. Father and son joined forces and thus began their heroic career of demon-slaying.

Many years later, when Li-Nezha was back in Heaven enjoying the rewards of his labours, mortals back on Earth began to worship him as a god of lotteries and gambling. Of all the Chinese gods, he's probably the only one mischievous enough to reveal the winning numbers.

LIU-HAI

A Daoist god of wealth and prosperity, **LIU-HAI** was a civil servant and alchemist in tenth-century China, but somehow became involved with a huge three-legged toad. It was his best friend, his magical pet, and would carry him anywhere he wished. Sometimes the toad would hide in a well and have to be coaxed out with a shiny gold coin. This must have had some deep mystical significance, as Liu-Hai is now revered as a god of prosperity. Images and carvings of him are everywhere, standing on his toad and juggling gold coins with a beaming grin.

A small statue of him (and his toad) in your house will bring the cash flooding in – and if you stick his image on your wallet you may well become a millionaire. (At least, that's what the New Age stores claim, and they've certainly made a packet out of him.) As well as doing conjuring tricks with coins, he is also the protector of needlemakers. This really needled us for a while, until we realised that traditional Chinese coins have holes in the middle – and thin string can be invisible from a distance. So we are neatly back to tricks with strings of coins.

PAN-GU

In the beginning, the Universe was like a huge black egg floating in the void. Who laid the egg? We don't know. Our research has so far failed to uncover a cosmic chicken. Trapped inside the egg was **PAN-GU**, by all accounts a hairy, shaggy critter. He had been sleeping for 18,000 years and was now looking forward to stretching his legs. Grabbing a handy axe, he bashed open the shell and watched in amazement as the Universe formed around him.

The light and lissom egg white floated serenely upwards and became the Heavens. The yolk, being heavier and rather lumpy, plummeted downwards and became the Earth. Pan-Gu thought this was wonderful, but what if the Heavens should fall or the Earth rise? The resulting scrambled cosmos was more than he could bear, so he resolved to stand between and hold the two apart like a Chinese **ATLAS**.

Now Pan-Gu was a growing lad, becoming taller with each passing year. At the rate of about 3 metres per day, after another 18,000 years he'd grown to almost 30,000 kilometres in height. This is not far short of the circumference of the Earth, and Heaven was now so far up there was no danger of it ever falling to Earth again. His mission accomplished, an exhausted Pan-Gu expired. His last breath became the wind, his sweat became the rain, his voice became the rumbling of thunder – and the rest of him was put to equally productive use.

Some legends tell that the fleas infesting his shaggy fur dropped to Earth and became the ancestors of the human race. But you can't believe everything you hear as Nu-Gua, the wife of **SAN-HUANG**, also claims responsibility.

SONG-JIANG

God of thieves and whistleblowers. Who says crime doesn't pay? After breaking every law imaginable, **SONG-JIANG** went straight to **FENG-DU**, the Chinese Hell. But then he spoke up: 'You may think I was evil, but all the bureaucrats in my province are ten times worse. I was only following their example.' He then proceeded to give names, places and dates. This evidence convicted many high-ranking officials and filled Feng-Du's punishment zone to overflowing. The gods were most pleased, gave Song-Jiang a free pardon and elevated him to deity status.

YI-DI

Chinese god of wine and alcohol. Prompted by Emperor Yu's daughter, who wanted to present her father with a gift, **YI-DI** decided to concoct a wonderful beverage. After much experimentation and fermentation, he arrived at the perfect brew. It was ricey, spicy, and very nicey. He offered it to the emperor, who thought it was delicious but far too potent. 'Of course I can handle my alcohol,' said the emperor, 'but what of future emperors? A sozzled ruler would be very bad for business.' Consequently Yi-Di was banned from making any more, but that didn't stop him reaching godly status.

YUAN-SHI-TIAN-ZONG

There is no way you can get an interview with a god who is eternal, limitless and invisible; there is no background to fall back on. His distinguished career has gone largely unnoticed in the Western world where titles such as 'The Celestial Venerable of the Primordial Beginning' are beyond the comprehension of those who have endured a comprehensive education.

Legend tells that he existed before everything, having formed himself from pure Qi energy. Then he created Heaven and Earth and ruled over all – at least for a while. At some point his reluctance to be scrutable led him to take on an apprentice so he could retire to perfect contemplation. So the young **JADE EMPEROR** learned the trade of Universal Mastery and became ruler of everything, while **YUAN-SHI-TIAN-ZONG** relocated to the Pure Jade Heaven for a million billion trillion years of navel-gazing. We understand he is still available for consultations and soul-saving, but only in an emergency.

ZAO-JUN

Domestic god of the fireplace. He had one Hell of a life as a mortal; it all seemed to be going so well ... until he fell in love with the wrong woman. From there it was the old, old story of losing his wife, going blind, losing his mistress, becoming a beggar and getting burnt to ashes in the kitchen stove. However, as luck would have it, there was a vacancy for a kitchen god and he got the job, helped by the piety of his grieving mistress. Now he can be found in every household, keeping an eye on things and offering protection. Something of a celestial snoop, he compiles an official report on every family which is sent to the **JADE EMPEROR** on New Year's Day. But he's not above a little bribery. Next time you have a Chinese takeaway, order some extra noodles or honey cakes to keep him happy. And he does like a drink.

ZHI-NU

The daughter of the **JADE EMPEROR**, she spends all her time spinning beautiful silk robes and lacy garments for the Heavenly host. She also makes the finest gossamer clouds and her tapestry of the constellations is a work of art. Her father was so pleased with **ZHI-NU**'s diligent work that he married her to Niu-Lang, the Heavenly official in charge of cowsheds (which may not sound like much of a reward, but then you haven't met him).

The two of them fell headlong in love and pretty soon she was getting behind in her spinning duties. So they were whisked off into the sky and separated by the Milky Way. You can still see them there; she is Vega in the constellation Lyra and he is Altair in the constellation Aquila. Now they are only allowed to meet once a year, when a flock of magpies swarm into the sky and create a bridge for them to cross. For the rest of the year they live apart and she is the Heavenly spinster in more ways than one. This is what comes of a marriage made in Heaven.

There are other versions of this tale, but they don't matter; the end of this story is far more important than the beginning. The seventh day of the seventh lunar month is when Zhi-Nu and Niu-Lang cross the magpie bridge. Their stars burn brightly in the Heavens, lovers hold hands and gaze into the night sky, and Chinese Valentine's Day begins.

ZHU-RONG

God of fire and Heavenly executioner. He was so proud of helping to establish Heaven and Earth that the authority went straight to his head. When Gong-Gong, a terrible water demon, came along boasting of supreme magnificence it was more than his ego could bear. Gong-Gong was a blundering evil black dragon type who was sick of performing menial tasks in Heaven. He foolishly challenged **ZHU-RONG** to a fight. They battled furiously for days and then fell out of Heaven, still throwing punches.

Upon hitting the Earth, Gong-Gong was much the worse for wear and admitted defeat. He decided to kill himself by head-butting one of the pillars of Heaven. This had the desired effect, but also ripped a great hole in the firmament, causing the Great Flood which devastated Earth.

It was up to Nu-Gua to put things right, but even she couldn't undo all the damage. The very Heavens were tipped sideways, and that's why the Pole Star is no longer in the centre of the night sky. Zhu-Rong returned to Heaven in triumph. No-one messes with the god of fire.

THE GODS OF EGYPT

Obsessed with the dead and gods with animal heads, Egypt had the world's largest mausoleums – the Pyramids. Ancient Egypt still holds its fascination in the modern world. In this internet age, we suggest the authorities rename the place E-gypt.

The language barrier can be a little tricky. As with most hieroglyphic translations, the old Egyptian names have many variant spellings in English. Seth is **SET** in his ways, and **RA** is also the eye of Re. There was a mysterious plague of missing hieroglyphs at the time of the New Kingdom (1550–1070 BC), when foreign influence made certain letters vanish from the language. Egyptian scribes valiantly tried to reinstate them by adding extra letters to the ends of words, which led to much confusion – and still does.

Having invented mummification, the Egyptians were very much into otherworldly preparations. This is not surprising as the many gods of judgement and death were waiting on the other side and would be most insulted if a soul turned up looking scruffy; the best-seller was *The Book of the Dead* afterlife instruction manual. The messy business of burial was looked after by a whole subset of undertaker gods. These were in charge of embalming – and handled many bits not normally on public view. This obsession with death may seem a bit morbid today, but the Egyptians viewed it all with healthy fascination and believed there was much to look forward to.

SEPA

Centipede god of fertility and protection – and centipedes, presumably. Known as 'The Centipede of **HORUS**', he does a similar job to **KHEPRI** the scarab, but with more legs. **SEPA** can also appear with the head of a donkey, or mummified with two short horns. Don't laugh. Protection from snake and scorpion bites is not to be taken lightly.

OGDOAD

The **OGDOAD** were the eight original beings before there were any beings. They come in husband-and-wife pairs. The males have frog heads while the females have snake heads. This may have deep symbolic importance, or perhaps they just felt like it and there was no-one around to tell them any better; they may also have evolved into baboons at some point. The legends tell how the Ogdoad got together and built a little island in the middle of Chaos. A cosmic egg was placed on this island and sun god **ATUM** hatched out. The Ogdoad greeted the first sunrise with howls.

There are many versions of this sort of creation story and there are rumours that **THOTH** himself may have laid the cosmic egg. There are other claims that he was a baboon at the time, making this slightly improbable but not to be ruled out. It is just as well the *Sun* newspaper wasn't around in Egyptian times or who knows what absurd stories would've been circulated.

And here are the Primordial Pairings: Amaunet wears a crown on her snake head and breathes life into new things, blowing fresh knowledge and wisdom into the minds of the elite. She does pharaoh guidance, imparting hidden rules for ruling. She is married to Amun but they seem to have led separate lives since Amun went further upmarket in his career and became the sun god. As a self-publicist he has insisted on an entry under his own name in our book.

Next up is Hauhet, goddess of immeasurable infinity. Her serpent head is all in order but jackal heads instead of feet seems to be all her own idea. Maybe she did it to impress her husband Huh, who with arms outstretched supports the Heavens. He is also in charge of the number 1,000,000, which must be the closest Egyptians got to infinity at the time. He likes to be known as 'The Infinity Frog' but this might be some kind of croak. Still, as a god in a million his tadpole glyph alone denotes 100,000.

This was a hard act to follow so Kuk settled for god of primal chaos and darkness. His wife Kauket also does whatever they do in the dark.

Nun seized the chance to travel and created his own solar boat which he takes on round-the-world trips with his consort. We can imagine him in Mr. Toad mode with a captain's hat perched at a jaunty angle on his frog head. His consort Naunet is goddess of primordial waters, and has very good sea legs – only her head is snaky.

With the arrival of Atum the Ogdoad withdrew. Now they mostly take a back seat while the newer gods get on with running things.

AAH

Old moon god. A shadowy figure who appears to work behind the scenes pulling strings. He's best pals with **OSIRIS** and **THOTH**, but seems strangely superior to them. Perhaps because he rules the 360-day moon calendar which governs the year. **AAH** is best known for gambling away five days of moonlight in a dice game. Because **RA** had laid a curse upon sky goddess Nut, she could not give birth to a child on any day of any year. So the sympathetic Thoth gambled with Aah and won five days worth of moonlight. (And as any cosmological person will know, moonlight is not measured in litres or kilograms, but hours and days.)

Thoth took this moonlight, divided it into five days and inserted it into the month of July. Because these extra days were not covered by **RA**'s curse, Nut discovered she could give birth during that time. So **ISIS**, Osiris, **HORUS**, and **SET** are all July babies. And the year has remained 365 days long ever since.

AKEN & AMENT

AKEN is the ferryman. He dresses in nautical fashion but spends most of his time sleeping at the wheel. Hobnobbing with the dead must have a soporific effect. Whenever a soul comes along asking for passage, they have a terrible time trying to wake him up. It's depressing to realise that public transport is subject to delay even in the afterlife.

AMENT is the goddess of Underworld hospitality. Daughter of **HORUS** and **HATHOR** she is the meet-and-greet deity for deceased spirits at the gates. You might expect her to be sitting at a desk when you arrive, but no, she perches in a tree and watches out for her husband bringing new recruits. When you arrive she offers you bread and water. With her regal demeanour you would expect something a little more refined.

AKER

God of earth and guardian of the gateway of death. His sphere of action is limited to a tiny patch of the world that joins the east and west horizons of the Underworld. Does this entitle him to be a horizontal god? His two lion heads face east and west, gazing into tomorrow and yesterday.

AKER guards the Gates of Death and lets the sun god **RA** through every day. Must be quite a monotonous job. We have it on good authority that a prayer to Aker can cure snake bites. He's also the god to turn to if you've accidentally swallowed a fly.

AMENHOTEP

God of architecture whose rise demonstrates the power of the priests in ancient Egypt. He started out as Pharaoh Amenhotep I, the second king of the Eighteenth Dynasty, but his many building projects were so popular that the priests elevated him to deity status upon his death. He proved very popular, with many festivals held in his honour each year. Most houses had a picture of him, depicted with black or blue skin to symbolise resurrection, which must have been a real inspiration to budding builders of the time. **AMENHOTEP** must be one of the very few gods to have left his mortal remains behind for us to poke at – his mummified body was discovered in 1881 in very good condition.

AMMIT

The devourer of souls. She's a demonic goddess who is part hippo, part croc and part lion, a scary combination that's put to good use when a soul's judgement day comes. **AMMIT** lurks under the Scales of Justice while **OSIRIS**, **THOTH** and **MAAT** weigh up the evidence. If your soul is deemed unworthy, she pops out and gobbles it up. And that's the end of you.

AMUN

One of the **OGDOAD**, **AMUN** started out as the god of wind and air alongside his wife Amaunet. But his remarkable staying power led to him becoming the great sun god in charge of everything. He really should be the god of self-publicity, opportunism and always having the last word. Long ago and far away, Amun went in for mystery and abstract ideas, but he always kept an eye on progress and was willing to go with current trends and fashions: a hawk's head when they were all the rage, colourful fashion accessories and a beard if they were in vogue.

He could be a trendsetter with his red, green and blue plumed headgear, bracelets and necklets. In his dressing room were heads and tails for all occasions – frog, serpent, ape, lion, ram and even a goose, beetle wings and claws. You name it, he would get it. He kept a low profile during the hassle of the years when **ATEN** became a dictator, but the moment monotheism was over he leapt back to prominence. As with any counter-revolution, a strong leader is needed, so he stepped in to become the great sun god of Thebes and his word was law.

With his increased importance, it wasn't much of a stretch for Amun to form an alliance with fellow sun god **RA**. The two deities joined forces and became Amun-Ra (note who has top billing there). Amun's publicity drive also extended to Greece, where he was worshipped under the name Ammon and had his very own oracle. As an Egyptian god of almost unique holiness and majesty, he's in a league of his own and has interesting parallels with the utterly holy **YAHWEH** of the Hebrews.

The wandering Israelites must have picked up a lot of cultural titbits from the Egyptians – and may even have borrowed the idea of monotheism from the short-lived Aten. But Amun, whose name means 'what is hidden', is name-checked on almost every page of the Bible. Whenever 'Amen' crops up at the end of a prayer, he is taking the credit.

ANKHET

Goddess of the Nile, **ANKHET** keeps the waters clean with fresh fertilisation, and consequently she's a very important goddess to the Egyptians. She's also good in a scrap – she carries a spear and doesn't hesitate to make her point. As far as family life is concerned, Ankhet is one corner of a love triangle involving her dad **KHNUM** and sister Satet. They're known as the Triad of Elefantine, but it's really more a *ménage à trois*.

ANUBIS

Egyptian god of the dead and lord of mummy wrappings. He's the famous funeral god with the black dog's head. But is he a doberman or a jackal? No-one really knows for sure. ('Down, Anubis down!' No, it must be a jackal.) He's the primordial son of spooky Nephthys and shining **RA**, and is far too profound to be the son of cow goddess Hesa as some sources claim. Death was a serious business to the ancients and **ANUBIS** ruled over it with grim majesty until **OSIRIS** took over the job. Nowadays he takes a back seat in funerary matters, but still likes to be involved in the judging of the dead. He holds the Scales of Justice steady while your soul is weighed, and if you're light enough he'll lead you to Osiris for the top prize of everlasting afterlife.

ATEN

A minor sun god who became top creator god of the world's first monotheistic religion. Thebes in Ancient Egypt was the bees knees – humming along happily with 500+ deities to choose from until one dreadful day Amenhotep IV came to power. He was obsessed with a little-known sun god named **ATEN**. Really obsessed. He changed his name to Akhenaten (He Who Worships Aten) and proclaimed henceforth there was only one god: Aten.

To prove his point, he abandoned all the old gods and temples, and moved everyone to a new capital at Amarna. There he built himself a magnificent new temple and palace where he could sit in the sun and worship all day long. Priests and suppliers of sacrificial succulents were forced onto the dole as the new religion was enforced.

To start with, the new sun disc god was balanced on the head of **HORUS** and **RA** was somewhere in the background. But as time went on, the other gods were forced out and Aten became more abstract – just a flat disc with a few ropey rays emanating from him, very similar to how small children illustrate sunshine. Despite his dedication, Akhenaten let things go sadly to pot, and after seventeen years of monotheism the populace was heartily sick of it. Being a pharaoh, there is no way he would have abdicated, but perhaps he succumbed to sunstroke or a slipped disc.

The next pharaoh was the much-revered Tutenkhamen, who restored all the delightful deities of yore. The world's first monotheistic god was hastily erased from public records. Aten became Aten-Ra for a mere twinkle, until Amun nipped in to oust him altogether as Amun-Ra. Now Aten is only preserved on disc via the computer and gets hardly a mention in the *Book of the Dead*.

This is not quite the end. Monotheism was such a momentous concept that it may well have been taken on board by the Israelites in their great Exodus – along with various Egyptian hymns and prayers. One final twist. Somebody, possibly even Akhenaten himself, composed a 'Hymn to Aten' which was actually set to music and written down. This, as far as we know, is the first ever example of written musical notation; but what's the heiroglyphic equivalent of a demi-semi-quaver? Is there anybody out there who can play it?

ATUM

Egyptian creator god who did it with himself, as in the phrase 'The Hand of Atum'. He was the first true god, arising from the **OGDOAD**s' waters of Chaos disguised as a hill. As the original creator god, he made the world and everything in it by performing a certain self-pleasuring act. (Those of an innocent disposition can take this to mean he was chewing gum.)

Top twin gods **SHU** and Tefnut were formed from the resulting bodily fluids. He was later amalgamated with **RA** to form Atum-Ra but still likes to keep his hand in. We know who his followers are, but we'll turn a blind eye.

ATUM is symbolised by the setting sun (is there an Egyptian god who isn't associated with the sun?). Sunsets are his particular thing, and when the sun rises each day he becomes reborn as **KHEPRI**.

BAST

Daughter of **RA**, **BAST** is the cat-headed goddess of fertility, sensuality and fire prevention. She also has a flair for avenging wrongs and is feisty enough for the Greeks to have identified her with **ARTEMIS**. Her official headquarters appears to have been at Bubastis on the Nile Delta, where she had an annual festival. A lot of water has flowed down the Nile since then and festivals are few and far between. Why not hold your own cat festival? It may do you and your cats the power of good.

Bast was a very useful goddess who performed a vital public service. In the event of fire, her cat servants would run into the flames to draw out the power. These were the original fire extinguishers – sadly this practice did lead to a few charred cats. However, cats were revered in Egypt and we're sure there was no deliberate cruelty involved. After all, with nine lives, they might come back, albeit slightly singed. The Egyptians must have been very grateful for these fire-fighting services, as dead cats were mummified and sent to join Bast in the spirit world.

There's a tendency nowadays to regard Bast as the goddess of sex and lesbians, but that has more to do with modern sex-

kittens. Cats are very sensual animals but you don't want to get scratched. We feel sure it is due to Bast's powers that we now have smoke alarms and catflaps, so never underestimate the power of the original cat-woman. Be kind to cats. And remember, kind to cats means tough on rats.

Sometimes she is referred to by the bastardised name of Bastet. It's all to do with hieroglyphic confusion and alphabetic pollution. As the Egyptian language changed, some letter-sounds were in danger of losing their pronunciation. So scribes fought a rear-guard action by nailing extra letters to the ends of words. Thus Bast became Bastet. But the 'et' at the end is, or should be, silent.

BES

God of domestic protection. Appearances can be so deceptive. Although seen as a repulsive shabbily clad bandy-legged dwarf, **BES** is one of the best. He is into home protection, music and mirth and can even come in amulet form as a talisman against evil spirits.

Every home should have a Bes to protect against misfortune. There are also claims of a female version called Beset.

DUA

Egyptian god of toilets, **DUA** looks after public sanitation and lavatorial cleanliness. This adds a new meaning to the phrase 'holy bowl'. Double action. Kills all known germs. Now wash your hands.

GEB & NUT

GEB is the macho Earth god, as opposed to all the feminine Earth Mothers out there. Oh dear. He had to be prised apart from his twin sister **NUT**, a big blue woman covered with stars.There is a crude illustration of them doing it which pops up all over the place. She is doing the upper bit and Geb, although very much smaller than her, is rising to the occasion. Later he was goosed by a goose resulting in the egg the sun was hatched from. It must have been the goose that laid the golden egg.

The son of **SHU** and Tefnut, Geb accepts any old spelling – Keb, Qeb and, when the letter 'S' was invented, Seb. His sacred beast is the goose and he is renowned throughout Egypt for his hilarious farmyard impressions. These are so side-splitting that they actually cause earthquakes. Believe it or not, Geb is such a laugh that his soubriquet became 'The Cackler'. Didn't we see him in a *Batman* comic?

Nut is never alone, even for a moment, as Shu the sky god holds her vast body in place. And every evening sun god **RA** enters her mouth and wanders around all night inside her body before emerging from a place you can probably guess. There were all sorts of problems when she wanted children and Ra was very much against it. 'If you become pregnant your children will never be born, not on any day of the year.' She turned to **THOTH** for advice and he said '**AAH**. I may have an ingenious solution…'

HATHOR

Egyptian goddess of happiness, which seems to have been in short supply in that part of the world. As protector of women, she's often described as a cow, but she is far more than that: she is seven cows all at once. Have you ever heard of such a thing?

The mother of Anhur under the name Heret, she certainly put herself about a bit. She was certainly a goddess of great complexity, associated with love, fertility, naughtiness, moon, music and cavorting. She has more associations with whatever was going on than you could shake a sistrum at. As a welcome passenger on the **RA** cruises, she had the hots for Ra or vice versa. You never know with sun gods. Once when Ra was being jeered at by Earthlings for looking frail after a heavy night, she took up a cudgel on his behalf. There was a rampage of frazzling which wiped out half the humans in the Nile Valley. She vowed to come back and take care of the rest after a weekend break.

Initially flattered, Ra was now horrified. To prevent further carnage he made secret arrangements with the brewing industry. Seven thousand jugs of red beer were poured into the Nile to look like the blood of the slain. Intrigued by the vast red lake, **HATHOR** stopped to peer at her red reflection. A finger to the lips of the image, and a little lick. Mm, tasty. One thing led to another and as predicted the biggest one-goddess binge of all time was under way.

Some time passed before Hathor woke up. She could remember very little. If there was any carnage it was nothing to do with her but she remembered she'd set out on this enterprise in the company of **SEKHMET**. She couldn't remember drinking all that beer, and that was probably Sekhmet as well. It was a pity that all the witnesses appeared to be dead. If it would help to compensate for any distress, she would be willing to donate a generous proportion of her godly time to take on the duties of revelry and quaffing. Furthermore she would also undertake the planning of the Nile Floods, so important to Egyptian agriculture. This could easily be calculated as she represented the Dog Star Sirius and, according to **THOTH**, if Sirius rose before the sun or some such thing, flooding was imminent. Sorted.

Now Hathor was popular and endearing and not given to ripping people apart, whereas Sekhmet was liable to bouts of being bloody-minded. We can only go with the theory that it was a prank that got out of hand thanks to Sekhmet. Her serpent head seems all in order, but jackals' heads instead of feet seems rather curious. But what do we know about how one goes about this type of measuring? She and **HUH** have it all figured out.

HORUS

The falcon-headed sky god from Egypt. His eyes are the sun and the moon, so he must be a bit starry-eyed. You've heard of the Eye of **HORUS**, haven't you?

Son of **ISIS** and **OSIRIS**, he fought **SET** tooth and nail to avenge his father's murder, and was eventually declared the winner on points in round 80. During the battle his moon eye was poked out, but he got it back afterwards and generously donated it to his shadowy undead father. We reckon this could be why the moon is always a little unreal and spooky.

Horus comes in many varieties and names and you never know what name he could be hawking around. He appears to have started out as Haroeris and as a finger-sucking baby godlet to become Har-Pa-Khered, and was even baby-snatched by the Greeks later to become Hapocrates. In midday sun mad dog scorching mode he becomes Heru-Behudti. Then he has to do guard duty and protect his dead father Osiris in the Underworld when his badge reads Har-Nedj-Hef. You can always carve his falcon symbol on your coffin or urn to be on the safe side. Finally he has to stand in as Judge Of The Dead under the name of Un-Nefer.

IMHOTEP

God of medicine and knowledge. A mere mortal, he was the chief architect of the Step Pyramid – the very first one. He also excelled in healing, medicine, magic and raising the dead. He was so damn clever and in such demand he could not be allowed to remain mortal, so godly status was bestowed upon him. As he might have said: 'A journey towards divine ascension starts with the very first step.' The Greeks identified him with **ASCLEPIUS**.

ISIS

The daughter of **GEB** and **NUT**, she went to the ends of the Earth to find the remains of her murdered husband **OSIRIS**. With cunning ingenuity she managed to reassemble the body for burial, and couldn't resist one last rite which was more fertility than funerary. In consequence, she became pregnant with glorious **HORUS**, and had to go into hiding before bad brother **SET** found out. Luckily her mothering skills paid off and Horus grew into a Set-beating superhero who became the first ruler of a peaceful united Egypt.

ISIS settled down to enjoy royal life, attending garden parties and state functions in her role as king's mother. She now has a fetching line in headgear featuring cow horns and sun discs. We've seen this before somewhere – Royal Ascot perhaps? Isis was one of the few Egyptian gods the Greeks took a fancy to, and she even went through to the Romans – there was a temple dedicated to her at Pompeii. The cult became very popular and her consort Osiris was probably the foundation of the Greek/Egyptian hybrid-god Serapis.

During the Cleopatra/Anthony affair, Cleo saw herself as the personification of Isis. With her departure, the Roman Senate did its best to demolish her Egyptian shrines, but you can't keep a good goddess down. By the time of Julius Caesar the cult was thriving and had its own festivals. All through this, Isis shook her sistrum – which she retained despite her classical look statue makeover.

With the Christians she happily became identified as the Virgin Mary. The Armenian liturgy even retained the rattling sistrum sound. Penitents crawling on a symbolic search for Christ were only replacing the earlier devotees on the symbolic search for Osiris.

KHEPRI

God of renewal and rebirth. If you believe the world is a great ball of dung, **KHEPRI** is the god for you – he's the sacred Egyptian dung beetle. Every morning, come rain or shine, he pushes his dungball up the hill to symbolise **RA**, the rising sun. In the evening he passes the ball to **ATUM**. We hope they wash their hands afterwards. Because baby scarab beetles are hatched from dung, the Egyptians surmised

that there must be something very potent in the stuff. So **KHEPRI** became the prestigious god of rebirth, and not, as you might have thought, the god of nasty smelly things.

KHNUM

Ram-headed god who creates everybody's bodies on his potter's wheel, shaping the clay as it turns round and round. If you ever get dizzy spells, that's probably why. His wife is the froggy goddess of childbirth Heket who knows all about the spawning game. When a clay baby is finished, they sneak it into the mother's womb and nature takes its course. Which shows that the ancient Egyptians weren't silly enough to believe all that nonsense about storks and cabbage patches. Tracking down the variations of his name has caused us no end of confusion. It's enough to make one's mind go knumb.

MAAT

Goddess of truth, justice, law and order. Despite her permanent head decoration of an ostrich feather she is far from a feather brain. The feather, which is always divided in equal halves, is her symbol of 'that which is straight'. She is heavily involved in the judgement of the dead along with **OSIRIS** and **THOTH**. With a permanent staff of forty-two assessors, **MAAT** has her own system of weighing souls.

A single feather is placed on the Scales of Justice. The ghostly heart of your Ka (i.e. soul) is placed on the balance and various spiritual tests are performed. Will it rise or fall? If your Ka's heart is lighter than a feather, you can look forward to a cheerful afterlife. But if it sinks below the threshold, **AMMIT** emerges from under the table and slurps you up. At least it's a quick end. Maat is a firm favourite aboard the Solar Boats of **RA**, and can hold her own with Thoth in any technical discussion. Kings adored her and she was always invited to coronations and royal parties as a welcome and respected guest.

MIN

God of lettuce and sex. This fertility god is a very popular phallic deity. He is mostly depicted as a stick man – with one of the sticks sticking out somewhat crudely. Taking part in a sexy threesome with Qadesh, a goddess of love and ecstasy, and Reshep, he has a plumed headdress and in his right hand he holds a whip – best not ask why, eh? There's more to lettuce than you might think. It was regarded as a powerful aphrodisiac – huge bunches of lettuce leaves were eaten in **MIN**'s honour in the hope that increased stamina would result. You can try this for yourself; lettuce is cheap and a few salad sandwiches may bring unexpected benefits.

Lettuces also feature in the conflict between **SET** and **HORUS**. Fed up with the never-ending fights, **RA** ordered them to be at peace. Seemingly compliant, Set invited Horus to stay with him for the weekend, but on the first night Set crept out of bed and attempted to sexually assault Horus, who awoke just in time and managed to catch Set's discharge in his hand, whereupon he fled home to his mother crying 'Look what Set has done now!' **ISIS** cried 'The filthy beast!', hacked off the sullied hand and threw it in the Nile. (She soon made him another one – replacement parts were her speciality.)

Isis planned revenge. She persuaded Horus to self-abuse himself into a jar, and sprinkled the contents over Set's favourite piece of garden, the lettuce patch. Every morning Set started off the day with a row of fresh lettuces, and he swallowed all the 'dew fresh' ones. When the story got out, how the gods laughed – 'How's the pregnancy going Set?'

So always wash lettuces very carefully before consumption.

MUT

Mother goddess of mothers and mothering. She is also the mother of **KHONSU**, the moon god. During the **AMUN-RA** ascendancy she was his female counterpart, doing her best to amalgamate all the great goddesses into her own identity. She liked to be known as 'Lady of Heaven' or 'Queen of Gods'. Ironically her symbol is that of a vulture. To get noticed in her early days, she helped **ISIS** collect the bits of **OSIRIS** and replaced his head and heart. This sort of thing is always a good career move.

NEITH

The great weaver goddess. Upset her and she threatens to unpick the woven Universe; bits of it already seem a little threadbare. She was asked by Banebdjetet to arbitrate in the fight for power between **HORUS** and

SET. Thanks to her, Horus was given supremacy and Set was given two compensatory goddesses, **ANATH** and **ASTARTE**. When she gets in a bad mood, she becomes the war goddess Anouke.

OSIRIS

Mr Big of the Underworld. Not a gangster as such but still in charge of the dead-end scenario. Married to the beautiful **ISIS**, he was quite content to rule vegetation and fertility until he was knocked off by his evil brother **SET**, who locked his body in a chest and chucked it into the Nile.

But nothing's ever that simple when it comes to the gods, and the chest was washed up on the shore, stuck in a giant tree, turned into a pillar and relocated to the palace of King Byblos where Isis, having searched high and low, eventually found it. Cursing his luck, wicked Set chopped the body into a zillion pieces and scattered them all over Egypt, so poor Isis had to search all over again, collecting bits and pieces of her dead husband until she had every last scrap.

Then **RA** took pity on her and sent **THOTH** and **ANUBIS** to help put the jigsaw puzzle back together. Set in his savage spite ensured there was one piece missing when **ISIS** came to reconstruct **OSIRIS**; his penis, which was thrown into the Nile, where it had been swallowed by a fish. But Isis,

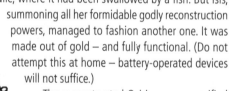

summoning all her formidable godly reconstruction powers, managed to fashion another one. It was made out of gold – and fully functional. (Do not attempt this at home – battery-operated devices will not suffice.)

The reconstructed Osiris was mummified for burial; and he looked so fine in his shiny wrappings that Isis couldn't resist one last fling. As luck would have it, her charms breathed new life into him and she became pregnant with Horus. Meanwhile, thanks to his Underworld connections, the resurrected **OSIRIS** was promoted to judge of the dead alongside Maat and **THOTH**. Consequently he now has little time for being non-judgemental. Osiris also found a new lease of life as part of the Serapis Project, a collaborative religious venture between the Greeks and Egyptians.

PTAH

Creator god with a sideline in masonry. The son of Nun and Naunet, he makes the breath of life. First you have to imagine – then you have to have a name for whoever, and then breathe out heavily and there you have it: a new soul ready to take up residence. Now a dignified older god, he is keen on stonework and crafts, and may have made his very own sandals; which do, we feel, detract slightly from his dignity.

RA

Egyptian top god, the Eye of the Sun. Previously known as **ATUM**, he's the most important Egyptian god. He created himself out of the mound formed by the **OGDOADs**' primordial Chaos, and then made **SHU** and Tefnut to form the world. Now he sails across the sky in his solar boat. Mankind was made from his tears and if that doesn't make you grateful, just go to Egypt and look at the midday sun. There he is – that's his all-powerful eye bearing down on you.

But is he all-powerful? There are times when he seems to be waning a bit and feeling his age. He has a very strange relationship with the sky goddess **NUT** (who arches backwards across the world and probably symbolises the Milky Way). In the evening he sails through her mouth and then has to battle through her nightmarish insides. As though in some sort of video game, he wends his way through twelve gates at the rate of one per hour without getting zapped by malevolent hideous monsters. And like some end-of-game baddie, the snake god Apep lies in wait hoping to gobble him up. Once these perils are transversed, he then surfaces via Nut's birth canal to greet the new day.

He's not alone in this enterprise – selected top gods come along for the thrill of pitting their skills and chilling out in no uncertain manner. **THOTH**, **MAAT**, **HATHOR**, **HORUS** are the top crew, with Abtu and Anet, a pair of life-size sacred fish who swim before the boat of sun god **RA** to warn him of any airborne crocodiles, hydrogen-filled hippos, or treacherous cloud banks he might encounter in his journey across the sky. Finally there's **KHEPRI** the dung beetle as a sort of morning mascot. The night boat is called Mantchet, and there's also a day boat called Semketet, where they probably laze around sunbathing and drinking cocktails as they recount their night-time adventures.

Shrouded in the mists of Chaos and speculation of cosmic genealogy, Ra may or may not have had parents. **NUT** is often put forward as his mother, but this is most likely due to his habit of popping out to be reborn after the night shift. Later in life there were some amalgamations. Ra was so much in the spotlight that many gods tried to get in on the act by adding his name to theirs for added glory. The most notable of these was Amun-Ra. Ra himself seems to have opted

for semi-retirement, although he remains very much in the public eye and has a full schedule of guest appearances.

SEBEK

Crocodile god of might and power – but only where pharaohs are concerned. The rest of us have to fight our own battles. **SEBEK** is depicted as a large crocodile, and has all the dangerous attributes you might expect: cunning, treachery, deceitfulness and sharp pointy teeth. Careful – it could all end in tears. He's possibly the husband of **TAWERET**, although it's hard to see what they have in common. And we're delighted to reveal that his biggest shrine was located in the city of Crocodilopolis. The Greeks liked him enough to give him a pet name: Petesuchos.

SEKHMET

Egyptian goddess of war and vengeance. She has a lion's head so is used to being lionised, and can be very fierce if upset. Always a controversial goddess, she finally came clean in a recent Godchecker interview: 'The destruction of mankind? Okay, I admit it. I did it and not **HATHOR**. So I'm **RA**'s daughter and I am the Eye of the Sun. Hathor thinks she is too, and we both wear sun discs to prove it. We get on fine, and hey, we both think the world of **RA**. We don't like to see people taking the mickey. Yes, I know I have the head of a lion and claws and I can flare up at times. I don't know what gets into me. Normally I'm Mrs Nice and Cuddly. Ask my hubby **PTAH**. Never a cross word. I do healing as well you know. It's not all searing flames of destruction. Anyway, I've got to go now. The cobra needs venomising.'

SESHAT

Queen of the bookroom. The daughter of **THOTH**, she's the head godly librarian. She keeps all the books for the gods, looks after tax returns and is a dab hand at architecture, astronomy and archiving. Her writing is extremely neat. Very literate, and would be of enormous help in maintaining our Holy Database. We must give her a ring sometime. She also wears a rather fetching leopard-skin robe, which so far hasn't really caught on in librarian circles.

SET

God of chaos. Also handles war, storms and deserts. His nickname is The Red God, but whether this is politics, hair colour or sheer embarrassment is difficult to ascertain. He's a bit of a mix and match, with donkey ears, a scorpion tail, and the head of a mysterious Egyptian aardvark. He can also turn up as a hippo with the jaws and tail of a crocodile. But one thing's for sure: **SET**'s a nasty piece of work. In fact, he's the god of evil chaos, and loves nothing more than creating mayhem.

Not content with constantly messing up the peaceful farms of **OSIRIS**, Set finally lost his temper and killed him. But not even scattering the remains far and wide could save him from retribution. **HORUS** son of Osiris came seeking vengance and the battle lasted eighty years. Not one to fight fair, Set tore one of Horus's eyes out, but Horus went straight for the testicles. The other gods cheered and awarded him the victory, banishing Set to the upper realms of **RA** where he became the voice of thunder.

He hasn't mellowed with age. If he enters the body of a human he can drive them mad. We're not surprised. It doesn't bear thinking about. His girlfriend was **ANAT** imported from Mesopotamia where she had had a bit of bother stealing a sacred bow, which helped her status as a warrior goddess.

SHU

Primeval god of air, along with his twin sister Tefnut. He deals in the dry dusty variety, while she's more than a little damp. She has a lion's head and spits a lot, and causes dew and wetness with other bodily fluids. **SHU** is the son of **ATUM** and fathered **NUT** (the sky), and **GEB** (the Earth), with a little help from Tefnut. But things didn't quite go according to plan. The sky wouldn't stay put and kept falling down onto the Earth. As gravity hadn't yet been invented, Shu decided there must be another reason. And there was: Nut and Geb were passionately in love and sneaking tight embraces at every opportunity. It wasn't so much a case of 'Did the Earth move for you?' as 'Did the sky fall on top of you last night?'

Shu put a stop to all this, but not before Nut had given birth to some very important new gods. And now Shu stands between Nut and Geb, holding up the sky like an Egyptian **ATLAS**.

SONS-OF-HORUS

Four dead good god brothers by the equally dead good **HORUS**. They undertake to help the deceased on their journey to the Underworld, looking after the embalmed bodily bits and wrapping up all the loose ends. They are:

DUAMUTEF, who has a jackal's head and looks after embalmed stomachs. These are kept in a jar until needed. Very useful in murder by poison enquiries;

HAP, who has a baboon's head and is in charge of embalmed lungs. At least smoking had not been invented;

AMSIT, who has a human head and is the keeper of embalmed livers;

and **KEBECHSENEF** who has a falcon's head and was in charge of, er, the lower bodily parts.

Come to think of it, calling someone a 'son of Horus' sounds like a terrible insult.

TAWERET

Goddess of maternity and childbirth. Very popular with those expecting a blessed event, she comes in the form of a pregnant hippopotamus. If you can believe this, just add breasts and a crocodile tail. (Make that several breasts – she was very well-endowed in that department.) Possibly the wife of **SEBEK**, she protects women and

children. Her alternative name, Thoeris, appears to mean 'Mistress of Talismans'. For added protection during maternity, put a picture of her on your pillow to keep the demons away.

According to the *Book of the Dead*, she nourishes the deceased and devours the wicked that are on their way to Hell. This must be for a taste of things to come. It would also seem the constellation of Ursa Major may be under her control. But there are lots of hippo goddesses and much confusion of names. When crocodiles come into the equation, as with **TAWERET**, and you get crocopotamuses and hippodiles, we tend to take the rest of the day off.

THOTH

Well-known god with the head of an Ibis. He's a good all-rounder for arts, science, music, astronomy, speech and letters. A good egg: if ever a god was greater than great it was **THOTH**. In one translation his name is prefixed with the word 'great' no fewer than eight times. Thith may have helped to reduce the embarrathment cauthed by having a name that lookth like a lithp. His resumé seems too impressive to be true – but most of the facts speak for themselves. He is the master of time, mathematics, astronomy, readin', writin', 'rithmatic and almost anything else you can point a pair of dividers at. 365 days in a year? Thank Thoth (see **AAH** for the full story). 12 hours of day and 12 hours of night? Thank Thoth. Circles having 360 degrees? Thank Thoth. His bestselling *Book of the Dead* is still in print and you will never be able to hitch-hike to Heaven on the Nile without it.

He does have his eccentricities – he sometimes likes to revert back to the good old **OGDOAD** days and appear as a baboon. Not just any old baboon, but one called Hedjwer that could probably have written the complete works of Shakespeare if it felt so inclined. Encouraging **RA** to call himself top god left Thoth free to run just about everything without any fuss or hassle. Pocket calculators? Thoth used the whole firmament, available to all on a grand scale. Think sky.

To make it easier, all the stars and planets required for calculation are associated with favourite gods. Need to work something out via Sirius? Log in and have **HATHOR** guide you. Need the moon for phases, time or tides? Go to Thoth; he chose to be top moon god alongside his best buddy **KHONSU**. Cool, modest, unflappable, and a brilliant arbitrator, Thoth has stood the test of time, time and time again. Full ticks and tocks to this tip-top god. He was also known to Greek god geeks as **HERMES** Trismegistus, possibly to avoid talking with a lisp. Although we are told the 'H's in the name of Thoth are silent. Whoever told us this has remained silent themselves. Perhaps it was **TOT**.

THE GODS OF FINLAND AND LAPLAND

Despite being a sparsely populated place, thick with forests and littered with lakes, Finland has been amazingly persistent and creative with its myths and legends.

For a mythology based on word-of-mouth tale-telling, Finland has better godly documentation than some other places we could mention. The rambling epics of **VAINAMOINEN**, the Finnish folk hero, and the publishing of *Kalevala*, the Finnish folk bible, give intriguing glimpses of a mythology centred around trees, animals, natural forces … and more trees.

The gods of Finland, although thin on the ground, are firm folksy favourites with spinners of spooky tales. When Christianity came and spread, Finnish mythology didn't turn a hair. It just mixed the two together with extra tales around the fire.

Note: Due to horrendously complicated issues with our database, the Finnish spellings are missing accented characters (such as Ä and Ö). We know this is wrong, we are deeply ashamed, but we're doing our best to fix it.

Also, at no extra charge, we include the gods of Lapland, aka *Sápmi aka Saamiland*.

JUMALA

JUMALA is so abstract that he barely exists at all. The name is the old Finnish word for 'god' – and this could be applied to any deity who fancied a boost. Particularly **UKKO**. Over time, the word Jumala came to be identified with the Christian god **JEHOVAH**, who more-or-less took over the position of top Finnish deity.

SAMPSA & PEKKO

'Little Sampsa Pellervoinen,
He's the lad to do the planting,
Sow the seeds and sow them thickly.'

Like a little Johnny Hayseed, **SAMPSA** wakes up in the spring and dances through the fields sowing corn and oats. Then **PEKKO** takes care of the crops while Sampsa has a well-earned rest. His favourite tipple is made from barley, which he probably sips as he hops through the hops.

AHTI

Water god of seas, lakes, rivers. Bit gloomy with a tendency to brood. **AHTI** lives a gloomy damp life in a wave-lashed, cloud-shrouded cliff, putting the whirl into whirlpools. He's jealous of the sky gods and feels he is not getting his fair share of godly worship from humans. But he hardly improves his public relations image by whipping up whirlpools and employing teams of spiteful sprites. His wife Vellamo is also a wet blanket and does a lot of sorrow-drowning.

ANTERO-VIPUNEN

A just-underneath Earth giant who used topsoil as a blanket so he could snooze undisturbed for simply ages. Things grew upon him and in his sleep he absorbed nature's secrets.

The Finnish hero **VAINAMOINEN** was building a magic boat and, badly needing a binding spell, was told to try the slumbering giant. When shouting and shaking didn't work Vainamoinen poked a stick down into **ANTERO-VIPUNEN**'s gullet. That didn't wake him either. The giant just yawned and swallowed him.

Making the best of a bad job, Vainamoinen managed to build a smithy in the giant's stomach. Quite how this was accomplished has never been adequately explained, but build it he did. Before long, the giant coughed and spluttered and Vainamoinen shot forth complete with regurgitated binding spells. We assume Antero-Vipunen slumbers on and that his digestion has recovered.

ILMARINEN

The divine smith and eternal hammerer. He was the brother (or possibly just a good friend) of **VAINAMOINEN**, for whom he forged a Sampo. This was a magic mill of amazing complexity which included the magic ingredients of a swan's quill tip, a barren cow's milk, a barley grain and the wool of one ewe. It was three-sided and could grind corn, money and salt, yet was easily portable.

This gadget was supposed to buy a bride for Vainamoinen, but things didn't work out with the prospective in-laws and they snatched it back. During a chase it got lost at sea, but it still grinds out all the sea's salt.

ILMATAR

Goddess of air, daughter of Ilma. In the beginning there was only **ILMATAR**, the void and a great deal of wind. Ilmatar, tired of counting rainbows and letting the wind play with her hair, began to long for a son. Her longing was so great that the east wind itself took pity. She found herself buffeted and tossed by the wind's tempestuous love-making until, exhausted, she could bear it no longer and collapsed. And there inside her was conceived **VAINAMOINEN**, the child of the wind.

Unfortunately he didn't seem inclined to make an appearance, and after seven centuries or so she began to give up hope of seeing him. Then one day she noticed a celestial eagle flying overhead. The poor bird was desperately pregnant and looking for somewhere to land. So Ilmatar helpfully raised her knee and the bird came swooping down. Half a dozen cosmic eggs were laid, followed by an egg made of iron. The bird then gathered them all up, sat upon them and went to sleep.

Ilmatar was faced with a problem familiar to anyone with a household pet: how do you move without waking them up? Her leg was aching, her knee was hotter than an incubator and she desperately wanted to go to the bathroom. Slowly, carefully, she began to stretch out her leg and slowly, inevitably, the seven eggs rolled off and fell majestically into the raging sea.

Now cosmic eggs are delicate things, and no sooner had they touched the water than the shells cracked and a vast cosmic omelette was formed upon the waves. Ilmatar watched in amazement as the churning mixture solidified into Heaven and Earth. One yolk slipped into the sky to form Paivatar, the Sun, while the egg white became **KUU**, the glistening Moon. Stars were made from pieces of speckled eggshell, and thus the world was formed.

You may be wondering what happened to the iron egg. Well, the black yolk became a thundercloud. Ilmatar was delighted with events, and busied herself shaping the lands and adding finnishing touches. And then she felt a stirring inside her. Vainamoinen had woken up after so many years and was eager to see the new world. He had quite a struggle to get out as no-one seemed very keen to help him, but he managed in the end and emerged, a bouncing bonny old man.

KIPU-TYTTO

Fin de siècle goddess of death. Sister of Kivutar, Vammatar and Loviatar, she lives in **TUONELA**, the Finnish Hell. Her name translates as 'Pain Girl' and she is the goddess of illness and sings you to the final sleep.

She has a black, pockmarked face and nine children with simple descriptive names like Gout, Ulcers and Scabies. I think we should stop there as I'm beginning to feel queasy. Her sisters are equally revolting.

KUU

Moon deity and/or personification of the moon. The Finns are at it again: they can't just have a simple moon god like everyone else. No, **KUU** was formed from the whites of duck eggs laid in the crook of the knee of **ILMATAR** (goddess of air), who had been floating in an ocean for 700 years. Then a lot of glittering and shining went on and Kuu became silver.

An impeccable source tells us that Kuu is not actually a god, but simply the Finnish word for 'moon'. It certainly seems to be the word for 'month', although our Finnish leaves a lot to be desired. Look, Finland is a weird place – all reindeer and Lapland dancing. They also know more about Father Christmas than they let on too (see **MARJATTA**).

LEMMINKAINEN

Trickster god, full of conjuring tricks. He came to a funny end – he was cut to pieces and chucked into the River of the Dead at **TUONELA**. Luckily for him, his anguished mum (whom some sources claim is **ILMATAR**) found the body and rescued it. Following assistance from Suonetar, the goddess of veins and blood vessels (only in Finland), she managed to glue the bits back together using top god **UKKO**'s amazingly adhesive honey. So **LEMMINKAINEN** is now sticky and tricky. He was a brave warrior but suffered from an overdose of anguish in his marriage to Kyllikki. She was a party girl until forced into  marriage, and despite vowing to be faithful and true, found housework so boring she just had to sneak out for a surreptitious dance.

Lemminkainen stomped off to war vowing never to trust a woman again.

MARJATTA

Christmas in Finland? **MARJATTA** is a virgin who became pregnant after swallowing a mysterious talking whortleberry. As told in the *Luojan Virsi*, a collection of religious songs, she gave birth in a stable to a god-like child who went on to supercede **VAINAMOINEN** as he sailed off into the distance.

With a worshipping stable boy, a bright new star in the Heavens, and a set of accompanying miracles, this all sounds very familiar. Where have we heard this song before?

TAPIO

Finnish forest god. Being in Finland he is probably evergreen rather than deciduous. With a beard of lichen and eyebrows of moss, you'll appreciate that he is made entirely of trees; consequently, he doesn't get around very much, but he doesn't need to as he can branch out and let knowledge whisper through his foliage.

The family tree includes his wife Mielikki, his son Nyyrikki, and his daughter Tuulikki, who makes sure the woods are well stocked with wild creatures of an edible kind. Then there's Tellervo, the maid. She is milkmaid of the forests, a lovely flaxen-haired girl, bubbly and comely. Just like all the other milkmaids you have met.

TUONELA

The Finnish Underworld. This is the rest home of the dead, managed by Tuoni and Tuonetar with the assistance of a team of hand-picked spirits. It's run like a very boring retirement home for those who've led very boring lives and are now content with a very boring death. The spacious grounds contain a protective river – and luxury accommodation means the straw is changed regularly every year. Each room has scenic views of the spot where **LEMMINKAINEN**'s remains were fished out of the water, and the nightly cabaret kicks off with Tuonelan Joutsen, the Swan of the Dead, singing a mournful dirge for your entertainment.

The proprietors claim that **TUONELA** is not an Underworld. The only complaint they have ever received is that the welcoming hospitality is sometimes a little too generous. At reception you are welcomed straight away with a tankard of frogs and worms.

So when planning your final vacation, consider Tuonela. A pleasant restful stay is guaranteed, and there's no need to book in advance. There are problems, of course: one of the oldest residents and part-owner Kalma has to be kept out of sight as she is the goddess of death and decay. Her name means 'Stench of Corpses' and she has her own abode in the grounds guarded by Surma, a monstrous hound with sword-blade fangs.

UKKO

Top management sky god who brought **ILMATAR** into being. He specialises in storms and lightning. He's also the source of a mysterious celestial beverage which drops from the skies. This is not so much manna from Heaven as honey from the clouds. It's not only sweet but also has amazing adhesive properties (see **LEMMINKAINEN**).

If you need more info, you could be out of luck. **UKKO** is somewhat aloof. There's no point in trying to reach him unless all other prayers remain unanswered. You could try his wife Akka, who as Earth Mother goddess is far more down-to-earth. As goddess of the harvest, she can provide in abundance. She is also very kind to Rowan trees.

Once the top god of Finland, Ukko found his popularity reduce as Christianity spread through the country. See **JUMALA**.

VAINAMOINEN

Folk hero god of the *Kalevala* and thousands of other epic poems and tales. They do go on and on … and on … and all in Finnish. Join the dots.

The son of **ILMATAR**, **VAINAMOINEN** spent 730 years in her womb and became so bored waiting to be born that he took matters into his own hands and crawled out. He discovered fire in the belly of a fish which was in the belly of a fish which was in the belly of a fish, and thus created the world's first three-course fish dinner. He also invented a vaguely harp-like musical instrument, using the bones of a gigantic pike and the hair of a maiden (who was presumably equally gigantic). This was called a kantele and proved so popular that it's now the national instrument of Finland. His kantele came in very handy for magical purposes, as Vainamoinen was a real whizz at singing spells. His musical duel with Joukahainen was probably the forerunner of the Eurovision Song Contest. He won the duel, but lost the prize as Aino, the young lady concerned, drowned herself.

That was always Vainamoinen's problem. He was a ladies' man, but had terrible trouble getting the ladies. His attempt to marry the very attractive daughter of ice sorceress Louhi was a disaster. He went to all the trouble of presenting her with the specially made magic Sampo machine as a wedding gift, but his potential mother-in-law was as cold as an icicle and the marriage was most definitely off.

SAAMI (LAPLAND)

ERLIK

This is a very unsavoury story. Sky god Ulgan, wishing to make a start with his creation project, made **ERLIK** from a chunk of mud to use as free labour. His mouth made an excellent hod. But Erlik had other ideas. While Ulgan was otherwise engaged making clay dolls, he spat out his very own landfills full of slime and saliva. Meanwhile, Ulgan had run out of life mix. Not wishing to leave the building site vulnerable to thieves, he got himself a guard dog whilst he went off to replenish supplies.

Wanting a play with the dolls, Erlik tried to bribe the dog with a mud bone. But the dog just snarled. So in a fit of pique Erlik spat over the fence and covered all the dolls in disgusting slime.

On his return Ulgan learnt what had happened and turned all the dolls inside-out. That's why we are slimy inside but dry outside, which on reflection is no bad thing. To teach Erlik a lesson, Ulgan slung him into the Underworld, but Ulgan managed to smuggle a few of the dolls with him. Left to his own devices, he turned them inside-out again, which is why the dead become so slimy on the outside while their bones dry on the inside.

MADDERAKKA

The mother goddess of childbirth responsible for baby welfare from the womb onwards – or should it be outwards?

Helping with the delivery service are her three daughters, Sarakka, Juksakka and Uksakka, who help choose baby names and prevent nappy rash. And she is married to Madderatcha who doles out the souls for the little darlings.

Together, they all help when it comes to inspiration for baby names. (Which one of them was responsible for the name Acker Bilk?)

We suspect **MADDERAKKA** may also be related to Akka, the wife of **UKKO**. But 'akka' means simply female, so our speculation continues.

THE GODS OF CLASSICAL GREECE

What can we say about the Greeks that they haven't already said about themselves? Consummate tall-storytellers, they have classy classic gods for all situations.

Greek mythology is a veritable blockbusting soap opera. What can **ZEUS** possibly get up to next – and with whom? How will **HERA** take her next revenge? Where will **APHRODITE** discard her nightie? Who has been barred from Olympus lately – and why? When is the next big punch-up? And will **HERMES** be sued for selling counterfeit sheep?

Full of twists, turns, plots within plots, wit, humour, satire, belly laughs and blood-curdling thrills, Greek gods have beginnings, middles, and ends without end. Coming soon to a temple near you! And they are all big stars – brawnier, more beautiful, and larger than any life you have ever known. The Romans couldn't improve upon them. So they just gave them a quick makeover and turned the whole pantheon into a spin-off sequel.

AETHER

The son of Erebus and **NYX**, he looks after the air the gods breathe. Not the polluted old rubbish we have to put up with; this is the supergrade five godstar variety. Very invigorating.

AETHER floats above Aer and is illuminated with Heavenly light. He's a very bright lad, and even on the clearest day we only see the merest trace of his splendour as it filters down to us. At night his mother **NYX** draws the curtains and the gloom of Erebus descends upon the world. When morning comes, his sister Hemera wafts away the murky mists and his radiant glow is seen again.

Attempts to discover traces of the aether on Earth were carried out by Michelson and Morley in a famous experiment of 1887. Did they find any? No. This non-result led directly to Einstein's Theory of Relativity, but dashed their hopes of selling bottled aether to the physics community.

AMPHION & ZETHUS

Twins of **ZEUS** via Princess Antiope. Between them they built the city of Thebes. **ZETHUS** drew up the plans with some help from **ATHENA**, and **AMPHION** (taught by **HERMES**) played a lyre with such resounding swing that the stones all leapt into place without any further aid to complete the building.

Zethus named the city after his wife Thebe and everything was hunky-dory until children came into the equation. Amphion was married to Niobe and his kids were so delightfully cute that Thebe was jealous. She crept into the nursery one night with a knife, and (as is obligatory on these occasions), the kids had swapped places and she cut the throat of her own son.

The gods were appalled and turned her into a nightingale to sing sad songs forever. Then poor Zethus woke up to one of those days when it didn't seem worthwhile to continue, so he did away with himself. Amphion and Niobe seemed strangely unaffected by these traumatic events. They carried on grooming their children for stardom until they reached the doting parent point of declaring that their half-dozen each of girls and boys were more radiant than anything **APOLLO** could offer. As for his sister **ARTEMIS**, 'Barren was she?'

That did it. Apollo reached for his bow. Zunk! Zunk! No more cutie-pie kids. Just one was spared after pleading for mercy: Chlorys. She went on to become goddess of flowers that bloom in the spring. The Romans turned her into Flora.

Amphion was definitely upset now, and raised an army to go and smash up the gods' shrine in Delphi. Zeus had no option but to confiscate his son's immortality and banish him to the Underworld.

APHRODITE

The beautiful goddess of love. Daughter of **URANUS**, she was born of sea foam and thus has a soft spot for surfers. So if you're surfing the net in search of love, remember **APHRODITE**, the goddess of chat room romance.

Whoever wears Aphrodite's magic girdle immediately becomes an object of love. But where can it be found? We've no idea. Try looking on eBay.

She was so beautiful that **ZEUS** married her off to the crusty old **HEPHAESTUS** to prevent all-out war among the randy gods.

APOLLO

Son of **ZEUS** and **LETO**. Sun god. Music god. Archery god. Poetry god. Painting god. Prophecy god. Plagues and healing god. Animal welfare god. God of radiance. God of ploughing. And much much more! Send for free brochure with no obligation. See him conduct the holy choir of **MUSES**; book now for **APOLLO** space missions. He also has undiminished beauty and virility. You name it, he has it, which is thoroughly sickening to us mere mortals.

But he is not entirely the Mr Nice Guy he would have us believe. There are women he pursued who won't talk due to transformation or worse. Daphne is now a laurel tree and Cllytia is a sunflower. Sudden deaths are not uncommon when he is around – and don't try to compete with him musically. It's all very well to play live but don't get flayed alive like poor old Marsyas, or be given the ears of an ass like poor old King Midas. Cassandra never got another chance either, nor was he very pleasant to the **SIBYL OF CUMAE**.

Apollo's son **ASCLEPIUS** was the result of another unfortunate lapse. Having had an affair with the mortal daughter of a king, Apollo was consumed with jealousy when he discovered she had another suitor, and, out of control, he killed her. In a fit of remorse he was just in time to rescue her unborn child and have him brought up with the best education to be Asclepius, the deity doctor. Apollo met his match in Zeus, and a tussle for power earned him a period in exile; but as Zeus had zapped his son Asclepius, zapping the cyclope thunderbolt makers seems justifiable. It can be very tough at the top and all in all Apollo handles it very well what with Zeus being his dad, having **ARTEMIS** for a twin sister, etc.

ARES

The son of **ZEUS** and **HERA**, he turned out to be a swaggering bully boy and yobbo god. He had the hots for **APHRODITE** and even after being caught in a net by **HEPHAESTUS**, in full *flagrante delicto*, this did not diminish his adulterous activities. The only thing he enjoyed more was war: **ARES** loved battles and violence. Never mind which side he was on, so long as there was plenty of blood.

His bloodthirsty sons Deimos and Phobos are in constant attendance, and if all is peaceful, it doesn't take long for his sister **ERIS** to knock up a little strife. Then there is Enyo, goddess of war and violence who may be a sister, wife or daughter.

Ares is not very popular with most of the other gods. He sided mostly with the Trojans in the Big Bust Up, and was wounded by a mortal with a little help from Athena who blatted him with a rock. He fled howling back to Olympus, and the Aloadae held him captive in a bronze jar for over a year because they could. His mortal sons were so vile **HERACLES** killed two, Diomedes and Cicnus, and **APOLLO** put paid to another, Phlegyas. Talking of Heracles, he also dealt with the iron-feathered Stymphalian-Birds which Ares kept as pets. When the Romans re-cast him, he was identified with **MARS**, the blood-red planet of war. It was only then that he got any respect.

ARTEMIS

ARTEMIS was the result of a wild fling between **ZEUS** and a lovely lady called **LETO**. He was married to **HERA** at the time, and not wanting his wanton ways to reach her jealous ears, changed himself and Leto into quails. Gods can do that sort of thing, especially randy Zeus, who must have experienced sex in the guise of almost every animal at some time or another. So Zeus laid Leto, and Leto laid Artemis – and it must have been a double-yolker as **APOLLO** was born at the same time.

Maybe it was the thought of having a sex-mad quail dad that put Artemis off men. When she grew up, she ran off into the wild and took to hunting with a band of women's liberation **NYMPHS** (particularly the **DRYADS**) such as Callisto, who joined her in a vow of chastity.

Despite the hunting, Artemis cares deeply for animals, but she has little respect for human males. When a prowling peeper called Acteon caught sight of her bathing naked in a pool, she hounded him to death with his own hounds. Then the great hunter **ORION** (who was up to much the same thing) got belted into oblivion with the aid of a large scorpion. We are not sure how, as eyewitnesses are understandably reluctant to come forward.

There are many 'hunting accidents' when the name Artemis crops up. But who wants to point the finger? It would probably be chopped off. But she wasn't a complete man-hater, as her efforts on behalf of **HIPPOLYTUS** show.

Her temple at Ephesus contained a statue of a female who, it seems, had undergone breast implants on a multiple scale: she was festooned with them. For a goddess so keen on keeping her nakedness private, that could just be someone's idea of a joke. But in fact the busty statue was actually Cybele, a goddess known for having lashings of lust (and bloodlust). It must be a feminist thing. Worshippers of Artemis revelled in their womanhood in all its forms. And they still do.

In due course the Romans came and revitalised ritualistic religion. They changed the name of Artemis to **DIANA** and her public relations were much improved. Now she is top goddess of the feminist movement, and an inspiration to animal rights activists, as long as quails aren't involved.

ASCLEPIUS

God of medicine. Also known as Asklepios and Aesculapius, depending on whether you are Greek, Roman or dyslexic. He's Dr Deity, having learnt his stuff from **CHIRON** (the medical centaur of all healing knowledge), but was struck off the register by a thunderbolt from **ZEUS** after raising **HIPPOLYTUS** from the grave. The dead were supposed to stay dead, and the gods did not approve of miracle cures. If all the dead came back to life, **HADES** would be out of a job.

So now **ASCLEPIUS** is a sort of Public Health Service god. Sleep at his shrine and you can take advantage of his healing dreams. We don't know if any beds are currently available.

We have it on good authority that the illegible inscriptions carved on Asclepius' clay tablets were the very first doctor's prescriptions – which have remained unreadable ever since.

With Epione he fathered Panacea, who attempts to cure with soothing sooths. Panaceas are still used to this day. And the modern symbol of medicine is based on one of his medical instruments, with the sacred snake of his daughter Hygeia wrapped around it. She of course was the goddess of hygiene. Why she kept a snake we don't know. Perhaps it swallowed viruses and bacteria.

ATHENA

Greek goddess of war, wisdom, art, technical skill and creative DIY. The daughter of **ZEUS** and **METIS**, she almost didn't get born at all after **GAIA** predicted that doom, woe and Olympian take-over bids would be the result. Zeus, remembering how he'd overthrown his own father, grew nervous at the thought of having a daughter with attitude. With the birth rapidly approaching, he finally hit upon a plan and swallowed Metis just before the crucial moment. But it wasn't long before strange tapping and banging noises began to emanate from inside him. What on earth was she doing in there? He was getting a headache.

A little while of this and the pain became unbearable. **HEPHAESTUS**, hearing the cries of agony, came running in and bashed his dad over the head with an Olympic wrench, and from the split in Zeus's skull sprang forth his daughter **ATHENA**. She was fully grown, fully dressed and fully armed with newly forged weapons and helmet. That's what all the noise was about.

Although wise and thoughtful, Athena is no shy maiden. Her best friend is **NIKE**, the goddess of victory, and she carries the Aegis, a flashy-looking device for zapping enemies. She is, of course, highly skilled in arts, crafts and matters of intelligence. Her symbol is the owl, and in matters of wisdom she is always right. After all, who's going to argue with a war goddess?

ATLAS

God of weightlifting and heavy burdens. He is often depicted with the whole world on his shoulders. This is incorrect, as he had to stand on the world and hold up the sky and Heavens above to stop them crashing down on us all.

During the war of the **TITANS**, **ATLAS** stormed Olympus and threatened the gods. As punishment for this war crime, **ZEUS** sentenced him to hold up the Heavens and bear their weight on his shoulders forever. Now the Heavens might be made mostly of cloud, but you'd be surprised how heavy they are. So Atlas was very relieved when the labouring **HERACLES** came along offering to give him a hand in return for a little help with some golden apples from the **HESPERIDES**.

Atlas nipped off to get the apples but wasn't inclined to resume his burden. 'Here, hold this a minute while I scratch my back,' said Heracles. And Atlas, not the brightest apple in the barrel, did so while Heracles made a sharp exit.

The awful burden was made slightly easier for Atlas to bear when **PERSEUS** came along and turned him to stone with the head of Medusa. He's now known as Mount Atlas.

CHARON

Ferryman of the dead. He's a sulky old git who transports souls across the River Styx to the gates of the Underworld. But not for nothing – oh no. First you have to pay him a silver coin. Don't forget to place one under your tongue before they bury you. And even then he might refuse if you haven't been properly buried. Isn't it time the old curmudgeon retired? He must have amassed an amazingly large pension by now. Still, with parents like Erebus and **NYX** what can you expect?

CHIRON

King of the centaurs, **CHIRON** was the son of **CRONUS**, who'd been horsing about with Philyra. With a tutorial by **APOLLO** and a degree in healing from the University of Thessaly, he was very good at the healing arts and renowned for his wisdom. He taught Dr **ASCLEPIUS** the secrets of medicine and thus put the beginnings of medical practice on a very sound footing.

Chiron then appears to have founded the school for heroes on Mount Pelion, with clients including **HERACLES**, Theseus and Achilles. Greek lessons and horse-riding were of course included as standard.

Sadly, Chiron came to an unhappy end when he was accidentally shot with a poisoned arrow by his old pupil Heracles. In frightful agony he roamed the world but, being immortal, could not die. Yes, the great healer could heal everyone except himself. Eventually he wandered to the place where **PROMETHEUS** was undergoing his own agony. Here at last he found freedom from his pain. Performing the world's first immortality-swap operation, Chiron donated his immortal nature to Prometheus and became mortal. Prometheus found himself free, while the old centaur dropped dead at his feet. But shed no tears as a sobbing **ZEUS** granted Chiron a second immortality and transformed him into the constellation of Sagittarius.

COMUS & MOMUS

COMUS was god of comedy, jokes and revelry. Always good for a laugh, and a bit of a practical joker. Son of Circe and **DIONYSUS** (or possibly **HERMES**), he must have inherited his parents' talent for brewing and sorcery because he invented a magic potion which gives anyone who tastes it the head of a beast.

He later found fame as Puck in *A Midsummer Night's Dream* ('Tremendous entertainment' – *Glasgow Herald*) and revitalised the sitcom industry.

MOMUS was more mockery, satire and sneering. Son of Erebus and **NYX** – not parents to father a son with happy jolly humour, the gods failed to find him funny and kicked him out of Heaven. It would be interesting to know if the pair of them formed a double act.

CRONUS

Father of the gods and one of the **TITANS**. He's known as the castrator, definitely a bad sign. His mighty father **URANUS** was terrified of the great ugly kids pregnant **GAIA** was producing and had them banished to the bowels of the Earth. In other words, Gaia's own bowels. She found this so painful (and not just emotionally) that she enlisted the aid of youngest son **CRONUS** to put an end to Uranus' machinations.

With a well-aimed swipe of a sickle, Cronus cut his father off in his prime. With Uranus out of the way, Cronus became top god, and with his wife Rhea he fathered all the other top gods. But it was a case of like father, like son. He was so fearful of his own powerful children that he gobbled them all up and only baby **ZEUS** escaped to save the day.

He is not to be confused with Chronus the grey-bearded wrinkly - the original Old Father Time.

DEMETER

Top crop goddess. She taught nomadic mankind how to plough the fields and settle down, thus making civilisation possible. Very popular with the rural folk. The daughter of **CRONUS** and Rhea, she was rather beautiful and the object of many gods' affections. But she had a liaison with a mortal prince called Lasion. **ZEUS**, who'd admired **DEMETER** from afar, was not happy. When she sloped off at a godly wedding for a fling, he flung a furious thunderbolt where Lasion happened to be standing. But before Zeus could take advantage, the equally horny **POSEIDON** leapt in.

To escape, Demeter changed into a mare and hid in the herd of King Oncus. But Poseidon changed into a stallion and she didn't resist. Jealous Zeus could stand it no longer and managed to pin Demeter down for a liaison of his own. A daughter was duly born, the beautiful **PERSEPHONE**. Now it was the turn of **HADES** to be jealous and one day, while Persephone was playing, he had the Earth swallow her up. When Demeter found her daughter missing she became demented. Tearing her hair, she ran round in the dark with flaming torches, but could shed no light on what had happened. Then **HELIOS**, sun god and right old nosy parker, had a quick word in **DEMETER**'s ear. He'd seen everything and told her that Persephone was now the consort of Hades in the Underworld.

Weeping and wailing, Demeter wandered far and wide. She refused to send as much as a postcard to the gods and in her absence crops became crestfallen, wheat withered and livestock limped to a breeding halt. The gods gnawed their fingers and beseeched her to return. But she refused to capitulate unless she could see her daughter.

One day she stopped for a breather on the palace steps of kindly King Celeus of Eleusis, who, not realising who she was, employed the poor miserable creature as a nurse and didn't ask for references. Demeter tended to Demophon, the son of King Celeus and Metaneira, who were amazed at how bonny the child became – and were even more amazed when they found Demeter about to wrap him in flames. She tried to explain this was only to make the child immortal – but they were not convinced until she turned on a bit of radiance and revealed her godliness. Thereupon she was held in great esteem and installed in her own temple at Eleusis. Here she started her very own secret society and mystery club. It's no good asking about it. Nobody knows – not even Helios managed to peep through the keyhole. Demeter taught Triptolemus, the eldest son of Celeus, to plough and sow and harvest, and gave him air miles vouchers for dragon-powered chariots to spread the news.

Meanwhile, the starving Zeus sent **HERMES** to the Underworld for negotiations with Hades and Persephone. A mother and daughter meeting was agreed, but Hades had a trick in hand. Because Persephone had eaten the mystic Underworld pomegranates, she was tied to the realm of death. But a deal was struck and she was allowed out for half the year.

Demeter was so pleased to see her that flowers bloomed and summer was born. But when Persephone was summoned back to Hades six months later, Demeter became very depressed. Leaves fell off the trees and along came the first winter. And it's been that way each year ever since.

DIONYSUS

God of sex, wine and intoxication – but not necessarily in that order. There are conflicting accounts of his genealogy and conception. The gods involved were probably too drunk at the time to remember. But although **ZEUS** may have had a one-night stand with **PERSEPHONE**, we plump for Zeus and Semele. Why else would **HERA**, the jealous wife of Zeus, arrange Semele's death by insisting he appear before her in all his robes of radiant glory? It was too much for Semele who sizzled away to a cinder, leaving an unborn baby to bounce around in a godly game of 'pass the parcel'.

The bouncing baby got slipped to Zeus who, full of remorse, popped it into his thigh. Gods are way ahead of any modern surgery. When it was born he called it **DIONYSUS**. Hera called it something else and sent some babysitting **TITANS** to tear the baby to bits and eat it. Rhea, bless her, managed to save the bits. Dionysus, disguised as a girl, was whisked off to be brought up in secrecy by Auntie Ino and Uncle Athamas. Not the best of step-parents. Hera discovered the plot, turned into a ram and gave him as a

plaything to a band of **NYMPHS**. If you think you
have troubles, consider being born twice with
a dadly birth, not knowing what sex you are,
and then suddenly finding you have
four legs, horns and an undetachable
woolly coat. Dionysus had many
wild and woolly adventures until
his godly status became apparent.
He put in for a god grant and was
given a more befitting body – and
a tutor. The tutor turned out to be a
fat, boozy, bald old buffer called Silenus.
They got on very well together, and under
tuition Dionysus made two exciting
discoveries: how to make wine, and
how to make orgasms which could
drive you to the brink of madness.

These new ideas brought him an enormous cult
following of wild young females (the Maenads), not to mention his
ever-attendant nymphomaniac Nymphs. Dionysus was a real whizz with
women, and set up a special 18–30 Club for them on Mount Cithaeron.
At some point he got involved with a Cretan princess named Ariadne, but
they drifted apart when she turned into a constellation. Even his aunt
Agave joined in with fervid enthusiasm as the crazy ravers danced and did
disgusting things.

The next few years were spent in hard drinking, and driving females
into a frenzy. This drinking and driving got him into a lot of trouble with
the authorities. News on the grapevine warned of police raids, and even
Dionysus realised it was time to stagger off to start afresh. He changed his
name to Liber and laid low until he emerged in Rome as **BACCHUS**. The
orgy-making was as popular as ever, but by now, with all the debauchery
and gluttony, Dionysus was starting to look more like the middle-aged and
balding boozer Silenus.

ECHO

Beautiful Nymph who had a most musical voice. She was employed by
ZEUS to divert **HERA**'s attention away from his illicit lovemaking. When
Zeus slipped out for a night on the town, **ECHO** would deluge Hera's ears
with a constant stream of babble, gossip and gibbering until he got back:

'…so anyway, I said, I said to her, oooh, I said, I don't believe it, and then she said to me, you won't believe what he said to her, she said, and so I said…'

Hera, driven half-insane by the mindless wittering, removed her power of speech and kicked her out. All **ECHO** could do then was wander the countryside repeating the last syllable of the last person to give utterance. After falling in love and being spurned by Narcissus, she took to living in caves where she had many a one-sided conversation. **PAN** was willing to overlook her affliction but she turned him down, so his shepherds tore her to pieces and scattered her all over the place. Now she's practically everywhere and will talk to anyone who raises their voice.

EOS

Daughter of Hyperion and Thea, she's married to the blustery wind god Astraeus and has four windy sons: Boreus (North), Eurus (East), Notus (South) and Zephyrus (West). She's a bit flighty herself, having been cursed with nymphomania by **APHRODITE**. She made the mistake of fancying **ARES**, which was the cause of the curse, and instead had to make do with a mortal husband, Tithonus. The shame of it.

She pleaded with **ZEUS** to grant Tithonus immortality, but forgot about the ageism clause, so poor Tithonus just got older and older and increasingly withered. Eventually the gods took pity and turned him into a cicada. Before this, **EOS** and Tithonus did manage to produce two sons, Memnon and Emathion. These did not bring any benefits. Memnon got killed by Achilles and Emathion by **HERACLES**.

So it's not surprising that poor Eos carries on weeping. But this in turn ensures there is never any shortage of dew. In Roman times she was known as Aurora, but we have yet to find a happy ending.

ERICHTHONIUS

Even old **HEPHAESTUS** has his moments of uncontrolled lust. One day he was chasing **ATHENA** and, becoming over-excited, a premature ejaculation occurred. A blob landed on Athena's thigh and fell to the Earth. Such is the fecundity of gods that a child instantly sprang up from **GAIA**'s fertile soil.

Gaia was somewhat irritated by this, as she hadn't included giving birth in her plans for the day, particularly not an ugly snaky child as this one was. So she gave the baby, named **ERICHTHONIUS**, to Cecrops for adoption and safekeeping. He entrusted the babe to the care of his daughters in a sealed basket. 'But whatever you do, don't look inside!' he said.

The moment you say that, feminine curiosity will prevail. So they peeked. And inside the child was curled up with two cuddly snakes. In fact, the baby appeared to be something of a snake himself. This gave the sisters such a shock that they leapt shrieking off the top of the Acropolis. They had obviously never seen their father's snaky bits.

ERIS

Goddess of strife and discord and sister of **ARES**. She stole one of the golden apples of immortality, given to **HERA** as a wedding present by **GAIA**, and turned it into the sour apple of discord. What caused the Trojan War? Thanks to **ERIS** and her apple, it was chaos, confusion and top quality bitching!

Miffed at not being invited to the all-star Olympus wedding of Peleus, King of Thessaly, and Thetis, future mother of Achilles, Eris sneaked in anyway. There's always a bit of bitchiness among the top Greek goddesses, but **ATHENA** and Hera were swanning around quite happily until Eris tossed the golden apple among them, bearing the label 'For The Fairest'.

Well, that upset the applecart. Forget the wedding – this was far more important. Who was the fairest of them all? The glamorous goddesses clamoured around **ZEUS**, asking who it should be. As he was already married to insanely jealous Hera, he wasn't going to fall for that one. Instead he passed the buck. 'This question must be decided by a mortal,' he said. And that really started the apple rolling. A dishy guy named Paris was chosen. Speedy messenger boy **HERMES** whisked them all off to Mount Ida. Paris, good-looking but crafty, suggested the apple should be shared. Hermes was having none of it. Fly them all that way for a bit of fun and have it fizzle out? No way. 'Look here chummy, there has to be a firm choice, or you'll get a thunderbolt up your whatsit. Do yourself a favour, you great mortal idiot. Go for bribes.'

So the gorgeous contestants lined up in their Olympic bathing costumes and Paris judged them, one by one. None of the goddesses wanted to travel the world and work for charity, so he went for the bribery option. Athena offered him wisdom. Hera offered him royal power. But **APHRODITE** offered him the most beautiful woman in the whole world, the daughter of Zeus and **LEDA**, whose name happened to be Helen.

You've sussed it, haven't you? He chose Aphrodite. Athena and Hera were furious. But what Aphrodite didn't tell him was that Helen was already married, to none other than the incredibly butch Greek ruler Menelaus. And Paris, who was a Troy boy, was therefore obliged to abduct her. This, of course, started the Trojan War.

Meanwhile Eris laughed like a drain. 'That Trojan Horse thing – what a cackle!' she shrieked as she shared the joke with her sisters. Who, we have reason to believe, just happened to be Nemesis and the **FATES**. Eris also had a daughter called Lethe who became goddess of forgetfulness. We can't remember who the father was.

Nowadays Eris is held in the highest esteem by Discordians, pranksters and those who like to set the cat amongst the pigeons. Little wonder that the solar system's 'tenth planet' – discovered in 2005 and the cause of much astronomical discord and argument – was immediately named after her.

Her daughter Ate is the goddess of mad impulses. She prompts people to do stupid things on the spur of the moment. If you've ever had an unfortunate fling with a complete stranger or run down the street naked to encounter your mother-in-law coming the other way, that's Ate at work.

EROS

God of love. Ancient legends tell how **EROS** was born of Chaos and helped **URANUS** (Heaven) and **GAIA** (Earth) get it together. Their offspring helped to populate the universe and fill the pages of mythology encyclopedias. Later legends claim he's the son of **APHRODITE**, but that's just too obvious, isn't it? Besides, he is probably older than her.

As the beautiful bittersweet god of love, he's in charge of the heart and carries a lethal love weapon which no-one can withstand. With two strings to his bow, he can fire golden arrows for love or leaden ones for indifference, so it's best to get on his good side if you're feeling smoochy. Warning: if you reject the love of another in a nasty manner, his brother Anteros will take his revenge. He was created to stop Eros from being lonely. He also has a bow but his pot shots are not for love.

The most eligible bachelor in the Universe, Eros finally married **PSYCHE** after accidentally pricking himself with one of his own arrows. This was a match made not in Heaven, but in the Underworld. He is also known as cuddly **CUPID** to the Romans and Profit to the manufacturers of Valentine cards.

After the Romans took over the Greek flowers and choccies empire, Eros went roaming to Londinium, where he now resides at Piccadilly Circus. If you feel there's something lacking in your love life, you should pay him a visit. We suggest you take a large bulls-eye.

FATES

Otherwise known as the Moirae, these timeless old entities weave the threads of destiny that control your life. The original spin doctors.

They are: **CLOTHO** the Spinner who does the thread of life; **LACHESIS** who allots the length of the yarn; and **ATROPOS** who does the final snip.

All the good and evil that befalls you is woven into your destiny and cannot be altered even one jot. You may find this a little unfair, but it's the stuff great Greek tragedies are made of.

As the daughters of primeval night deities Erebus and **NYX** (though some claim that **ZEUS** and **THEMIS** should be held responsible), the **FATES** control the destinies of all. Even the gods are subject to their decisions.

Under the Romans they became just as popular under the name **PARCAE**.

GAIA

Big vista Earth Mother. Born of Chaos, she gave birth to Pontus, the sea, and **URANUS**, the sky. Then she married Uranus and became the unfortunate mother of the huge **TITANS**, the Cyclopes and the **HECATONCHIRES**. Her husband was shocked at the nature of their offspring, so she hid them all inside herself to protect them, which was terribly uncomfortable for all concerned. Luckily her youngest, **CRONUS**, came to the rescue armed with a large cutting tool.

But all that's behind **GAIA** now. She became best friends with **HERA**, giving her the golden apples of immortality as a wedding present, and always gathered the utmost respect. As fertile as they come, her offspring also includes Acheron, the god of rivers, Python, and who knows who else?

HADES

God of the Underworld and son of **CRONUS** and Rhea. When the family fortune was divvied up, he got the Underworld share while his brothers **ZEUS** and **POSEIDON** were given the Earth and sea. There's nothing wrong with nepotism as long as you keep it in the family. They even named the place after him.

Unlike many Underworld gods, **HADES** is quite affable provided you treat him with respect. And although a dingy and dull place, Hades itself seems to be a very popular joint – Greek heroes are always nipping down there to rescue their mates or consult the dead. But Hades doesn't really approve of these shady goings-on. The Land of the Dead is supposed to be for the dead, alright? Even if you get past **CHARON** and **STYX**, there's a whole team of demonic officials to fend off enquiries, including Thanatos and **HYPNOS**. Watch out for their bureaucratic dead tape. And don't eat any pomegranates or you'll be trapped there like his wife **PERSEPHONE**.

Hades, known to the Romans as **PLUTO**, has an enormous guard dog named Cerberus keeping watch on the entrance to the Underworld. The sign on Hell's gate does not read 'Beware of the Dog'. It reads: 'Beware of the Three-Headed Serpent-Maned Monster Hound with Slavering Jaws and Deadly Halitosis'.

HECATONCHIRES

These hundred-handed giants were the sons of **URANUS** and **GAIA**. They were not too bright, not having twigged they were mostly tree. After naming them **BRIARIUS** the Vigorous, **COTTUS** the Furious and **GYGES** the Big-Limbed, the parents decided they had done enough and hurled them to the world below the Underworld. There they stayed for a million or so years knowing no better life, until the time came when **CRONUS** put paid to the fatherhood of Uranus and the big gods vs **TITANS** dust-up started.

Mother Earth Gaia was trying to be neutral, but she kept getting stomped and trampled on by both sides. She moaned to **ZEUS** that this wouldn't happen if her lads could join in. In action the brothers had the mindless violence and loyalty that ensured victory for the gods, and as a special reward Zeus said they could go back to the lowest Underworld and guard such Titans as had surrendered.

HELIOS

It's sunshine sunshine all the way as he shines through the sky in his golden-winged chariot. From up there he sees everything that happens and is often called upon to shed light on events. Son of Hyperion and Thea, he has a frankly staggering number of children. By turning the tables and following the sun from behind a cloud we have peered into his love life – and it seems to be 'Go for it sunshine, all the way'.

With his wife Perse he bore four Aeetes of the Argonauts, and a little Perses and Pasiphae and Circe. Next there was a liaison with Rhodos, one of the **NYMPHS**, who bore seven sons and the daughter Electryone. Does it stop there? Not at all – he's the father of Acheron by **GAIA**, there's an affair with the Oceanid Clymene and another seven daughters called the Heliades and his ill-fated son **PHAETON**. Then he moved nearer to someone called Neara and two daughters, Phaethusa and Lampetia, arrived in time to prove most useful in looking after his sacred cattle flocks.

Then he had the hots for Leucothea, but Clytie who had already enjoyed **HELIOS**' favours was jealous, and told her dad King Orcharios of Babylon – who condemned Leucothea to be buried alive. Helios arrived too late to restore her and so changed her into a shrub. In remorse, Clytie exposed herself to nature until she faded away, gazing all the time at Helios zooming through the Heavens. She was transformed at last into a heliotrope, which as you should know is a sunflower.

We last see him chasing after Anaxibia, another of the Nymphs, who seems so far to have eluded him. Phew!

HEPHAESTUS

Differently abled son of **ZEUS** and **HERA**. 'Well,' said the disappointed Hera, 'with legs like those he is never going to play for Olympus,' and tipped him over the edge of a cloud.

He fell into the sea but two Goddesses, Eurynome and Thetis, rescued him. They taught him to make seaside souvenirs from seashells and coral and he turned out to be an amazing craftsman, graduating from this to greater and grander things.

Apart from his ugly mug and withered legs, he became a muscular hunk. With his strength went strength of purpose and he went for Blacksmithery in a big way. If you can run an underwater forge you have unassailable skills. Such was his fame, he was allowed back to Olympus and Zeus had him making thunderbolts and supervising the Cyclopes when the war with the **TITANS** was in full swing.

Peace came and with it new demands as he could make just about anything: clockwork tables, armour of invincibility, wrought-iron pub signs and robotic statues. He even got to marry **APHRODITE**; quite a consolation – even if she did cheat on him a lot. But he did have a small revenge when he caught her and **ARES** *in flagrante* in a net of his own devising and put them on display for a bit. This made him even more popular.

For all his strength he is not a god to go about causing trouble and smiting folk. Like his works, he is well-tempered, and has acted as a role model for smithery the world over. The Romans couldn't wait to commit forgery and sign him up as **VULCAN**.

HERA

Mrs **ZEUS**. Supreme Greek goddess and the queen of Olympus. She's also a goddess of marriage and birth, which is somewhat ironic considering that her notoriously unfaithful husband Zeus produced an incredible number of illicit offspring with an entire pantheon of lovely ladies.

If he wasn't liaising with **LETO** and **LEDA**, he was getting friendly with Danae, **THEMIS** or Mnemosyne – all behind **HERA**'s back. He used every trick in the book to mislead and divert her away from his affairs.

Although as regal as they come, Hera is not the most godly of goddesses. She can be spiteful, vicious and extremely jealous, but who can blame her with all the carrying-on Zeus did? Their arguments and fighting make Mount Olympus shake to its roots. And when Hera starts throwing the Holy Crockery you know it's time to make a rapid exit.

Even Zeus is scared of his formidable wife. After seeing what she did to his illegitimate son **HERACLES** we can understand why. The one time he managed to get the better of her by force, by chaining her to a mountain with horrifically heavy weights, Zeus didn't hear the end of the matter for centuries. No wonder he spends most of his time delayed at the office.

We have to admire Hera's strength and determination. She certainly gives as good as she gets. And if you're lucky enough to be in her good books, she can be wonderfully gracious and charming. But she's best avoided at parties unless you happen to be carrying a sacred pomegranate in your pocket.

HERACLES

Not a god to start with. Just an old-fashioned heavy. The Sylvester Stallone of Greek mythology.

One day **ZEUS** declared that a descendant of heroic **PERSEUS** would become King of Mycenae, a city of great splendour and power. Zeus being top god, his word was immutable, and thus was it so. But not quite the way he intended. Alcmena's child **HERACLES** was almost due to be born. He was full of Perseus genes – and just happened to be Zeus's illegitimate son.

Heracles means '**HERA**'s Glory', but after she drove him mad and forced him to kill his own children it was more like 'gory'. Hera detested most of Zeus's extra-marital kids, but she hated Heracles with a divine vengeance and plotted the most evil plots against him. Poor Herc, reeling from the murder of his children, went to the oracle of **APOLLO** for psychological counselling and was told that a bit of physical labour would take his mind off things. Thus began the Labours of Heracles.

These tasks, in truth devised by Hera and implemented by his half-brother and rival to the Mycenaen crown Eurystheus, lasted many years -- and were designed solely for the purpose of wiping him out. But he didn't know that. 'Complete those labours and immortality shall be yours,' the oracle had said, and poor Herc didn't know any better.

So he went off and battled monsters, cut heads off things, and went on quests devised by Eurystheus to cause maximum trouble. From battling Typhon and Echidna monster productions to performing whiter-than-white washing day miracles with the Augean Stables, he was certainly kept busy. He even had to nip down to the Underworld to take Cerberus for walkies. Rival Eurystheus devised every setback he could imagine to put Herc off, including declaring several labours null and void. But whenever our triumphant hero returned with a slavering beast under his arm, Eurystheus would run off and hide under the bed.

Although Heracles succeeded in every quest, this only made Hera hate him the more. The poor guy travelled everywhere doing his best to right wrongs, but she plagued him with storms and evilness for many years afterwards. Finally, after many more adventures, including being sold as a slave, becoming a pirate and fighting for Olympus against the giant sons of the **TITANS**, he died in a mix-up over a magic potion, and was accidentally tainted with the blood of the Hydra from one of his own arrowheads.

But as a reward for all his trials and tribulations, he was offered a grudging kind of immortality and a share of the film rights. Reconciled to Hera at last, he married her daughter Hebe and now lives happily ever after. And then did it all over again for the Romans under the name **HERCULES**…

HERMAPHRODITUS

His and hers. Tits and bits. Greek up the creek. Handsome man meets beautiful nymph in lakeside liaison and she ends up moving into his place. Literally. Two can live as cheaply as one when you share the same body.

HERMAPHRODITUS started as the handsome son of **HERMES** and **APHRODITE** until he got jumped by one of the **NYMPHS** who was very persistent. She wanted to be with him body and soul, and clung on until some sort of cloning took place. The first example of genetic modification? That kind of thing is all very well until you have your first real argument. And then you realise that you have to throw the crockery at yourself.

HERMES

Messenger of the gods. He's also the god of merchants and commerce, athletics and travel, public speaking, shepherds and thieves. The son of

ZEUS and Maia, he was barely a day old before he was stealing **APOLLO**'s sheep, bartering goods and contemplating the small print of manufacturers' warranties. A very musical lad, he invented the lyre and the pan pipes and had what may have been the world's first jam session with music buddy Apollo. His gift of the gab made him the perfect choice for messenger duties. Zeus made him a herald and kitted him out with a winged hat and sandals. Powered by these he can zoom all over the place delivering news that's worse than it sounds. **HERMES** then made a vow to Zeus: 'I will never tell lies – although I cannot promise always to tell the whole truth.'

Despite wheeling and dealing by the seat of his pants, Hermes always manages to leave his customers perfectly satisfied, mostly due to his incredibly cunning sales talk. He's such a persuasive salesman he could sell pyramids to the Egyptians. (Wait! He already has!) Those sandals make him fleet of foot and an expert runner, which is why he's also the god of racing and athletics. Perfect for chasing after new clients, or running away from old ones.

His dodgy dealing tactics were also passed down to his son Autolycus. Under the Romans he changed his name to **MERCURY** and floated himself on the stock market.

HESPERIDES

Three Golden Ones. Daughters of **NYX** and Erebus who look after the very rare apple tree Golden Immortalitus, not to be confused with Golden Delicious. This shines with the golden radiance of a glorious sunset, which is why the **HESPERIDES** are also sunset goddesses.

AEGLE does the shining, **HESPERA** 'Light of the Evening' does the watering (she was also known as Arethusa but took on an alternative name to avoid confusion with the well-known nymph), and **ERYTHEIA** 'The Red One' pores over the best times for pruning and picking. Hestia pops in from time to time to tend the flowerbeds.

The Hesperides are best of friends with **ATLAS**, who is a close neighbour. Some legends even claim he is their father by Hesperis. Other legends give **ZEUS** the credit, and one or two cynical folk claim the Hesperides are simply a flock of golden sheep.

HIPPOLYTUS

Son of Theseus the Minotaur slayer and his mistress Antiope. He was not a happy lad and did not like life in the palace where he grew up. When a trumped-up charge of attempting to rape his stepmother Phaedra reached his ears he fled in a chariot. Theseus prayed to the gods to stop him, and **POSEIDON**, being nearest as the chariot was hurtling along a coastal road, sent a huge wave, which startled the horses into causing a crash with fatal results.

For a time, anyway. When **ARTEMIS**, **HIPPOLYTUS**'s patron goddess, heard about it she was livid. She demanded that her client be restored to life as he was innocent of any crime and Poseidon had not been asked to destroy him anyway. She raised such a commotion that **ASCLEPIUS** rushed to the accident spot with his first-aid kit. A shot of ambrosia had **HIPPOLYTUS** sitting up and twisting his broken neck until the pain subsided.

This in turn upset the **FATES**, who had not been consulted on this emergency raising of the dead. It meant taking in a lot of extra sewing and having to unpick lots of threads – and someone would have to pay. They threatened to go on strike unless someone was stitched up, so **ZEUS** had to kill Asclepius with a thunderbolt to keep them happy.

Artemis took Hippolytus away, declaring she would make a new man of him. He is now an ancient hippy sitting in the sun and enjoying the simple life forever.

HORAE

Goddesses of the seasons and, later, of natural and moral law. They were three very beautiful and talented daughters of **ZEUS** and **THEMIS**, despite bearing the almost unbearable names of **EUNOMIA**, **DIKE** and **EIRENE**. At least this was an improvement on their earlier ghastly names of Thallo, Carpo and Auxo. Their numbers are often exaggerated as they got around a lot and some scholars feel there must be almost a dozen. This is because they went partying with the Graces and could do chorus girl routines. On the other hand, their name means 'Hours' and there are twelve hours in a day.

Amongst many other things, they look after the Gates of Heaven. When undesirables approach, they slide a cloud in front so no-one can get through or get hurt. So much nicer than a board proclaiming 'Trespassers Will Be Thunderbolted'. The **HORAE** do lots of fruity and blossomy things, and also offer services such as babysitting for the gods and feeding the horses. No-one has a word to say against them, and we certainly don't wish to hear any such thing.

HYACINTHUS

Flowery god of male love. Like politicians and celebrities, the gods have their little foibles that they try to keep quiet. **APOLLO**, for instance, was mad about **HYACINTHUS**, who was a prince and not a princess.

One fine day they were playing frisbee with Apollo's discus when the west wind **ZEPHYRUS** and the north wind **BOREAS** became a teensy bit jealous. These were given to whispering sweet nothings into the lad's ears, but this time they both took a quick puff and oh horror, the frisbee went spiralling out of control. It came down and hit Hyacinthus a blow on the head. The discus being made of heavy metal, nothing much could be done for the boy after the blood had been mopped up, but Apollo commemorated his memory by turning the mortal remains into a hyacinth. Isn't that sweet?

HYPNOS

HYPNOS is the god of sleep, which he induces with purest opium smoked through a horn. Obviously the god of hippies. He could also be the god of dangerous addictions, as he works for **HADES** with his brother Thanatos, the god of 'everlasting sleep' – death.

Luckily, he's recently found a better use for his talents and given his name to hypnosis, the mesmerising modern miracle of psycho-physiological somnambulism. You are feeling sleepy … sleeeeepy. You are going to sleeeep … Does it work?

LEDA

Daughter of King Thestius, she was notorious for swanning around with **ZEUS** during one of his bird impressions. Zeus had turned her into a swan to avoid detection by the jealous **HERA**, and in that form she had a lot of fun, until she discovered she'd conceived and that instead of giving birth, she'd have to lay eggs – which subsequently hatched into godlets.

LEDA was married to Tyndareds, a banished heir to the throne of Sparta, and when the eggs arrived two of the yolks were his: Castor and Clytemnestra. The other two, Pollux and Helen, were Zeuslings.

There is another ending to this story. Check the website for details.

LETO

Daughter of Coeus and Phoebe and mother of the twins **ARTEMIS** and **APOLLO**. She's quite a bird, and we're not being sexist – she was a quail at the time. Blame **ZEUS** – it was his doing that the twins were born with egg on their faces.

Disguising themselves as birds and getting intimate on a floating island was the only way for **LETO** and Zeus to escape the attentions of a jealous **HERA**. Which helps to explain why Leto was known as The Hidden One.

METIS

The first Mrs **ZEUS**. She was the goddess of wisdom and Zeus was warned that any resulting children would be much smarter than him. Now any sensible god would have abstained from sex, but randy Zeus was so turned on by her shape-shifting abilities that he couldn't resist. So when she became pregnant he remembered the prophecy and decided to take precautions, a little late. He swallowed **METIS** whole – but himself gave birth to **ATHENA**, goddess of wisdom, making him sadder but wiser.

MINOS & HIS MINOTAUR

MINOS was king of Crete and, what with being a love child of **ZEUS** and owner of a maze containing the bull-headed bloodthirsty **MINOTAUR**, offspring of the Cretan Bull, he was determined to get into the godly record books. The bull was a prezzie from **POSEIDON**, and was supposed to be used for a sacrifice but ended up having a fling with Minos's wife Pasiphae and the Minotaur was the result. Plenty of tabloid fodder there, and more once Theseus became involved.

After he died, Minos was given a new lease of life. Sitting by the side of Aeacus and previously estranged brother Rhadamanthus, he gives the casting vote in tricky cases of Soul Judgment.

MORPHEUS

God of dreams. 'I met at eve the Prince of Sleep, his was a still and lovely face.' Son of **HYPNOS** and Pasithea, **MORPHEUS** is also the nephew of Thanatos, the god of death. This gives him a very good pedigree in Greek slumberland.

While his brothers Phobetor and Phantasos veer toward the more bizarre scenarios and violent nightmares, Morpheus specialises in ultra-realistic dreams – the kind where you find yourself naked at the office party. When he stands beckoning in the twilight of your dreams, girls looking for nocturnal pleasure will be unlucky, for they will be very much on their own. We reckon further research needs to be done on this beckoning business.

Of his private life, very little is known. Morpheus sleeps in a darkened cave with Poppy, but who is she? Vague rumours circulate that this could be Opium Poppy. Which explains a lot. Yet in most tomes of Greek geekishness he is a sadly neglected figure. Scholars appear to have dozed off at the very mention of his name and indexes bear witness to this indolence. Perhaps Morpheus himself has encouraged this fading dream memory with his metaphorical metamorphosis into a shadowy handsome figure waiting in the wings of the dusk.

His legacy is Morphine, named after him and found in most medical works, so think of him as medical history. He is also known as the Sandman, but you can call him Sandy for short.

THE MUSES

Born of **ZEUS** and Mnemosyne, they inspire poets, musicians, writers, philosophers and website designers.

The world would be a far poorer place without **CALLIOPE** – she has a beautiful singing voice and makes even the wimpiest poetry resound with epic meaning. The lover of **APOLLO** she gave birth to **ORPHEUS** and Linus. She took a shine to **ACHILLES** and may have taught him rowdy drinking songs.

CLIO was probably the muse Homer turned to when he needed substance for his epics. Apart from history and poetry she introduced the Phoenician alphabet.

ERATO champions smoochy love songs and erotic poetry, and after a few glasses of wine her party trick is impersonations.

EUTERPE invented the double flute to give double the pleasure.

MELPOMENE does the tragic bits with doomed lovers and lingering. Always in demand, then.

POLYHYMNIA is usually found writing and singing hymns which she does not seem to enjoy. She sings mournfully and even her dancing is miserable. Sometimes she just sits around looking worried.

TERPSICHORE does dramatic dancing, barefoot with bangles.

THALIA does stand-up comedy routines, pastoral sitcoms and nights out.

URANIA is really spaced out and does astrology and astronomy. She carries a globe, and wears a cloak decorated with stars. You can't beat a bit of cosmic mystery.

Their sublime choir is conducted by Apollo, who ensures they perform everything in perfect blissful harmony.

NEMESIS

Goddess of retribution and vengeance. She knows where you are. Don't try to get too clever, too lucky or too rich. **NEMESIS** particularly hates arrogance and offences against the natural order of things. Jaywalking may carry divine penalties – and don't even think of running a red light.

Her parentage is obscure. Daughter of **ZEUS**? Oceanus? Erebus? No-one is certain and we'd rather not risk getting it wrong. There's also a possible twist involving **LEDA** and a clutch of eggs. Nemesis is depicted as a stern-looking woman holding a whip, or sometimes a pair of scales. In the Hellenistic period she was occasionally shown holding a steering wheel – which just proves what we were saying about the red lights.

NEPHELE

Ixion, the wickedest man in the world, was invited to a Heavenly Olympic banquet. But he intended to repay this generosity by raping **HERA**, the wife of **ZEUS**, whom he fancied rotten.

Seeing through this little plan, Zeus made an exact replica of Hera from clouds. The cloned Hera was called **NEPHELE**. She was very life-like and Ixion was completely fooled. Having caught out his wife's would-be assailant, Zeus tied him to a flaming wheel and sent him off for everlasting punishment in the Underworld.

This left Nephele very confused. As she could not be un-created, and kept being mistaken for Hera, she tried to avoid further bewilderment by weeping in corners. But that didn't work as passing gods kept asking: 'What's the matter Hera?' Zeus got a bit fed up with it all and married her off to Athamas, the most stupid king in the world, making her queen of Boeotia. It went well at the start but after two children Nephele got the miseries again and kept turning into a drizzling cloud. Athamas got fed up and set up a secret love nest with **INO**. Not too good a choice as Zeus was having an affair with her sister Semele, and Athamas had to let him have a spare key.

Then of course Hera found out. After telling Athamas in no uncertain terms how stupid he was, she whisked Nephele back to Olympus to work in the stables – filling the water trough with tears.

NYMPHS

Frolicsome female nature spirits. These are beautiful young ladies who inhabit trees, rivers, fields and other pastoral places. As guardians of nature, they protect the ecology of the countryside. And let's face it: **GAIA** needs all the help she can get. But they still find time to frolic. We present the Good Nymph Guide:

AURAI – breezy Nymphs

DAPHNAIE – laurel tree Nymphs named after Daphne, a Naiad plagued with unwelcome sexual advances until Gaia came to her rescue and turned her into a laurel tree.

DRYADS – collective name for tree and forest Nymphs. They are shy and inhabit a specific tree. They can emerge and do a bit of frolicking and **ARTEMIS** takes them for days out.

HAMADRYADS – oak tree Nymphs

HYDRIADS – water and sea Nymphs

LIMONIADS – meadow and flower Nymphs

MELIADS – ash tree and fruit tree Nymphs. It is said the ash trees came from fertile Gaia soil which had been pollinated by blood from the recently liberated testicles of **URANUS**.

NEREIDS – sea Nymphs

NAIADS – river and stream Nymphs. They like running waters, silvery streams, babbling brooks and rippling rivers.

OCEANIDS – cloud and sea Nymphs

OREADS – mountain pine Nymphs

Although, like angels, they are spiritual beings somewhat below godly status, the Nymphs are not immortal. They just live for a very long time. A tree nymph lives as long as her tree, a river nymph likewise. Although some are the daughters of specific gods, most of the Nymphs have no easily defined parentage. They mostly seem to be young human ladies who have fallen into rivers or been accidentally slain by passing heroes. The gods don't like all that beauty going to waste.

NYX

Being a real night person, she loves the dark. Which explains why she is the consort of Erebus, the god of darkness – or at least likes him enough for the odd fling which has resulted in the births of **AETHER**, Hemera and the **FATES**.

Every evening she coaxes him out to spread his gloomy darkness, which obscures the shining Aether and lets the stars come out to play. It's up to daughter Hemera to waft away the darkness every morning to let the sun shine. Like many other Greek deities, **NYX** has lent her name to a celestial object. Previously known as S/2005 P1, this gloomy moon circles the remote planetoid Pluto in a suitably shadowy and mysterious manner. Strangely, astronomers have decided to spell the name 'Nix' instead of

Nyx. We imagine there must be a Disney character with a similar nixname waiting in the wings.

OMPHALE

Queen of Lydia, she bought **HERACLES** at a slave auction for one year. She dressed him up as a woman to humiliate him, making him follow behind her in dress and veil carrying a sunshade. Then she dressed in his lion-skin and took to brandishing his club at the peasants.

Then she realised he was enjoying it as much as she was, and the cross-dressing became sexually stimulating.

PAN once came across **OMPHALE**'s nightie in a grotto sans the Oomph girl. He leapt under the duvet only to find himself clutching Heracles, who kicked him out in no uncertain fashion.

Pan still limps whenever he thinks about it. Heracles was not having any funny hanky-panky threesomes thank you very much, even if he was having to labour as a devoted slave.

ORION

The hunter, giant mortal son of **POSEIDON** and Euryale. He must have been very big once as you can see his belt in the sky. Where the rest of him is we don't know. Try joining the dots.

His life was filled with unhappy love affairs, mostly because he couldn't help falling for girls above his station. If you're a king and **ORION** pays a visit, our advice is to lock up your daughter and call the police. He's a typical macho hunter type, and he mostly hunts females. (See **ARTEMIS**.) He may also have been involved in the motor industry at one time. Is he anything to do with safety belts? There is another rumour that he is in Ireland and has changed his name to O'Ryan.

ORPHEUS & EURYDICE

ORPHEUS was the son of the silver-tongued **CALLIOPE** and when he played his lyre even the rocks and trees would stop what they were doing and listen.

When his wife Eurydice, who started as a **DRYAD**, was poisoned by a serpent, she had to descend to the Underworld. Orpheus went to the rescue and sang such heartfelt ballads that even **HADES** shed a tear. Unfortunately he slipped up on the small print: that she could follow him out but on no account was he to look back. He did and Eurydice remained among the dead.

Poor Orpheus was so miserable that he tried to become a hermit, but a pack of wild Maenads kept pestering him. Adding injury to insult, they bombarded him with sticks, stones and rotten tomatoes before realising that not even the smallest twig would dare to interrupt his wonderful lyre. So they beat him to a pulp instead and sent his head floating down the river, still singing of his woes.

PAN

God of shepherds, flocks and fornication. What does that tell you about the ancient Greek countryfolk then? The son of **HERMES**, and possibly a goat, **PAN** was one of the **DIONYSUS** drinking crowd, with all the leering lusty living this entailed: woodland glades; **NYMPHS**; orgies; flutes. That sort of thing. You get the picture. As a god with his hooves firmly placed on the ground, Pan was (and still is) worshipped as a potent deity of fertility and earthiness.

He was known as Faunus by the faunicating Romans. In time, his carefree lifestyle began to upset the early Christians, who saw his earthy temptations as a manifestation of the Devil. Who would've thought that the horny old goat would become the blueprint for popular conceptions of **SATAN** – cloven hooves, horns and all?

PANDORA

Don't open that box! If she were a goddess, she'd be goddess of curiosity. But **PANDORA** was the first woman, invented by **HEPHAESTUS** on the orders of a bored **ZEUS** (who'd run out of goddesses to seduce). The gods showered her with all the gifts of womankind, including beauty, intuition, persuasion and the ability to pack suitcases.

But when **PROMETHEUS** stole fire from Heaven, the gods were angered and decided to teach mankind a lesson. Pandora was given to

his dozy brother Epimetheus, along with a mysterious box. 'Whatever you do, don't open it,' they said.

With amazing restraint, Pandora resisted the temptation for almost twenty minutes before having just a little peek inside...

And BLAM! All the evils of the world burst out, much to Pandora's surprise. First out was Apate, goddess of lies and deceit. What a sneaky underhand trick! The misfortunes of mankind zoomed off to cause havoc, leaving a guilty Pandora to discover Elpis (hope) lurking at the bottom of the box – along with a little note saying 'Fooled you!'

Pandora might be blamed for all the world's problems, but without her daughter Pyrrha the human race would be extinct. So try to think outside the box.

PERSEPHONE

Queen of the Underworld. She is the illicit daughter of **ZEUS** and **DEMETER** and grew into such a beauty that men would look at her open-mouthed and say 'Cor!' or in Greek 'Kore!' – which is what she came to be called. Although she always insisted her proper name was **PERSEPHONE**.

With Zeus and his brother **POSEIDON** always getting the pick of ravishing beauties, the third brother **HADES** felt very left out, what with being stuck in the Underworld. So Zeus promised him a beautiful woman named Kore when she was old enough. What he neglected to do was let Demeter or Persephone know. Persephone was engaged in the innocent pursuit of picking flowers when a black-horsed chariot came surging up from a chasm and she was snatched. To all intents and purposes she had vanished without trace.

There is an unbreakable rule that those who partake of food in the Underworld are tied to it forever. Hades, who fancied Persephone rotten, tricked the silly girl into nibbling a few pomegranate seeds.

This caused some concentrated arbitration but Zeus, being the wily old diplomat he was, brought Rhea into the equation and stitched up an agreement whereby Persephone could stay with Demeter for the spring and summer to help with the growth industries and then pop down to live with Hades for six months or so, creating a winter break and season ticket for nature to take time off.

Demeter's never been happy about this, and that's why winters are so bleak. So think of Hades when you are cuddled up cosily in front of a fire.

PERSEUS

Son of **ZEUS** and Danae, but sadly a mortal. Granddad Acrisius had read a horoscope warning he would be killed by the child of Danae. So he shut them both in a box and chucked them in the sea. Wooden boxes float and fishermen catch all manner of odd things in nets – they ended up on a tiny island just big enough to have a king, Olydectus, and all went well.

PERSEUS grew up and, being a get-ahead kind of fellow, set off in a boat to have adventures. Naturally to do this he'd put in a grant for Heavenly aid. The Stygian **NYMPHS** provided suitable equipment: a helmet of invisibility from **HADES**, a shiny diamond sword from **HERMES**, and … a scruffy old bag from the tool shed. This last item proved by far the most useful, as he used it to carry off the freshly severed head of Medusa, most notorious of the Gorgons.

From this exploit he gained Pegasus the Winged Wonder Horse, born from the blood of Medusa. (Somewhere along the way he got into an argument with **ATLAS** and used Medusa's head to turn him to stone. For which Atlas was very grateful.)

Finding he was very good at this sort of thing, and having great confidence in his equipment, Perseus went in for the full thrilling hero career, rescuing Andromeda from a frightful sea dragon (so many years before that copycat St George). He became extremely popular, never refusing to sign autographs or speak to reporters, and was always hoping this would ensure the possibility of being taken on an Olympian trip.

His grandson Eurystheus became king of Mycenae and was an utter coward, to the embarrassment of all concerned.

PHAETON

Secret son of sun god **HELIOS** by Clymene. He managed to track down his old man and tried to drive his sunny chariot, but hadn't passed his driving test and made a right pig's ear of it. **ZEUS** zonked him out of the sky to prevent him scorching the Earth when he went badly off course.

PLEIADES

More daughters of **ATLAS** who sought stardom after nearly having their careers ruined by **ORION**.

They all had casting couch affairs with leading directors of the day except one, Merore, who was propositioned by Sisyphus, a pushy mortal, so she doesn't get to shine as brightly as the others.

MAIA, **TAYGETE** and **ELECTRA** were chosen by **ZEUS** giving a three-star rating. **ALCYONE** and **CELONEO** got **POSEIDON** and a two-star rating. **STEROPE** got **ARES**, so we only give her one star.

Constellations and stars were exceedingly useful to Greek Mythologists. They could stick gods surplus to requirements on Earth up there, where they could bask in Celebrity Status, and be looked up to without causing any scandal or confrontations. In fact, they have been of great use to astronomers who have used Greek god names for Star Charts, and then used Roman gods for planets.

It is good they can all be stars but it is a shame they are not allowed to sing or dance or anything.

PLUTUS

God of riches. The son of **DEMETER**, he made the Horn of Plenty from one of bull-headed river god Achelous's horns, which had been snapped off by **HERACLES**, and filled it to the brim with goodies.

To avoid favouritism when it came to doling out the cornucopias, **ZEUS** blinded him. So now he can't see a thing and wealth is dispensed to good and bad alike. But you could try writing him a begging letter in braille.

POSEIDON

God of the sea. Took charge of the waves while his brothers **ZEUS** and **HADES** plumped for the earthy bits. Feared by sailors, he can cause storms and shipwrecks with the aid of his three-pronged trident, but if he's in a good mood he can soothe the sea to sleep.

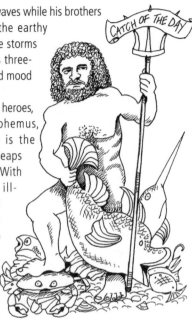

He is the father of many gods and heroes, including Theseus, Triton, Polyphemus, **ORION** and Pegasus. His wife is the reluctant Amphitrite, but he still leaps from one lusty affair to the next. With Iphimedeia he produced the ill-fated **ALOADAE** twins Otus and Ephialtes. **DEMETER** presented him with Arion and Despoena. And so on. Sea air is obviously good for the libido. Check out his flowing beard and ruddy complexion.

Under the Romans, **POSEIDON** was poised and ready to become **NEPTUNE**.

PRIAPUS

Long-standing god of virility. He's the brother of Hymenaeus and the son of beautiful **APHRODITE**, but there's some confusion over his father's identity. Zeus, **APOLLO** and **DIONYSUS** are the most likely candidates. But we incline towards Zeus because it was his wife **HERA** (a jealous rival in the beauty stakes) who put a curse on the unborn baby which resulted in him being delivered plug-ugly and impotent. He was so utterly revolting that the gods kicked him out and **PRIAPUS** fell to Earth. The unhappy child was fostered by **NYMPHS** and shepherds, which brought him during his formative years into contact with the piping hot band of **PAN** and the Satyrs, a group well known for their wild animalistic behaviour and outrageous sexual exhibitionism.

He was always well-attended by Nymphs and their nymphomania. But sadly, however much Priapus lusted, he could not come up with the goods. Until one day something amazing happened and his male appendage grew to enormous size. Could there have been a god named Viagra lurking behind the scenes? Unfortunately this erection was permanent, and so huge that he couldn't move. He was rooted to the spot. Pan carried him off and stood him at the entrance of the woods as a sort of minder. Whenever unwanted visitors wandered by, Priapus would lift his tunic, brandish his weapon, and scare them away.

Following this, statues of Priapus became very popular for guarding gates, estates, crossroads and doorways. He was employed as a sort of sleeping policeman, or traffic hump. And before passing his figure, it was deemed wise for passers-by to stroke the willy for luck. (This kind of career opportunity is sadly lacking in modern times.)

Somewhere along the line some wag (or graffiti artist) added a winged helmet and sandals to some of these statues, thereby causing identity confusion with **HERMES**. Basic phallic statues began to appear and these were known as Herms. (Eventually, the Romans promoted Hermes to **MERCURY**, so it must have done his reputation some good!)

Meanwhile, Priapus rose fairly high in the public's estimation, and was later given responsibility for harvests and fruitfulness. But one disturbing fact remains: he never had any progeny.

PROMETHEUS

Son of Iapetus and Clymene. He was a rival to his brother Epimetheus in the creature creation game. He was eventually punished for stealing fire from the gods and bringing it to mankind. In **ZEUS**'s eyes, this was the most terrible crime, almost as bad as giving scammers access to high speed internet.

Zeus was furious, and dished out a terrible punishment. **PROMETHEUS** was chained to a rock with goddess Bia's patented god-bonds which only an immortal could break. He was left there to suffer agony and torment forever, having his liver pecked out every day by an eagle. Next day another liver would grow back. The punishment was supposed to last for all eternity, but as luck would have it **CHIRON** the centaur came along…

PSYCHE

Personification of the soul, goddess of beauty and wife of **EROS**. Princess **PSYCHE** was the most amazingly beautiful mortal ever. She was almost as beautiful as **APHRODITE** on a bad hair day. People were known to forget their own names and swoon at her feet. Aphrodite wasn't happy. Her temples were being neglected by Psyche fans and that just wasn't on. So she conspired with Eros to make the princess fall in love with the ugliest man they could find. That would soon get her out of the public eye.

Eros fluttered off and got ready to launch an arrow of love at the innocent Psyche. But by chance, he pricked his finger on that very arrow and fell hopelessly in love with her himself. This caused all kinds of problems for all concerned, and eventually Psyche found herself cut off from mortals and gods alike as Aphrodite's wrath pursued her. She contemplated suicide by drowning, but even the waves refused to take her.

The only way to salvation was by passing Aphrodite's cruel and unusual tests. The ultimate challenge: go down to the Underworld and steal **PERSEPHONE**'s beauty cream. Her heart quailed, but Princess Psyche made her radiant way down the gloomy steps. Seeing the approach of loveliness, Cerberus, the ill-tempered hound of Hell, rolled over like a puppy. One sweetie from her maidenly hand and he was friends for life. And grim **CHARON**, taking one look at her youthful beauty, blushed to his boots and gave her free passage. So finally she arrived at the throne room of **HADES** himself.

Now Hades is very proud of his domain, and doesn't tolerate the living turning up. It spoils the atmosphere of gloom and despair. So he would've killed Psyche there and then, but his wife Persephone saw this was no

ordinary interloper and asked why she'd come. As the story unfolded, Persephone took pity on Psyche and gave her a big jar of her finest beauty cream. Hades sighed and allowed her to return, making a mental note to cancel Cerberus's doggie chocs for the next hundred years.

Psyche struggled back to the land of the living with the jar of beauty cream. What did Aphrodite want with beauty cream anyway, she wondered. It must be something really potent and special. Surely a little dab on her cheek wouldn't do any harm...

So Psyche opened the jar, poked her finger inside, and instantly fainted away. It was very powerful beauty cream indeed. In fact, it could have transformed Medusa, ugliest of the Gorgons, into a chart-busting sex kitten with the three **GRAEAE** sisters on backing vocals. Psyche was about to wither away under the influence when Eros turned up and whisked her off to Olympus. With **ZEUS**'s blessing, they were at last married. Aphrodite didn't mind too much as she now had a goodly supply of face cream to play with.

SELENE

Silvery goddess of the moon. Her brother is **HELIOS**, the Sun, and her sister is Eos, the dawn. Secretive and shy, she enjoys flitting silently through the night with a pearl-white or silvery chariot. But she quite likes being glimpsed through the clouds – and her coyness is somewhat calculated. For **SELENE** also enjoys romance, and has shared kisses with more people than you could count on a long winter's night.

Who spread the rumour that her reflection in water could be trapped and that if you kept very quiet she would draw nearer and nearer – until you could snatch her from the sky and make her your servant? We tried that and it didn't work. What a tease.

SIBYL OF CUMAE

This was the Sibyl of all Sibyls, females blessed with the gift of prophecy and second-sight. She was much fancied by **APOLLO** who offered her anything in exchange for sex. She chose immortality and then didn't keep her side of the bargain. But Apollo was not a god to be ripped off and when she looked at the immortality contract she found the clause: 'Youth and Beauty not included.'

After a few hundred years she was a tiny, wrinkly little thing. The priests hung her on the wall in a bottle and charged extra to see the talking curio.

By this time the only words she would come out with were: 'I want to die.' This may not be the end of the story, as 700 years later the Romans inherited her.

SILENUS

God of beer buddies and drinking companions. He's fat, bald, hairy and drunk. **SILENUS** is the teacher and debauched buddy of **DIONYSUS**, and taught him such tricks as balancing a goblet on your nose and how to open a jar of wine with your teeth. We don't know exactly what happened to Silenus, but we do know he was granted immortality by the gods. We have the feeling we might have seen him here and there over the years; the fat, bald, bearded character who is always seen drunk and incapable slumped in the corners of pubs. If you see two of these characters at once, one may be Dionysus or Bacchus – or you may just have been over-indulging.

STYX

Goddess of the Underworld river. 'Styx and Stones may break my bones but words will never hurt me.' Well, they will if you swear by the River Styx and then break your oath. The River Styx goes through the Underworld and is in the charge of the goddess of that name. She's the daughter of the ocean and had four children: Force, Might, Victory and Zeal who helped the gods in the war against the **TITANS**.

She was rewarded with her own ten-channel river, a palace in the Underworld and dominion over the oaths of the gods. Anyone swearing such an oath has to drink from her ice cold waters to bind their vow. Quite a chilling experience as these drinks can freeze the blood and destroy mere mortals.

TARTARUS

Primeval god of Hell, and the place of ultimate punishment. One of the first gods to arise from the void of creation, **TARTARUS**, like his siblings **NYX** and Chaos, personifies ultimate formless gloom. Little is known of his personality but as the first god of Hell we assume him to be a dour and depressing being.

Tartarus lives in the bowels of the Earth, many miles below as the anvil falls, and holds together the bottomless pits of the world. Presumably

HADES rents the Underworld from him on favourable terms. As Greek Mythology developed, Tartarus sank into oblivion, giving his name to the dark places of punishment for those that have been judged guilty of unspeakablenesses.

TITANS

The twelve giant offspring of **GAIA** and **URANUS**. They come in brother-sister pairs: Cronus and Rhea, Oceanus and Tethys, Hyperion and Thea, Iapetus and Themis, Crius and Mnemosyne, and Coeus and Phoebe. (The six sisters are also called the Titanides, by the way.)

They were so big and painful in labour that poor Gaia couldn't bear to bear any more. So she got **CRONUS** to help with some radical birth control and newly neutered Uranus was overthrown.

After the deed was done, Cronus and Rhea ruled over the gods and the world entered a golden age of peace and prosperity. Of course this didn't last as the gods warred against them and a disgruntled **ZEUS** banished them all to Tartarus Prison.

TYPHON

The son of Earth Mother **GAIA** and **TARTARUS** the Fathomless Gulf, **TYPHON** is one baaaad baddy. In comparison, Mike Tyson in his heyday was a cuddly kitten. A smokey black colour, he had a hundred dragon heads with flame-flashing eyes. He liked to spit molten rock, and his snake arms and legs were too numerous and writhy to check out. He scared the Hell out of the gods, who fled from Olympus and hid out in Egypt.

When **ZEUS** could no longer take the 'cowardy custard' jibes of **ATHENA**, he was forced to fight. And got his ass badly whipped. Typhon then took the badly battered god off to his cave to tear him to bits at leisure. He started by hacking out a few sinews so Zeus could not move. Typhon then took a few days off to go clubbing and left a monsteress called Delphyne to keep an eye on his prisoner. 'Call yourselves friends?' sneered Athena at the cowering gods, who were all disguised as animals to avoid involvement. Eventually **PAN** and **HERMES** volunteered to go and suss things out.

They found the cave and saw Typhon wasn't in. So Pan let out one of his wild echoing panic-inducing cries. Delphyne panicked, ran up a wall and clung to a dark corner. Hermes rushed in and hurriedly popped Zeus's sinews back into what he hoped were the right places, leaving the healing process to immortality – which is pretty foolproof and almost instantaneous. After all the humiliation, Zeus was more than somewhat peeved. The return fight was on in almost no time. It would have been a sell-out if the gods had bothered about such stupid things as money. Zeus trained hard, and various supporters of his plied Typhon with drink…

Wham! Bam! Slam! This was one of the ding-dongs of all time. No blows barred. Forget the *Rocky* films – this was a battle with real rocks. Not to mention torn-up trees and mountaintops. Zeus eventually decked Typhon with the whole of Mount Etna. It's doubtful he will beat the count of ten, which for a fight this big is measured in years. Ten thousand years to be exact. But Typhon still left a lot of trouble behind – his wife Echidna gave birth to the nastiest set of horror monsters ever to crawl across the pages of Greek Mythology. Try not to think Nemean-Lion, Chimera, Hydra, Sphinx, Medusa, Cerberus and Orthrus. Her children could chew the living daylights out of all but the toughest heavyweight champion deities.

URANUS

Great primeval god of the sky. Born of **GAIA**, the Earth, he covered the world in the form of a vast bronze dome and ruled over everything. Taking Gaia as a wife, he impregnated her with many children but was not prepared to deal with the consequences. In fact, he was terrified of the monstrous brood of **TITANS** forming inside her and threatened terrible reprisals should they ever pop out. Gaia, wanting to protect her children, kept them inside herself as long as she could, but pretty soon the pain was unbearable. Relief only came when their youngest son **CRONUS** stepped in. Or rather, popped out.

Armed with a sickle, he lopped off **URANUS**' … er, well, let's not go into details. Suffice to say that Uranus was cut off in his prime and Cronus took over as supreme being.

ZEUS

Top god of the Earth and ruler of Mount Olympus, the lofty cloudland where the Greek gods live and look down upon mankind. He is a real high-flyer, an Olympic champion, battling with the giant **TITANS**, casting thunderbolts and engaged in all manner of gut-busting glorious godly pursuits. His father **CRONUS** was so terrified of the newborn baby **ZEUS**'s awesome power that he swallowed him up – and lived to regret it. It was left to Amalthea (and her goat) to protect the budding supergod while he learned to walk, talk, and rule the Universe. Since then he's never looked back.

Zeus is married to the long-suffering **HERA**, but spends most of his time lusting after goddesses, mortals, animals, and indeed anything that will keep still long enough. It's tough at the top, being the most fantastic hunky irresistible god of all time and having constantly to prove it. Never a quiet night in with slippers and a mug of cocoa because he has to keep his wife happy too. Their trials and tribulations form the basis of half the Greek entries in our database. Zeus has had so many mistresses and fathered so many children that there's no point in giving a list here. Just take our word for it. See also Cronus, Rhea, **HEPHAESTUS**, **ATHENA**... and in fact most of the other Greek gods.

Moving on to more godly matters, Zeus was also known to the ancient Greeks as Epiphanes, the Magnificent One, whenever a certain star appeared in the east. This was celebrated with piph-ups known as epiphanies.

When he's not running around after nubile goddesses in the form of a lusty animal, Zeus looks after law, upholds justice, and casts thunderbolts on those deserving it.

THE GODS OF
THE INCAS

Once a mighty empire stretched over the central highlands of the Andes, way down south past Mexico, ranging from Chile to Peru where the capital city of Cuzco prevailed.

After 400 years and much personal sacrifice to keep the sun shining and the gods contented they had it all. Mighty buildings without the aid of cement mixers, metal casking, weaving, pottery, paved roads, suspension bridges, amazing art and sculpture, some quite abstract, and a thriving music scene. Agriculture flourished although there were no horses. They didn't bother with things like wheels, and reading and writing – all their records were done with knotted string.

Naturally it couldn't last. The Spaniards came and under Pizzaro used all his cunning, treachery, greed and cruelty to seize power after the Incan ruler Huayna Capac had just died and there was a state of indecision as to who should be the next divine ruler. It wasn't long before all the Inc ran out.

But just when you thought it was all over, the Incas had one secret city, Machu Picchu, hidden high in the mountains which the Spaniards never found. Or anyone else until 1911 when Hiram Bingham of Yale University stumbled across it, by which time it was deserted but still magnificent in its desolation. Adventurers have been searching for other secret cities and El Dorados ever since.

APOCATEQUIL

God of lightning. He's also chief priest for the moon god – an obvious case of moonlighting. To keep him happy, statues of his noble self were erected upon the mountaintops. He is responsible for the birth of twins when he becomes a lightning bolt and participates in mortal lovemaking. This does not sound like safe sex to us.

His dad was Guamansuri and there was a twin brother called Piguerao. With such a pig of a name he preferred to be known as 'White Bird'. We also think he was in partnership with Apu-Illapu, the god of thunder.

AYAR

The family of sun god **INTI**. They were some of the survivors from the cave of refuge at **PACARI**. It was all the rage at the time.

There were four brothers and four sisters. Ayar-Cachi got himself walled up again when he became a troublesome pest, Ayar-Colo turned himself into a sacred stone, and Ayara-Car became landed gentry with vast estates.

Of the brothers this left Ayar-Manco who became **MANCO-CAPAC** and went off with the last remaining sister Mama-Oullo (we can only assume the others chose other brothers), and they went on to find and found the civilisation at Cuzco.

CHASCA

Goddess of the dawn and twilight. In other words, she's Venus. And like the Roman Venus, she's a lovely young thing, and the protector of virgins. She is very fond of fleecy white clouds, and would no doubt have been a great Barbara Cartland fan. We imagine she favours a particularly extreme shade of pink. Could be married to…

CHASCA-COYLLUR

God of flowers and protector of maidens. Could be husband of the flowery **CHASCA**, but there's no proof apart from a similarity of names and a fondness for petals.

COCOMAMA

Not the goddess of chocolate! In fact, she was a flirty female who was cut in half by jealous lovers and subsequently transformed into the world's first coca plant. Men who managed to satisfy their woman's sexual needs were rewarded with a munch on the coca leaves afterwards.

Although the coca plant does contain a tiny amount of cocaine, it also contains many other nutrients and stimulants that are extremely good for you if you want to keep on the go without dangerous after-effects. (At least, according to this month's scientific reports – next month there'll be another with opposing views.)

We could also mention a certain well-known brand of soft drink, but we don't want to get sued. If you live in Peru at a high altitude it is up to you – coca leaves are not illegal as far as we know. Who needs chocolate?

CONIRAYA

God of instant fecundity. Trees, animals, plants, humans – life sprang from everything he touched. Without any of the pleasures usually involved in propagation, though, as sadly he could not find a mate.

ILYAPA

Thunder god of mischievous pot shots. Fires a sling at a water pot carried by the Milky Way, who happens to be his sister. The cracking of crockery is what produces thunder and deluges.

In times of dire drought, simply tie up a black dog until it's wilting with thirst. **ILYAPA** will take pity on the poor creature and send rain in abundance.

INTI

Mighty Incan god of the sun. Very important and powerful, he's the father of legendary **MANCO-CAPAC** and the sunny son of **VIRACOCHA**. His name is so sacred that even those permitted to utter it must do so soundlessly. Obviously we can't give you any help with this. His moon goddess partner is Mama-Quilla. Her face is like a full moon and she is interested in women's welfare, and sorting out calendars and feasts.

INTI is represented as a golden sun disc with a shining face. Incan emperors were believed to be the manifestation of Inti on Earth and were thus hot-tempered and prone to sunspots.

KA-ATA-KILLA

Moon goddess. She lived around Lake Titicaca in pre-Incan times. No jokes please or you could be turned into rock, like some of her followers at Tiahuanak, who now appear to have joined the ranks of the Huanca. Meanwhile, the Incans came and **KA-ATA-KILLA** was nudged aside in favour of Copacati.

KHUNO

High-altitude weather god who got fed up with humans messing about with his nice clean snow. He also didn't see why they should be burning things to keep warm. Some kind of compromise was reached when he directed them to the cocaine plant. After a few nibbles of that, they didn't care how high they were or what the weather was like. They also became very protective of the snow. So it looks like **KHUNO** was the world's first drug dealer. Is it any coincidence that 'snow' is a nickname for dodgy powdery stuff?

MAMA-PACHA

Earth goddess. She's great at getting to grips with the soil. Take her step-by-step seasonal advice and you will win all the awards at your local village produce show. Somewhat unusually, she has the form of a large dragon. If you mess with her crops, or make corn circles, may the gods help you. You could end up with an earthquake. She had her own earthquake at some point and **PACHACAMAC** emerged.

MANCO-CAPAC

Creator god with a golden rod. Aided by his sister Mama-Oullo, he poked the ground with his holy implement looking for somewhere suitable to start the human race going again after the mysterious worldly cataclysm (see **PACARI**). Not too rocky, not too soft, not too wet, not too dry. The place they came up with was Cuzco.

As well as giving rise to the entire Incan race, **MANCO-CAPAC** is also the god of fire and **PACHACAMAC**'s brother.

PACARI

The cave of refuge from which bottled-up gods emerged after some unmentionable disaster. Maybe they caused it.

Accounts are very confused and conflicting as they were still gods in shock. The twins Piguerao and **APOCATEQUIL** were there at the time but have always refused to comment. The **AYAR** family was also in residence. There was no *Incan Echo* reporter on hand at the time and there is nothing that can be verified.

Recent research suggests that **PACARI** may have been located at the Mayan city Teotihuacan. This was old before even the Mayans showed up, and is full of mysteries. Signs of fire indicate some earlier disaster, and its Pyramid of the Sun covers a chambered cave which may have been the Place of Emergence. Were the gods huddled inside while Teotihuacan burned?

PACHACAMAC

Not waterproof clothing but the all-powerful Earth creator god. Mark you, there is nothing to say that he couldn't have given his name to a Pacamac. After all, he had a brother called Kon who was a god of rain and the south wind, and one of **PACHACAMAC**'s jobs was to drive it north.

The brother of legendary people-producer **MANCO-CAPAC**, he was filled with the desire to create a race of humans. But his attempts at people-making were short-lived as he forgot to provide food and had to face a charge of neglect from the starving masses. His unpopularity was increased further when, in an attempt to rectify the food situation, he turned the first woman's son into an enormous potato. It was downhill all the way for Pachacamac after that. And then a vengeful Vichama turned all his people into rocks, sparing only the potato.

URPIHUA-CHAC

This was a goddess who owned the biggest fishpond of all time containing the world's stocks. She also had beautiful daughters which **VIRACOCHA** kept chasing, until they were forced to turn into doves to escape him.

Poor old Viracocha – he doesn't have much luck with his sex life. He was so frustrated he kicked down the pond walls and all the fish escaped into the sea and rivers so he didn't even get a fish supper.

VIRACOCHA

Supreme god and creator of all things. In the beginning he created in the dark; no Sun, no Moon or stars. Just the planet Earth and a handful of giant beings wandering around trying to make sense of it all.

This wasn't so easy. **VIRACOCHA** had decreed a Rule Which Must be Obeyed, but it apparently wasn't as the giants were pretty soon wiped out by a giant vengeful storm. Opting to try again, Viracocha went to Lake Titicaca and commanded the Sun and Moon to rise from the waters. Thus he became sun god as well as storm god.

With light and warmth to inspire him, he created the Human Race Mk II. This version was much more successful. He then nipped down the road to Tiwanaku, otherwise known as the centre of the world. Here he carved the names and locations of every tribe and nation on a great piece of stone and bid his servants to create civilisation as we know it. We presume he must have taught his servants to read.

At some point he found time to hitch up with Mama-Cocha, a sea goddess who was popular with sailors and fishermen, which must have ensured some fish suppers. Several godly adventures later, Viracocha retired to the sky. But he often takes trips to Earth disguised as a beggar to check up on the state of the world. This usually causes him to cry a lot. If you see a ragged figure weeping in the streets, be generous of spirit – it might be him. One day, if we are all too wicked, his tears will cause a flood of total destruction.

THE GODS OF INDIA

It's India for glitzy, glittery gods who are much larger than life – especially the Hindu gods. They are the Bollywood celebrities of eastern mythology. After all, what's the point of being a god if you can't be a bit flash? So the gods of India have more arms, legs and heads than most other pantheons put together, from a modest four up to a million. **INDRA**, for example, has a thousand testicles. That should make your eyes water.

Hindu gods are without doubt some of the sexiest around. Colourful, wild and over-the-top, they ride on exotic peacocks, elephants, tigers, turtles. They wave exotic objects and dance around outrageously. They wear more beads, baubles, bangles and gems than any deities from elsewhere. Their temples are adorned with sexy carvings that make Puritans foam at the mouth. Indian mythology has mightier deeds, more heroic adventures, dirtier demons – and a thousand transmogrifications are par for the course. So let yourself go and join in the cosmic dance with **SHIVA** and the gang.

ADITI

Godmother of the sky. Being a goddess of fertility and motherhood, **ADITI** is very much associated with sacred cows. We're not quite sure of the connection between sky and cow. Does she commute to Earth or is there a herd of Heavenly flying bovines?

Her name means 'without limit', which seems appropriate enough. As the mother of the Devas, including **AGNI**, she is venerable and vital, but somewhat elusive and vague.

AGNI

Hindu fire god. He certainly looks the part, with fiery red skin and coal-black eyes. He has three legs and also rides a ram – presumably side-saddle. **AGNI** is a bright young spark who symbolises the fiery rebirth of each new day – either a reference to the blazing dawn or an expression of relief that the campfire didn't blow out in the night. To keep him aflame, holy maidens twirl a wooden fire drill to ignite and reincarnate him on a daily basis. We have no idea if there are any holy Zippo lighters.

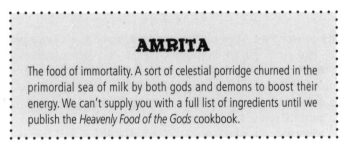

AMRITA

The food of immortality. A sort of celestial porridge churned in the primordial sea of milk by both gods and demons to boost their energy. We can't supply you with a full list of ingredients until we publish the *Heavenly Food of the Gods* cookbook.

AVALOKITESVARA

Lord of compassion, fondly known to us as 'have a look it's Vara'. And there is a lot to look at, for he comes in many forms, from the basic one head, four arms model to one with eleven heads and a thousand arms.

We do not know who does the counting or if it is before or after the bars close. But we do know that this **BODHISATTVA** is very popular, being identified with Amitabha, **GUAN-YIN**, **KANNON** and Chenrezig.

AVATAR

Deities in disguise. This is the form of a god coming down to Earth in a mistaken identity mode. Sometimes when visiting the planet you just need to go incognito. If you can wear a completely different body it all helps. Do you know that Clark Kent is really Superman? Gasps of surprise from Dr Watson: 'Is that really you Holmes?' That sort of thing.

BUDDHA does this sort of thing quite a lot but **VISHNU** is the best known, having ten special costume changes. Humans catch on to everything eventually. Now the internet is packed with **AVATAR**s of people pretending to be rich, handsome, sexy – or normal.

BALIN

Son of **INDRA** and a monkey queen. Half-brother of Sugriva (both monkeys). He started out well giving the demon **RAVANA** a thorough pasting, tying all his arms and legs with his tail and dragging him around the world for laughs for a dozen years.

Ravana survived to fight another day, but not with **BALIN**, who next had a falling out with his half-brother, and they fought in single combat to the death. Sugriva had the help of **RAMA** who was also **VISHNU**, and by using Rama's bow had the power to shoot Balin dead.

BHISMA

A poor semi-divine soul caught up in the Pandavas vs Kauravas conflict. Dad a king, mum the River Ganges, **BHISMA** would have been the eighth child except that she had drowned all the rest, and then turned herself into total water. The king married again with the agreement that Bhisma relinquished any claims to the throne and never had children.

Then what happens? Bhisma takes on tutoring for both Pandavas and Kauravas, teaching military skills. This encourages them to beat Hell out of each other as they grow up. For much more look up Queen **KUNTI**.

BODHISATTVA

Beings who are just the merest gnat's whisker from **BUDDHA**hood. They are so enlightened they can dive into the final Nirvana any time they wish. But they are kind enough to wait a bit and help others reach the same position. Therefore the **BODHISATTVA**s are the most compassionate figures in all creation, putting their spiritual ecstas on hold for the sake of others.

BRAHMA

The great Hindu creator god. With four heads looking to the four corners of the world, **BRAHMA** remains aloof and aloft. He is the do-it-yourself god of meditation. So, after much meditation I ask myself: if the world is round, how can it have four corners?

BUDDHA

The wise one and original enlightened Buddhist being. Siddharta realised the truth as he sat under a Bho tree: you can either go on tiresomely being reincarnated forever, which eventually becomes a real drag, or you can opt out, take the Holy Eightfold-Way and float enigmatically around in Buddhahood.

As soon as he discovered this, he became **BUDDHA**, the enlightened one, leaving the rest of us floundering. Now Big Buddha is watching you – and lots of little Buddhas are too – but in a serene and peaceful manner. He is hoping you too will take the path to enlightenment.

Buddha has been and gone and come more times than we know. Before he was Siddharta, he may have been biding his time as the ninth **AVATAR** of **VISHNU** and lots of **BODHISATTVA**s who are Buddhas-Who-Have-Been or Maitreya, the Buddha-To-Be if he has not already come and gone. But definitely when he comes back as **KALKI**, the horse that's the end of the Universe. It would be too much otherwise.

Wherever you go his smiling benign features and air of blissful relaxation can only have a beneficial and calming influence. Furthermore, he can also be Chinese, Tibetan, Japanese or almost any East Asian nationality. In which case he may not have been Siddharta at all – or maybe only a little bit.

CHAMUNDA

A terrifying skeletal goddess dancing and brandishing many horrible things. She seems to be leading some kind of punk band, including a braying hound. We won't mention the flayed elephant's ear.

DEVADATTA

Evil cousin and rival of **BUDDHA**. He did everything he could think of in the way of dirty tricks and booby traps to kill Buddha, but he was always thwarted. Mercenaries got converted, rogue elephants paid homage. Nothing ever went according to plan. As he made a last personal attack on Buddha armed to the teeth, he was booby-trapped himself and vanished into a fiery mouth hidden in the ground, which opened up and swallowed him.

DHANVANTARI

A mortal who held the first cup of **AMRITA** – or was it **SOMA**? He was not allowed to drink it so it was probably Soma as Amrita was a sort of porridge of immortality. I suppose it could be slurped. Anyway, never mind that. **DHANVANTARI** was given the status of Heavenly physician with special dispensation to teach mortals. 'This is Amrita – this is Soma.'

DHRITARASHTRA

Blind king and father of the Kauravas. He was blind due to Karma – in a past life he blinded a swan and killed its kids for a laugh and now Karma was getting its own back. And then some – he also lost his hundred children in the great Kauravas vs Pandavas war. At least he couldn't see it happen.

DITI

Mother of a giant called Daityas. One day, a notice appeared on the gates of Heaven: No Giants Admitted. Then **INDRA** proclaimed all giants were to be banished to the Underworld. **DITI** was not at all happy, and asked her husband **KASYAPA** to make her pregnant with a son strong enough to destroy Indra. To shut her up he agreed, but only on condition that the pregnancy would last 100 years, and she must remain pure in mind, body and spirit for the duration.

Much much later … the baby was due! Overcome with excitement Diti broke a rule and forgot to wash her feet before bedtime. Woe, disaster, red alert – Indra sent an embryo-destroying thunderbolt. The baby came out in seven pieces, all crying. Well, even Indra has his soft side, or maybe **SHIVA** and **PARVATI** intervened. All seven bits were restored to become Maruts; these are storm gods which have iron teeth and roar like lions.

DURGA

Warrior goddess. She has lots and lots of arms and armaments! You name it: disci, thunderbolts, flares, skulls, words, snakes and drums. She is a goodie at heart, but when you take on 120 million demons at a time all mounted on elephants you can't afford to mess around.

GANDHARVAS

Godly musicians. They often perform at festivities, with complementary dancing, singing and swinging. They come in many mistily mystical shapes and forms, but they have never had a recording contract.

GANESHA

Elephant-headed Hindu god of wisdom and prudence, known as the 'Lord of Obstacles'. But he only puts obstacles in the way of those seeking a shortcut to Heaven, to prevent overcrowding and illegal immigration. All in all he is very much loved and there are many images of him. He is rather greedy and overweight though, and just loves yummy fruit and drink sacrifices. He does come with a good pedigree – parents **SHIVA** and **PARVATI**. He is the sort of god you can talk to – very user-friendly.

He has four arms but an elephant's head with only one tusk, possibly due to Shiva's habit of surprising Parvati in her bath which she found very annoying. From her bodily scrubbings she created a guardian figure and brought it to life with a sprinkling of Ganges water. Shiva took one look at the figure barring his way and just lopped its head off. 'That was our brand new son!' wailed Parvati. Servants were dispatched to find a new head without delay. The first head they found was that of an elephant. Better than no head at all, thought Parvati, and that was that.

There are other stories about the head. Did **RAMA** lop off a tusk when **GANESHA** was back on guard duty? Did he break it when falling off the rat he used for transport after a bout of binge-drinking? Or did he snap off his tusk to use as a pen when he needed to jot down something really important? (We've all done it, haven't we?) This sounds the most plausible to us as Ganesha is a god of wisdom and prudence, but is never seen carrying a pen. He does indeed like to carry a few artefacts around with him: a shell, a discus, a club and a water lily. But these are purely symbolic and are of no practical value. Gods never carry useful stuff like flashlights or penknives. Ganesha has two wives, Siddhi and Buddhi. They have to share the tusk.

GANGA

Daughter of Himavat god of the Himalayas. She is the goddess of the sacred River Ganges. 145 million Hindus can't be wrong.

HANUMAN

The Hindu monkey god, son of monkey mum Anjana. And what a monkey he is! Always fighting and helping his mates in battle.

INDRA

Deva leader and supreme ruler of the Vedic gods. He's in charge of war, storms and fighting, and also invented the curious practice of drinking water. However, he prefers the hard stuff, drinking huge quantities of **SOMA** which seems to set him off with thunderbolts and things. He rides a white elephant (which may be pink by now), and runs his affairs from the world's only portable Heaven (patent pending).

He's perhaps best known for battling the evil Vritra, who'd nicked all the world's water and could only be defeated by a massive boozing session. Sadly, **INDRA** seems to have faded into the background now and may even be in a clinic for gods with problems.

One more thing. We are told on good authority that Indra has a thousand vaginas. We haven't actually seen or counted them. There are some limits to our researches.

INDRANI

Mrs **INDRA**. We have chosen not to intrude.

JALANDHARA

A very powerful and ambitious demon born of the River Ganges and Primordial Ocean. **JALANDHARA** was on the brink of taking over Heaven when **SHIVA** came to the rescue. He sent his wife **PARVATI** to use her feminine wiles and flirt with the demon. He did one of his quick-change acts which was a perfect impersonation of the demon itself and had sex with the demon's wife Vrindha. Shiva then leaked the news everywhere. Vrindha killed herself and Jalandhara went ballistic.

Meanwhile the gods had been developing a secret weapon – a sun disc so sharp that it had to be kept under wraps when not in use. So when the demon came storming in to tear Heaven apart, there was a ziiish as the disc took the demon's head off – then boing! The demon grew a new head.

This kept happening – a ziiish/boing! stalemate until it was noticed that each time there was a ziiish a small drop of the demon's blood was falling into the Primordial Ocean which triggered off the reconstitution process. So a team of goddesses put on demon fancy dress and licked up and caught any drop of blood before it could reach the ocean. One final ziiish! And yes, the headache was over.

JUGGERNAUT

Hindu god of road clogging, hogging and gridlock. His holy vehicle contains the bones of **KRISHNA** and is a real danger to other road-users. For starters, it's 50 feet high and takes several days to accelerate from zero to crawling pace. The truly devout used to throw themselves under the wheels, which we believe gave rise to the world's first road accidents with not a scrap of motor insurance. **JUGGERNAUT** has the alternative name Jagganath, but this could be a dodge to avoid paying his vehicle licence. His name is not taken in vain amongst the heavy goods vehicle fraternity.

KADRU

Snake goddess. She was the the wife of Kasyapa, who also had another wife **VINATA**. There was great jealous rivalry between them. **KADRU** asked for a thousand children, and amongst them were Shesha and Vasuki. Vinata asked for just two children, with the stipulation that they must outrank those of Kadru. The two children were Varuna and Garuda.

Thwarted, Kadru took to crawling into the wombs of pregnant women who then produced more snakes, or worse, humans with snake-like propensities such as cold-blooded cunning and evil. This is why we have so many people with these characteristics slithering about the world today. Many seem to go into politics and seek positions of power.

KALI

The Black One. She is goddess of darkness, blood and thugs. **KALI** has three eyes, four arms, vampire fangs and is bloated with the blood of victims. She is awful, terrible and horrifying. However she does have some good points. We just don't know what they are at present. Kali is also Mrs **SHIVA**.

KALKI

Horse god, or at least a part of **VISHNU** horsing about. Sometimes he is a horse with four arms, sometimes he rides a white horse when we presume he is in a more human mode, but possibly with the addition of hocks and hooves. Anyway, when the human race reverts to a bestial state, his job will be to gallop through the world with a sword, purging and purifying us so we can start anew.

KAMA

Love god. He is a beautiful Hindu youth who rides an elephant or a parrot (yes, a parrot) and has a **CUPID**-like bow made of sugar cane. He is a somewhat open-minded god of desire. It is just as well we don't all desire the same things. This is what comes of having **VISHNU** and **LAKSHMI** for parents.

KARNI-MATA

Goddess of rat reincarnation. Although she was a fourteenth-century historical figure known as Ridhubai, she is still going strong and has a plush temple crawling with cuddlesome plague-carrying vermin. Her devotees believe her to be an incarnation of **DURGA**.

The story goes that she was so upset by god of death **YAMA**'s refusal to restore a storyteller's dead son to life that she took matters into her own hands. Result: The son was reincarnated as a rat – whether he liked it or not. And now her temple is full of rodents, all of them the sacred souls of minstrels, storytellers … and perhaps even writers of entertaining mythology websites. There are perks if you want to return as a rat. Free cheese for life, a very appreciative worshipping audience, and if you do meet an untimely death, a little golden statue to remember you by.

KRISHNA

One of the most popular Hindu gods, a dashing, daring, blue-skinned hero who drove women wild and demons into despair. **KRISHNA** is not just a top Hindu god, he's practically a superhero. But he had to work for it. Most of his formative years were spent avoiding death at the hands of jealous nasties.

The eighth child of Devaki, he and his brother Balarama were due to be killed at birth by wicked uncle Kamsa, but **VISHNU** saved the day by transferring them to a womb with a view in a quieter neighbourhood. Sweet little godlet **DEVA** was substituted in their place. Wicked Kamsa would have killed her instead but the gods whisked her away to Heaven.

Once Krishna was safely born, his troubles really began. A succession of baby-killing demons tried their best to dispatch him, but the innocent little lamb was really an indestructible godly lump with a thousand sneaky demon-dispatching tricks. See what happened to **PUTANA**, for example.

Once grown up, Krishna parted company with his womb-mate Balarama and went to chase girls in the countryside. This suited him down to the ground and, with his good looks and charm, Krishna soon found himself with 16,000 girlfriends. This was not entirely due to his good looks and charm; he came to the rescue of the lovely maidens and was forced to marry them all to prevent moral complications.

This idyllic lifestyle was cut short when it was revealed that he was really the eighth incarnation of Vishnu, and was therefore supposed to be doing important godly work instead of messing around in the hay all day. So Krishna left to start a new career as demon destroyer and hero, pausing only to kiss goodbye each of his 16,000 wives.

Many tales have been told of Krishna's amazing adventures: how he rescued Rukmini from a devilish marriage; how he feuded with the villainous **SISUPALA**; how he grappled with fate and dodged death the way some people dodge the tax collector; how his bones ended up in **JUGGERNAUT**, the god of heavy goods vehicles. But you get the picture.

Krishna is truly a supergod. He's clever, sexy, cunning, and blessed with outrageous good fortune. In the Bollywood of Heaven, he is a rich and famous celebrity. Now the star of epic philosophical action-adventure *Mahabharata* and creator of the sublime poem *Bhagavad-Gita*, his name is revered all over the world.

KUBERA

God of riches. A hideous dwarf dripping with jewels, he has three legs but only eight teeth. Still, we don't think being beautiful has ever been high on any tycoon's agenda. Taking another look, we notice he has only got one eye. But it's the trappings of success that count. Only the richest of rich gods can afford a sky chariot called Pushpaka which is large enough to contain a whole city. Where he parks it we can't imagine, and no-one could ever push it. But now you know who helps the rich get richer.

KURMA

VISHNU in cosmic tortoise form. That's cosmic and not comic. It's the cosmic egg again, and this time a Vedic tortoise popped out – only he may have been a turtle because he does a lot of swimming around. **KURMA** helped out when the gods were making ambrosia from the Primordial Sea of Milk. Well, it's very good for the skin.

LAKSHMI

Wife of **VISHNU**, mother of **KAMA**, and good luck wealth goddess of seven inside deals. She can pop into your feet, thigh or naughty bits, or your bosom, heart, neck or face. All these will bring good fortune appropriate to the part involved. We can hear you muttering 'that's only six', but she will also do your head in if that's where she enters – and that is bad fortune. So the odds are six to one.

MAHAKALA

The Great Black One. With a name like that you can tell he's the god of death. This is **SHIVA** as The Destroyer, charging in on a lion with rattling skulls and three fierce eyes frowning.

MANASA

Hindu goddess of snakes. She leads a sleazy fertility cult of snake worship. It must be love at first bite. During her festival, basketfuls of the wriggling love creatures are tamed by smoochy flute music, rising from their baskets and swaying hypnotically to the tune. Then they do magical feats while their devotees slip into a sexy trance. It's all to do with that mystic snake energy which coils around the Universe. She's possibly the goddess of copper wire, too.

MANU

A sort of celestial Noah. He looked after **VISHNU** when he was a tiny fish, and nurtured him to full fishliness. Afterwards, Vishnu repaid him by warning him of the mighty flood and how he could be the only human to survive it. Apparently there are supposed to be fourteen wash-it-all-away floods before the world ends. Each time it happens, **MANU** will be there to man the boat. So far we are about half way; the floods can be millions of years apart, so there is no need for immediate panic.

NANDI

White bull god. He is **SHIVA**'s right-hoof bovine and stands guarding him in temple situations. Of course, being a bull, there is a fertility connection too. That explains why Shiva acolytes need to touch his testicles before entering. If you're thinking of upgrading your home's front door, bull's balls might make an interesting alternative to doorbells or lions-head doorknockers.

NARASIMHA

VISHNU in man-lion mode. There is a story of him appearing in this form to defeat the demon Hiranyakasipu who had been upgraded to total invulnerability. Apparently this complete impregnability did not provide enough in the way of indestructibility, as **NARASIMHA**'s claws shredded him to bits. Vishnu had found a clause where the invulnerability did not apply to animal claws.

PARVATI

Wife of **SHIVA**. She may also have been **LAKSHMI**. At one time she was very worried about the darkness of her skin and hid herself away in a forest practising austerities and praying to **BRAHMA**. He rewarded her by giving her a golden skin and allowing her to become Gauri if not Devi, the 'Yellow' or 'Brilliant One'. In this guise she is pretty good and benevolent, but there is a **KALI** side to her nature as well. Watch out if her eyes go red.

PRAJAPATI

Hindu lord of creation. Born out of **BRAHMA**'s right thumb, he had one thousand sons and fifty daughters and thus single-handedly populated the planet. There was also an incident involving a lake of semen, but we won't go into that at the moment.

PURUSHA

Very old creator god and later an **AVATAR** of **VISHNU**. He has put himself about a bit. His eye is the Sun, his breath the wind, his head the sky ... and other of his bits are everything there is or ever has been. He did all this chopping and changing by making great sacrifices of himself. If he ever decides upon reassembly the world will end.

PUSHAN

God of some stars. Poor old **PUSHAN**: benign, plump, benevolent, in charge of nourishment and welfare of cattle, and popular at banquets. He didn't deserve to be in the way at Daksha's banquet when uninvited **SHIVA** stormed in and went apeshit. Poor old Pushan got all his teeth kicked out and they are now stars in the Milky Way. He can now only feed on milk and slops. When your teeth are in stars they can't be in jars.

PUTANA

A demoness who tried to make a sucker out of the baby **KRISHNA**. Getting a job as a wet nurse, she put poison on her nipples. Krishna sucked so hard he sucked her inside out, and left nothing but an empty skin. How the baby chuckled – poison indeed! He had the digestion of an immortal. We hate to think who had the job of changing his nappies.

RAMA

Major heroic figure and **VISHNU** incarnation number seven. **RAMA** tales have all been immortalised in the *Ramayana Epic* and he pops up in the *Mahabharata* and comic strips. Lots of battles with demons and exciting adventures for kiddies of all ages. His wife Sita was abducted by **RAVANA** leading to an almighty punch-up, but Sugriva and **HANUMAN** came to our hero's aid with a monkey army to attack the demon fortress. Rama is usually portrayed with a huge golden bow, a fabulous weapon donated by **SHIVA**.

RATI

Goddess of sex. Of course she is, being the girlfriend of **KAMA**. To put it in common vernacular, 'She's a bit of a goer'. She'll try sex with anything that takes her fancy, and she fancies just about everything – gods, mortals, beasts, trees and plants.

RAVANA

Once an angel, he was banished from Heaven with a choice of redundancy packages. He chose three mortal lives devoid of any godly assistance so he could go to the bad and become the worst demon ever. For his first life he chose to be Hiranyakashipu who even tortured his own son until dispatched by **VISHNU**.

But that was just a trial run – now he was back as **RAVANA**, the raging pillaging king of demons. Ten heads, twenty arms, teeth like knives, he could be any size he wanted. He was also immune from death by gods, and he battled with them all. Vishnu's Sun disc and **INDRA**'s thunderbolts were a little wounding at the time but they soon healed up. The tusking by Indra's four-tusked elephant put him in a very foul mood indeed.

The very elements shrank from his approach: the sun dimmed, tides stopped flowing and the winds went chill. Something had to be done and it was Vishnu using all his ingenuity to create himself as **RAMA** that ended it all. Even that took a struggle of epic proportions with help from many quarters of the godly kingdom. Legions of Indian artists have kept poverty at bay for centuries depicting large and lurid scenes of the final battle. But wait – this was not the end – there was one life to go and he became **SISUPALA**.

RUDRA

Temperamental storm god known as 'The Howling One'. Not nice. He is red-faced and has many of them, all frowning and scowling. His neck is blue. Despite the terrible sartorial consequences he dresses in grotty animal skins. When he's out and about, he spits with rage if anyone gets in his way as he charges along on his wild boar – and then he will zap you with arrows of death. Thousands of poisonous offshoots of him cause misfortune at any opportunity.

His wife is **PRISNI**, goddess of compost, and he also has a girlfriend called Rudrani, a bloody goddess of anger. She likes a drop of the red fluid does Rudrani. This means battlefields, sacrifices, woundings … she goes where it flows. She even takes a sober interest in women's monthly cycles, surely making her a goddess of premenstrual tension.

SAMBA

KRISHNA's son, who turned out to be a right pain. Fond of stupid pranks, there came a time when a piece of his folly backfired badly. Dressing up as a pregnant woman, he taunted some Brahmins by asking: 'Which one of you is the father?' There was a rapid joint response. He was roundly cursed and told he was now indeed pregnant – with an iron club. If that wasn't bad enough, he was told the club would be the cause of his father's death. Horrors! Instant early morning sickness. The weight in his belly grew until in due course it split and a club cub popped out – just a small one. Terrified it might grow **SAMBA** broke it into pieces and threw them into the sea.

A new scene. Krishna sitting under a Bho tree at the seaside meditating in the lotus position. A fleeing deer rushes past and a hunter's arrow hits the god's exposed foot. The arrow is tipped with a sliver of iron as hunters and beachcombers don't waste anything. Krishna didn't seem too bothered. After all, he could just return to being **VISHNU** full time.

SARASVATI

Goddess of wisdom and creative artistry. She rides a peacock or swan or sits on a lotus and is rather desirable to look at apart from having four arms. But she's not just a pretty face – she's into all the arts including poetry, music and writing. She is said to inhabit libraries so the extra arms must be useful for replacing books on shelves.

SATI

She fell madly in love with **SHIVA**, which was opposed by her father Daksha. This led to bitter enmity. **SATI** was so upset by it all she threw herself into a sacrificial fire. Grief-stricken Shiva whirled off on a self-destructive dance of death, which would destroy the Universe. **VISHNU** leapt in and brought Sati back to life as **PARVATI**, who became the wife of Shiva forevermore.

SHIVA

Lord of the cosmic dance. And how **SHIVA** dances; he whirls and propels enemies to defeat and his dancing creates or destroys the Universe. Until you have seen him in action you really don't know what break-dancing is. He appears to have four arms and five heads, but this could be the blurring effect of his high-speed gyrations. In his destroying mode he is known as **MAHAKALA**. He also has a pet snake called Shesha with a thousand heads.

SISUPALA

Drastically dangerous demon previously known as **RAVANA**. He was vanquished, but like any villain worth a film script came back again for a sequel under the name **SISUPALA**, with only four arms and three eyes this time. He was only a baby. He came with the warning that he must be loved and adored, and would only turn really nasty if he got to sit on the knee of someone who wanted to do away with him. Getting used to being loved he would run to strangers and climb onto their laps. Furthermore, he now had mortal parents who lived in a palace and were visited by celebrities.

One day **KRISHNA** came visiting. The moment he sat down Ravana rushed to him and clambered onto his knee. Krishna muttered something extremely uncharitable and the baby's extra arms and eye disappeared. Sisupala was not happy about this – he enjoyed being a little devil and always being noticed. He brooded a lot but grew up seemingly normal and even found a prospective wife, Rukmini. She was not at all keen but arrangements went ahead against her wishes, so she wrote to Krishna. He came flying to the rescue, whisked her off and married her himself. After that Sisupala plotted and planned to ambush and destroy Krishna who smiled and enjoyed it all. He just loved a grudge. What were another hundred failed attempts on his life?

Then, at an important sacrifice held by King Yudhishthira, Sisupala insulted Krishna to his face and also drew his sword with the aim of slaughtering the king. This was too much. Krishna cried 'Drop the Disc!' and down came the Sun disc, slicing Sisupala neatly in two. His blood gushed out in a fiery pool and lapped over Krishna's feet. Part of his spirit is now absorbed into Krishna so the demon did get a partial revenge.

SKANDA

Hindu war god. If two heads are better than one, this god is a bit of a godhead because he has about a dozen. He also has a spear and rides into battle on a peacock at the head of whichever army he is currently supporting.

SOMA

God of the sacred drink named after him. He brews the potent Indian booze of the gods which guarantees immortality. Or is it immobility? It also has many other amazing properties and was even used as a fertility treatment by Sumitra, wife of King Dasaratha. Anyway, **SOMA** is a god too, but it gets a bit confused as we don't know if he was named after the drink or vice versa. He had some connection with the moon or maybe it was moonshine. This Soma is pretty strong stuff and neither gods nor mortals can remember much after a few noggins.

TVASHTRI

Handyman god who tackles all those pressing godhold jobs. A god of all trades, his job spec includes weapons, chariots, thunderbolts, and he'll even have a go at a palace. **TVASHTRI** is fairly abstract in appearance – sometimes seen as a disembodied hand with or without a power drill gripped in its fingers. Best of all, he invented a bowl of everlasting booze which can never be emptied. Strangely, not much has been heard of him since.

UMA

Mrs **SHIVA** and goddess of light and beauty. She can turn into **DURGA** or **PARVATI** at a moment's notice.

VAMANA

VISHNU in dwarf mode. Evil fellow Bali was planning to take over the whole Universe. There was a little dwarf in his court which amused him – and when the cheeky little chappy asked if he could have a little bit of land for his very own, Bali laughed and said he could have as much as he could cover in three strides. Whoooooosh! The dwarf expanded to unbelievable dimensions. Yes, it was supergod Vishnu all along. And with a hop, skip and jump he had encircled the whole Universe. This left Bali nowhere to go but down – to the Underworld. With **KRISHNA**'s foot on his head he didn't argue.

VARAHA

VISHNU as a boar. All to save the world from the demon Hiranyaksha, who was dragging it down into the Primordial Ocean. **VARAHA** dived in after it and flipped it out with his tusks so swiftly that not a drop of water had time to harm anything. He proceeded to give the demon a total tusking. Vishnu was then free to stop making a pig of himself. We are told that he got the original idea from **BRAHMA** himself who had used the boar thing to bring the world up from the Primordial Ocean in the first place, except that he had to dry it out and stock it with livestock.

VISHNU

Top Hindu god, one of the creator triad along with **BRAHMA** and **SHIVA**. He rules the Universe on a day-to-day basis. As necessity demands he switches shape with his ten **AVATAR** modes:
1. A fish called Matsya
2. A tortoise called **KURMA**
3. A boar called **VARAHA**
4. A man-lion called **NARASIMHA**
5. A dwarf called **VAMANA**
6. A bruiser with a battleaxe called Parashurama
7. A prince called **RAMA**
8. A god called **KRISHNA**
9. A Buddha called **BUDDHA**
10. **KALKI**, the rider on the white horse at the end of the world. Or he might be just the horse. He hasn't used this one yet.

He's always on the turn, changing shape and form every time he pops down to see us. It makes your head spin. Where is he going to pop up next and how will we know? But he is a pretty good demon destroyer so we should not mock. The last thing we need is an infestation of demons. He's also the husband of **LAKSHMI** and father of **KAMA**. His camp bed is Vasuki, the World Snake.

YAMA

Buffalo-headed lord of death. Takes evil-doers to Hell or guides them to rebirth. He also thinks fleshly passions block enlightenment

THE GODS OF JAPAN

The Japanese have 800 myriads of gods which must cause a few congestion problems on their islands. Many of the best gods have now been absorbed by modern worshippers into the Manga and Pokemon cabals. They appear to have a tendency to worship anything if it stays still long enough and looks interesting. Photography has replaced iconography and pilgrims can often be seen in London recording taxis and street lamps for possible deification.

Major Japanese beliefs are Buddhism, Shinto, Yamaha and Objectism. They also have some very endearing gods of good fortune.

BAKU

'Eater of Dreams'. He will come if you call him and devour your nightmares. He has the head of a lion on a horse body which has tiger feet. Don't look if you do invite him – he may have caused your nightmares in the first place.

BIMBOGAMI

God of poverty who doesn't help the poor – but rather makes them poor in the first place. He is filthy, scruffy, ragged and bearded and you will find it very difficult to get rid of him if he gets inside your home. The clicking of deathwatch beetles is a warning sign he is with you…

CHIMATANO

Signpost god. If you ever arrive at a crossroads marked by his symbols you will find them exceedingly phallic. You are supposed to stroke them for luck. Shades of **PRIAPUS** there.

EMMA-O

King of Hell. He lives the good life in a large castle covered in gold, silver, pearls and jewels. His judgement is relatively simple. If you have killed an innocent human being you go into a cauldron full of molten metal. There is a get-out clause: if, after your crime, you made a pilgrimage to all thirty-three shrines of Kwannon, you may be excused.

FUDO

God of fire, wisdom and protection from disaster. He lives on top of a mountain surrounded by flames. You can go to consult him on tricky issues and obtain fire insurance, but be very very careful because anyone who looks upon him is instantly struck blind. Probably best to send a postcard instead. **FUDO** is known as 'The Immovable' and, being Japanese, probably resembles a sumo wrestler.

FUTEN

Wind god. He is buffeted and under pressure. This ancient deity stands on mountaintops with his white beard swirling and his wind banner whipping every which way. How he gets from one mountaintop to another is a mystery; perhaps a primitive type of hang-gliding over which he has little control. How he must long for calm windless days.

HOORI

Otherwise known as Fire Fade, he's a god of hunting, a great-grandson of **AMATERASU**, and the younger brother of Hoderi, known as Fire Flash. One day they got bored and decided to do a job swap. But when **HOORI** used Hoderi's fishing tackle, the line snapped and he lost his brother's favourite magic fish hook.

Hoderi was not of a forgiving disposition, and it was nag, nag, nag all the way home. 'That was my favourite hook and I want it back. Don't stand there waving your arms – go and get it. Don't come home until you've found it – I'm not cooking for you. I didn't catch anything with your stupid hunting ear anyway.' Then he took to throwing stones if Fade came near their domain. Hoori donned a wetsuit and tried diving about in the sea, but it was hopeless. 'Why am I doing this?' he asked himself, 'am I a god or a sardine?' But all was not lost. He had been spotted by Otohime, the sea dragon's daughter, who thought 'Oooh, he's gorgeous'.

Wearing her most seductive swimwear, Otohime managed purely by chance to collide with his canoe. They hit it off at once. 'Do you come here often?' she asked. 'Only in the canoodling season,' he replied. With such repartee how could things go wrong? When he confided about the missing fish hook she beamed with delight. 'You've come to the right place. My dad is the ruler of the sea and if you come home to tea with me I'll butter him up and get that silly hook back for you.' Now she knew she had him hooked.

At first Ryujin, dragon king of the sea (the handsome fellow pictured overleaf), was not too pleased when his daughter brought home what he presumed to be a fisherman. Being the protector of aquatic species he had 'No Fishing' and 'Fishermen will be Devoured' notices all over the place. Hoori assured him he hated fishing as much as Ryujin did. 'I only tried it once – I hated every minute of it and I won't ever do it again – and if it will help I'll say sorry to the poor brave fish that got stuck on the hook and kiss his mouth better.'

After that the two of them got on like a dragon on fire. Three actually, as the daughter was planning wedding gongs. Everything was going so swimmingly she was in no hurry. Life was good in the palace and the wedding did eventually take place. But there came a day when Hoori remembered the fish hook and his brother and became strangely homesick. By now his wife was expecting a child, so with Ryujin's blessing and a gift of two tide jewels – and the fish hook of course – he planned a triumphant return to reclaim his half of the Hoori and Hoderi kingdom.

Was Hoderi happy to see him? Not a bit. 'Where the bloody Hell have you been? Gallivanting around getting married – not even so much as a postcard in all these years. Oh, we're going to use the no postal service as an excuse are we? Too much trouble to put a message in a bottle then. Anyway where's my hook? No, I don't want to meet her. She can shove off and have your baby. I don't care where. It's none of my business. There's plenty of empty sheds around. They should be full of fish, but you lost my best hook didn't you? Anyway, I'm going fishing even if the hook is bent and you haven't bothered to straighten it out properly.'

Hoori scratched his head and got on with the matter in hand – settling his wife. She refused the services of a midwife and did not want him to

be present at the birth. She wanted to be entirely
alone. Hoori was very unhappy about this and was
determined to keep an eye on her, so he peered
through a crack when he heard a cry. He should
have listened to her. At the first labour pang his
wife changed into a monstrous dragon. Hoori
shrieked in fright and dismay, and she did the
same, scuttling off swiftly into the sea leaving
him holding the baby. She never did return but
sent a sister in a nanny's uniform to care for the
child. 'Serves you right,' said his brother.

This time the easy-going Hoori had had enough
of these jibes and decided to test the tide jewels.
These are the equivalent of microchips for sea
control. Jewel one – Whooooosh! Tide out out
out. Hoderi was stranded in a boat with no sea
underneath – no fish. Jewel two – Whoooosh! Tide
in with tidal wave, boat sunk and Hoderi up to
his neck in water. Unfortunately he never learnt
to swim. Hoori controls tide to creep mode, and
does not stop until only Hoderi's mouth is above
water screaming and begging for mercy and
promising to be ever so nice from now on.

What happened to Hoori's son? Well he grew up and married his caring
aunt Tamayon-Hine and they in turn had a son called Kamu-Yamato, and
then a second, Toyo-Mike-Nu who grew up to be the first human emperor
of Japan; but this may not have happened until after he died and was
called Jimmu-Teno. So you can save time and think of him as Mike and
Jimmy.

IZANAGI

Shinto creator god who begat the islands of Japan and most of the
contents therein via his wife **IZANAMI**. Unfortunately the strain proved
too much for Izanami and she died in childbirth. **IZANAGI** tried and failed
to rescue her from the Underworld, but while cleaning himself up after
this very messy operation, he unexpectedly gave birth himself. Sun goddess
AMATERASU was born from the tear in his left eye, Moon god Tsukiyomi
was born from the tear in his right eye, and storm god **SUSANOO** was
born from his dripping nose.

IZANAMI

Shinto creator goddess. She is very Heavenly with the Heavenly floating bridge, and the Heavenly jewelled spear used to stir the celestial porridge. But then it becomes a little incomprehensible: something about wagtails giving birth to a leech – or it may have been a jellyfish. There was some sort of split-up and she ended up in Yomi, the land of gloom. Further details can be found in the *Book of Ancient Matters*, written in AD 712. This account, being in ancient Japanese, has to be read back-to-front and probably in very small doses.

JIZO

A protector of mankind. He appears to jingle a lot – he has rings on his staff to warn of approach. **JIZO** is capable of rescuing souls from Hell and is therefore extremely popular. He is especially protective towards children, which is nice to know, and will always help those in need.

KAMI

Gods of incomprehensible things. There are over eight million of them, so if you find something you don't understand, there's probably a god for it amongst the Kami. They're divided into Heavenly incomprehensibles (Amatsu-Kami) and Earthly ones (Kunitsu-Kami) if that's any help. We find the whole idea pretty incomprehensible ourselves, but we don't know if there's a Kami of Kami.

KANNON

Goddess of compassion and mercy. She's the Japanese version of China's **GUAN-YIN**, who is really a female manifestation of India's **AVALOKITESVARA**. Being a Bosatsu, she spends her time tending to tormented souls who haven't yet seen the light. If you're lost in Japan and looking for Nirvana, **KANNON** will put you straight. If anyone can, Kannon can.

KAPPA

Water demons. They will lure you into rivers and suck your blood. They are, however, extremely polite. So here is what you do: you will recognise a **KAPPA** from the bowl-like depression on top of its head filled with water. This is its power source. So you bow to a Kappa in the approved Japanese fashion, and naturally, having to return the courtesy, it will bow back and the water tips out. It is then powerless until the water can be replenished. That is not all: they are crazy about cucumbers. They prefer cucumbers to blood. Bribe them with a cucumber and they will promise you almost anything. And once a promise is made they are honour-bound to keep it.

MARISHA-TEN

Goddess of war and victory. She means business. Never mind her eight blade-wielding arms and cavalry of ferocious boars – she has the ultimate means for making an army invincible. She can turn them invisible. You can't beat that.

MUSUBI-NO-KAMI

God of love and marriage. Sometimes female in appearance but mostly appears in the form of a handsome young man. Visits earth once a year and leaps out at unsuspecting girls from inside a cherry tree to offer them blossoms of future love.

NINIGI

God of rice and of the Japanese imperial family, so he's a bit starchy and hard-boiled. The grandson of **AMATERASU**, she passed on to him the sacred items that are the Japanese equivalent of the Crown Jewels, only more so: a mirror, a necklace and the sacred sword.

OKUNINUSHI

God of healing and sorcery. As the youngest of eighty brothers he had a few family problems with a lot of bullying – but he got to be a god. Teamed up with Suku-Na-Biko, a tiny god with moth wings and feathers who was into curing and cultivation. It was a very good alliance as Oku knew his own family were incapable of such things and had no intention of 'keeping godliness in the family'.

RAIDEN

God of lightning. He has a very striking appearance: flames for skin, a demon's head and eagle's claws. He owns a thunder beast called Raiju which he sends in the form of a fireball, leaping through trees and clawing at things.

It is not advisable to sleep out of doors in thunderstorms as, apart from getting terribly wet, Raiju can join you when he gets tired. He curls up in your belly button for a snooze and **RAIDEN** has to wake him up with fire arrows. This is not a good way to have your navel pierced. In calmer moments Raiju can take the form of a badger, weasel or cat to sharpen his claws and leave scratch marks on trees.

SAMBO-KOJIN

Kitchen god with three faces and two pairs of hands. Just what is needed in a busy kitchen.

SHICHI-FUKU-JIN

These are the seven gods of good fortune, a *very* special package deal. Book a cruise in the treasure boat they all share. It's super value and the trip of a lifetime with.

Benten: goddess of love, music and literature.

Bishamon: the Enemy Basher and Big Time Minder, dressed in armour.

Daikoku: expert in wealth counselling. He has a big sack which he hits with a hammer and it becomes full of goodies for you. (This never happens when we hit the sack.) He is far superior to Santa Claus, since you don't have to wait until Yuletide and he does not mess about with chimneys and reindeer. He is still fat and jolly, but no hiding behind a beard to go 'Ho! Ho! Ho!' His son is Ebisu, god of fishing and good catches. Probably in charge of navigation.

Fukurukoju: responsible for good health and keeping fit. He certainly keeps in shape, but not the shape most people would want to be with an elongated head and short bandy legs. This is so you won't give up or be jealous – you will always feel you are in better shape. It is possible he has been made a spin-off for the Chinese Feng-Shui Brigade as part of their Fuk, Luck and Shou package.

Jurojurin is god of longevity and although he is fond of rice wine and is accompanied by such diverse creatures as a crane, a stag and a tortoise, his dignity is not impaired as he clutches his sacred staff to which is attached a scroll of wisdom. He also seems to have a Chinese counterpart called Shou-Lao. Then in case you missed the first goodies sack there is rotund, happy, smiling Hotei with another one. He is sometimes known as the 'Laughing Buddha' and likes to have his roly-poly tummy tickled.

SHOJO

Orangutan-like gods who live on the sea bed. They could even be sea monkeys. The **SHOJO** wear skirts made of green seaweed and they make white wine. What can they make it from? Is it brine wine? If you are a good person, it will be a fine wine and taste delicious. But to bad folk it will taste like poison – and work as such unless they give up their evil ways. We've heard of seaside trips and the dangers of sunstroke but this is Bizarre-on-Sea.

SUSANOO & AMATERASU

Being born from the snot of **IZANAGI** was not an auspicious start to life and could be the reason **SUSANOO** was prone to behaving like a bit of a bogey – especially towards his sister **AMATERASU**. She was born from the left eye of Izanagi, presumably after wiping a tear away after sneezing. He had just come back from the Underworld and was covered in gloom dust. Another god, Tsukiyomi, was born from a tear in his right eye.

Amaterasu was given the Sun, Tsukiyomi was given the Moon and Susanoo was given the ocean, which he rejected. He then argued with his sister saying the one who could produce the most godlets instantly should have the most power. He snatched her fertility beads, bit them open and spat out five godlings, shouting 'I've won.' Amaterasu counter claimed saying as the beads belonged to her so did the godlets.

This caused Susanoo to have endless tantrums, rushing about the world and throwing things all over the place. He ended up by throwing a flayed horse through the roof of Amaterasu's sewing room, which scared the daylights out of her, so she ran away and hid in a cave. This caused no end of commotion as the sun couldn't shine again until she was coaxed out with an all-singing and dancing performance by Uzeme the goddess of joy and mirth, a jewelled necklace and her reflection in a mirror when curiosity tempted her to peer out.

Susanoo was then thrown out of Heaven and mooched about Earth rather at a loss until he met an old couple weeping copiously. 'What's up?' he asked, and they told him they were due to be visited by an eight-headed dragon. He had already eaten seven of their daughters and now he was coming to scoff the very last one. When Susanoo saw the daughter he realised what was missing in his life, and said 'Give your daughter to me – I'll look after her don't you worry – now tell me about this dragon and have you got any booze?'

Susanoo changed the girl into a comb, as he still retained some godly powers, and stuck her into his hair to keep her out of harm's way and then filled eight bowls with rice wine inside a palisade he built which had eight holes in it. The dragon came sniffing along its usual route, came across the neatly concealed wine and thought this is my day. Eight heads popped through the holes, eight tongues lapped, eight brains became befuddled and the whole dragon conurbation fell into a slumber. Enter Susanoo with a sword, and a swish, and a lop and a chop, chop, chop, chop, chop, chop, chop. Just for good measure he gave a few extra strokes and something dropped out of the dragon's tail with a clunk. It turned out to be a sword.

The sword is called Kusanagi and supplies proof to all you sceptics that this tale must be absolutely true as this is the Imperial Sword of the Japanese Royal Family and may be viewed today providing you can get the necessary permission. And Susanoo? From then on he always kept his nose clean.

UKE-MOCHI

Fast food goddess of nosh, grub, scoff and instant dinners. The wife of Inari, she avoided cooking like the plague. One day Tsukiyomi, the Moon god created from a tear in **IZANAGI**'s eye, invited himself over for dinner with **UKE-MOCHI** after hearing she had been proclaimed a gastro goddess. When he popped his head round the kitchen door, he was disturbed to find his hostess vomiting into the dishes. She had planned to serve this up on a bed of rice with a delicate garnish and a bottle of house wine.

Disgusted and insulted, Tsukiyomi killed her and stormed out. However, the corpse of Uke-Mochi continued to propagate food like some uncontrollable growbag. From every orifice poured the ingredients for daily bread, rice pudding, soya beanfeasts and much more, including the odd cow and other edible animals. Ever her fame grows and fast food chains should offer everlasting prayers. Her husband Inari – the god of rice

– still holds a rice distribution concession. He feels in the circumstances it all turned out for the best as he does not have to face his wife's cooking anymore.

UMASHIASHIKABIHIKOJI

A primeval reed from which sprouted various gods. These were all concerned with creating the world. We wonder how it came by this name. Is it possible the gods play Scrabble? You would score 1,316 points exactly if you put it down right. Of course no dictionary could prove you wrong. Bit of a shame you can only have seven letters at once.

THE GODS OF
THE MAYA

South of the border, down Mexico way, reaching as far as Guatemala, Honduras and El Salvador, this amazing civilisation started with the Zapotecs and included the Olmecs and Mixtecs before ending with the Toltecs. Their city, Teotihuacan, preceded Mayan culture and is full of mysteries from an earlier civilisation. It seems to have suffered fire at some point, but parts of it were in use up to Aztec times. With its pyramid of the sun built over a chambered cave, this may even have been **PACARI**, 'The Place of Emergence', where the Incan gods hid during a terrible disaster.

Unfortunately, Mayan books were unspeakably fragile and only four precious volumes have survived the ravages of time for us to consult. No wonder the Maya are so enigmatic – imagine if mankind was wiped out and all a visiting alien had to go on was a couple of Harry Potter books and half a telephone directory. If anyone has the original *Popol Vuh* and can return it to the library from whence it came, all fines will be cancelled.

Yes they did like sacrifice on a huge scale – but we still have wars and terrorism. As for European terrorism, the Mayan Empire had already dissipated and it was the poor old Aztecs who got the full brunt of Spanish aggression.

ACAT

God of tattoos. The Maya often decorated themselves with body art which was of deep mystical significance. No cheesy anchors or 'I luv Prudence' for them – they favoured designs of the utmost godliness. Having the symbol of a god tattooed on their flesh would, they believed, give them just the faintest whiff of godly essence themselves.

Tattooing can be a nerve-wracking business. It's all very well scribbling a wobbly picture of Marilyn Monroe on someone's elbow, but what if you're inscribing the utterly holy face of a god and get the nose wrong? It's enough to make anyone's hands shake.

Luckily, tattoo artists can call upon **ACAT** for assistance. He blesses the ink, the needles, the skin, and the funny buzzing machine. More importantly, he guides the hands of the tattooist at every stage of the operation – for perfect results every time. We see many tattoo artists who would greatly benefit from Acat's help.

AH-BOLOM-TZACAB

God of aristocracy. Also known as God K, for Kings. He's the god with the long nose and a leaf sticking out of his nostril. He has something to do with picking the right lineage for the upper crust of the ruling classes. Note the posh double-barrelled surname.

AH-CILIZ

God of eclipses. Although everyone knows that eclipses are caused by a supernatural being eating the sun, in Mayan mythology there's a twist. **AH-CILIZ** is actually a servant of the sun and waits upon him at table. Why he should occasionally take it upon himself to devour his master is unclear. Pay and conditions not good enough? They should try for arbitration.

AH-CUXTAL

God of birth. There are usually goddesses for this kind of thing but the Maya always liked to be different. **AH-CUXTAL** protects the unborn child and ensures its safe passage into the world. Then he washes his hands.

AH-PEKU

God of thunder who spends most of his time taking it easy on hilltops and mountaintops. But when a storm cloud happens to be passing overhead, he flags it down, jumps in and drives off making the most terrible thunderous noises.

AH-PUCH

The ruler of Mitnal, level nine of the Underworld: the deepest, darkest, dreadfullest department of Mayan Hell. At some point it became associated with **MICTLAN**, which was the Aztec version. Identified by the Aztecs with Mictlantecuhtli, the grinning god of death, **AH-PUCH** is also known as God A, the first of the **ALPHABET GODS**. A is for 'Argggggghh!!'

Ah-Puch likes to surface at night and skulk around in really scary mode. A putrefying corpse with an owl's head is his favourite outfit. Wishing to look the part he uses the eyes of the dead to add the finishing touches to his headgear. One of his nicknames is 'The Flatulent One', which is not something we care to investigate further.

For some reason Ah-Puch often has bells tied to his hair, but he is not being cute. What he does when he homes in on a victim is worse than you need to imagine. There is only one way to escape his attentions. How!! Shriek! Moan! Scream! Give it your best shot. Sound utterly convincing. Ah-Puch will then assume you are already being dealt with by some of his lesser demons. He will stop outside your door to sigh 'Ah…' and pass by with a grim smile.

But Ah-Puch, the lord of death and patron god of the number ten, will get you in the end. He uses the screech owl Muan, the evil bird of bad tidings, as his messenger. To this day the legend persists that when an owl screeches, someone nearby will die. If you hear a hoot, take a deep breath and count to ten.

Kam, also known as God A, is an emergency back-up death god for when Ah-Puch is on vacation. Little is known of Kam – his existence is hinted at by codex glyphs but his attributes and personality remain a mystery. But he does appear to favour death by violent means – such as stabbing, decapitation and Mayan chainsaw massacre.

ALPHABET GODS

In the early days of archeological exploration, when glyphs and codices were still a complete mystery, no-one had a clue what the god's names were. So for administration purposes, they were identified by letters of the alphabet. 'This is a picture of God A, and underneath is God B. Please insert God C into Slot D and connect to God E using the tool provided.'

This godly A-to-Z was first compiled by Paul Schellhas in 1904, with various revisions appearing over the years. As more information came to light, godologists were gradually able to work out the names of each god. But the A-to-Z system is still in use today so we've incorporated it thus:

God A: **AH-PUCH**
God B: **CHAC**
God CH: **XBALANQUE**
God D: **ITZAMNA**
God E: **YUM-KAAX**
God F: **BULUC-CHABTAN**
God L: **VOTAN**
God M: **EK-CHUAH**
God N: **UAYEB**
God O: **IXCHEL**
God P: **FROG GOD**
God S: **HUN-HUNAHPU**

BACABS

These are the four gods of the cardinal points of the compass. As the Maya didn't have any cardinals or compasses, just think of them as giant brothers who hold up the four corners of the sky. The sons of **ITZAMNA** and **IXCHEL**, these are the deities to point you in the right direction.

BACKLUM-CHAAM

God of male sexuality and masculine horniness; usually depicted with the relevant section of his anatomy standing to attention. We assume he is the god to call upon should you have any trouble in that department. Far more reliable than those unsolicited emails promising more inches than could safely be accommodated in anyone's pants. Go for **BACKLUM-CHAAM** every time – there's no need to be embarrassed.

BULUC-CHABTAN

One of the **ALPHABET GODS** known as God F, for fire. This pal of **AH-PUCH** is not Mr Nice Guy; a god of gratuitous violence, he torches houses and roasts people on a spit. And if someone unexpectedly drops dead, **BULUC-CHABTAN** is probably to blame.

CABRAKAN

The son of Hell-god **VUCUB-CAQUIX**, he's a mountain giant Hell-bent on catastrophe. But the hero twins **HUNAHPU** and **XBALANQUE** stopped his destructive ways by giving him poisoned fowls to eat. Then he was buried alive. His giant brother **ZIPACNA** came to a similar end.

CAMA-ZOTZ

God of bats. Not as in bat-and-ball, but flappy wings and pointy teeth. Naturalists and godologists believe him to be a leaf-nosed vampire bat. He has his own house of bats in the Underworld, and caused no end of trouble for the **HERO TWINS**.

CHAC

One of the **ALPHABET GODS** known as God B. B is for 'bursting clouds'. **CHAC** is a reptilian critter with fangs and a rather droopy snout. His hair is a permanently knotted tangle of confusion, which we find quite endearing. Very important for harvests and growing, Chac sends rain into the world by weeping from his large benevolent eyes. He's very good like that, even teaching the secrets of farming at no extra cost. Chac comes in four fashionable colours symbolising the four corners of the world: red (east), white (north), yellow (south) and black (west). He owns the colour-coordinated **BACABS**.

CHACMOOL

Mysterious laid-back god of handouts. These are the reclining statues with a bowl or container on their laps waiting, with head cocked to one side, for a votive offering. Or are they? No-one really knows. Buddy, can you spare a dime? Or possibly a heart?

CIT-BOLON-TUM

God of medicine who appears in the form of a wild boar, rather than the white coat and stethoscope you might expect. **CIT-BOLON-TUM** is known for his nine precious stones treatment. What this involves appears to be confidential, but it seems to work.

EK-CHUAH

One of the **ALPHABET GODS** known as God M, for 'merchants'. **EK-CHUAH** started off as a god of conflict, which could explain a lot about door-to-door vendors and telesales tactics. He has black-rimmed eyes and a large droopy lip … or is it a nose? That would explain why his name sounds like a sneeze. Ek-Chuah! Either way, he has a real nose for business. He is usually depicted as a dark brown or black deity, appropriately enough as he's the patron of the Cacao bean. Yes, Ek-Chuah is a god of chocolate!

FROG GOD

Frog god or god of frogs. He's also known as God P (P is for 'pond life'). He nearly escaped the net, but not the world wide web, where he was found hiding from mythologists on an obscure web page. He has froggish fingers and is fond of growing things in damp places against a blue background. We only have someone's word for this as we haven't yet come across any snapshots yet.

HERO TWINS (XBALANQUE AND HUNAHPU)

XBALANQUE and **HUNAHPU** are the sporty **HERO TWINS**. They grew up keeping their eyes on the ball seeking vengeance for the loss of their father **HUN-HUNAHPU** until at last the day came when they were in the premier league. Following in their father's footsteps, they successfully negotiated the tricky tests of Hell and challenged the Xibalba team to a match.

From the kick-off it was a tough one. The twins ignored the ball and kicked the life out of the monstrous **VUCUB-CAQUIX** and his two giant sons **CABRAKAN** and **ZIPACNA**. But **CAMA-ZOTZ**, the bat god, was passed a knife and managed a magnificent header by lopping **HUNAHPU**'s head off.

The game seemed to be a draw, so the brothers asked for extra time. Hunahpu borrowed a turtle's head while his own head took an early bath and was hung above the court to dry. Nevertheless the head still managed to participate in the heading, which really threw the Underworld side. They were totally disorientated in the last minute when **XBALANQUE** caught the head and kicked the turtle top knot into touch. Victory to the **HERO TWINS**!

Xbalanque replaced Hunahpu's head so you couldn't see the join. 'How do you do that?' asked the defeated team. 'That's us,' grinned the twins, 'we always stick together. Chop anything off and we just stick it back.' The losers pleaded for a demonstration. So the brothers chopped them into pieces. But they decided against the joining together bit and left the Underworld to face the sports press. Further exciting adventures followed, starting with their monkeying around with the **MONKEY TWINS**.

With many exciting adventures under his belt Hunahpu was elevated to Sun god while Xbalanque became Moon god. Every day when the Sun goes down, he tosses the stars across the dark empty Heavens. This is good practice for his throwing arm.

HUN-HUNAHPU

ALPHABET GOD S. S is for 'sport'! A wizard of the dribble, he was unfortunate enough to come up against Xibalba, the Underworld team, in the cup final. It all started when he was playing football with his sons **HUN-BATZ** and **HUN-CHOEN**, and his brother Vucub-Hunahpu in goal. They made such a noise shouting to each other – 'pass it this way' and 'get into him sonny' and 'that ball was never off-side' – that they disturbed the Underworld beneath the field.

VUCUB-CAQUIX, lord of the Underworld, was very irate and sent messengers summoning **HUN-HUNAHPU** and his brother to the Underworld cup final. Along the way there were many dangerous intelligence tests which, being more brawn than brain, they failed miserably. But more humiliation was to come when the Xibalba team walked onto the field.

Their star player Vucub-Caquix bent the rules and cut off Hun-Hunahpu's head. The referee didn't like to say anything or even admit to being there, and who can blame him? Vucub-Caquix hung the head on a calabash tree. One day an Underworld lass called Xquic fancied a calabash and picked what was left of Hun-Hunahpu by mistake.

Game to the last, he managed to pass some sacred spittle into her hand. We did say he was wizard of the dribble. Xquic must have swallowed because she gave birth to **HUNAHPU** and **XBALANQUE**, otherwise known as the **HERO TWINS**.

ITZAMNA

Reptilian top god. He's the son of the Sun, creator god **HUNAB-KU**, and was heavily involved in the development of Mayan culture. He brought agriculture and farming to the masses, and invented books and writing. He's also known as **ALPHABET GOD** D for 'doctors'. Old and ragged with a bulbous red nose, he has a red-hot healing hand ideal for doctors needing quick cauterisation facilities. **ITZAMNA** had a quick fling with **IXCHEL**, which resulted in the birth of the **BACABS**. In the daytime he is Sun god Kinich-Ahau. His feathery serpent mode Kukulcan was identified with **QUETZALCOATL** by the Aztecs.

IX-CHUP

The young moon goddess. She often poses with the cuddly rabbit of the moon, although this looks more like someone's holiday snaps. Her name is often taken in vain by scholars who confuse her with **IXCHEL**. A sad mistake.

IXCHEL

Moon goddess of pregnant women and mother of the **BACABS** by **ITZAMNA**. She invented weaving and, being partly waterfall herself, takes charge of downpours. Her hair is very snaky – it's made from real snakes. If humans upset her she can get quite grumpy. If you see her wearing her crossbones skirt and writhing serpent hair do try not to be noticed. Then again she has a softer side as a rainbow goddess of childbirth.

IXCHEL is also known as God O (or rather, Goddess O). O is for 'obstetrics'. She is the wife of **VOTAN** and, like him, is knocking on a bit, red-faced and wrinkly. She's into all the crafts: weaving, watercolours and probably bottles her own chutney.

I✳TAB

Moon goddess of suicide, **IXTAB** dangles from the sky with her neck in a noose. This seems terribly morbid, but she does gather up the souls of suicides and take them to Heaven, so there is some happy ending.

MONKEY TWINS (HUN-BATZ AND HUN-CHOEN)

HUN-BATZ and **HUN-CHOEN** were the ill-fated sons of sporty **HUN-HUNAHPU** and his wife Xbaquiyalo. They started off as highly regarded creative kids; artistic, musical and full of knowledge. They were top of the class in everything, until one day their dad Hun-Hunahpu introduced them to football. Suddenly school was forgotten, homework was ignored and daily football practice became their only interest.

One day dad went off to the Underworld to play an away match, but never returned. After many moons, some strange Underworld girl called Xquic popped up with two kids and demanded a place in the family. It turned out that after the ill-fated match, Hun-Hunahpu had managed to father two more children – the **HERO TWINS**. These new step brothers were dashing, daring, brave, resourceful and cunning. Naturally the **MONKEY TWINS** hated them.

The daily football matches became a hotbed of argument, vicious tackling and constant fouls. The Monkey Twins used every dirty trick in the codex, and pretty soon the Hero Twins decided to send them off the pitch for good. The Monkey Twins were lured to a particular tree and told there was a nice collection of juicy birds up there. So up they climbed expecting a dinnertime treat. But as they climbed, the tree grew taller and taller. They couldn't get down; they could only go up. There was no escape until they discovered that they'd been turned into monkeys.

Because of their former skills they were much venerated, and everyone tried not to laugh, but grandmother Xmucane got the giggles and they fled in embarrassment.

PADDLER GODS

There are times when even gods have to paddle their own canoe. Well, some cargoes are too precious to end up the creek without a paddle. When there are souls to be ferried and corn distribution to be taken care of, you need to run a tight canoe. Corn gods don't do water, and without wheels it's waterways all the way. And guess who has right of way at all times? Old Jaguar Paddler sits in the bow and streams through the night shift, and Old Stingray Paddler dabbles away from the stern to the daytime doddle.

UAYEB

Also known as God N. N, alas, is for 'not lucky'. One of the Pauahtun, he is the god of five unlucky days; when they are or how often they occur is not clear. Once a year would be tolerable but every week would be a bit over the top. He may also be the first god to wear a shell suit, as a snail shell seems to be his principle abode. **UAYEB** is also often portrayed as a drunken sex-maniac. There's obviously something we don't know about.

VOTAN

God of warfare and death. Married to **IXCHEL**, **VOTAN** is the old black god, and my goodness, he is old. He's so old that no-one quite remembers who he is. He was very very old with no teeth even when he was first worshipped, which was so long ago it may have been before time began.

We don't know how black he is either. His face may be painted black, or he might just have been cleaning the chimney or living in a cave for too long. But perhaps it's the fumes from the potent black cigars he smokes. If you like the good old days and haven't yet given up smoking, Votan could be the god for you. He's also known as God L. L is for 'live percussion'! Yes, Votan is the god of drums! He invented the art of drum solos in his skin-tight and drumboogie days.

YUCUB-CAQUIX

Demonic deadly death god of Xibalba, the Mayan Underworld, along with his second-in-command Hun-Came. His name means 'Seven Macaw' and he's the gigantic bird god monster who set himself up as the Sun god but lost at darts to the **HERO TWINS** – who cheated and used blowpipes. His sons were also troublemakers, being the giant demons **CABRAKAN** and **ZIPACNA**.

According to legend, **VUCUB-CAQUIX** carried the false sun in his beak and was shot down in flames at the end of the last creation. Interestingly enough, in the constellation of Cygnus his beak holds the mysterious star X-1, which became a supernova and now seems to harbour a black hole.

XAMAN-EK

ALPHABET GOD C. For 'copal tree', of course. He has a black monkey head. You may think there is worse to come – but no, he is all peace and benevolence. In fact, he's a god of holiness and godliness, a real god's god. His symbol is the North Star, used for guidance and direction, so he's the one to call upon if you get lost. His only indulgence, if you are offering, is incense from the resin of the copal tree.

YUM-KAAX

God of agriculture and maize. He's a promising youngster with a trendy corn headdress, but is always getting into fights with bad weather, famine and drought. Also known as God E. Does that stand for Vitamin E? Maize is full of goodness. Try a bowl of nutritious yummy Kaax today! He is usually depicted holding a small pot of maize plants and looking extremely displeased about something.

ZIPACNA

Evil mountain god, son of the Underworld god **VUCUB-CAQUIX** and the giant brother of giant **CABRAKAN**. He was extremely arrogant and nasty, and thought nothing of killing four hundred brave young warriors by sitting on them. Okay, so they'd been sent by the g ods to kill him, but it's still a nasty way to go.

ZIPACNA came to a dead end thanks to the **HERO TWINS**, who set a devious trap. They made an enormously juicy and mouth-watering artificial crab and told Zipacna his dinner was ready. While he was salivating over it, they chopped down a nearby mountain the way lesser mortals would chop down a tree. Timberrr! The mountain toppled and crushed Zipacna beneath its weight.

THE GODS OF ANCIENT MESOPOTAMIA

Mesopotamia, the cradle of civilisation. Nurtured by the Tigris and Euphrates rivers, the lands of Sumer and Akkad bloomed with fertile thought. It was Sumertime and the living was easy. Of course, this new-fangled writing did have its downside. For the first time in human history, intelligent people could earn a living by making little squiggles on pieces of clay instead of chasing animals across the landscape, which soon led to the rise of accountants, lawyers and bureaucracy. The world's first rule book was written by King Hammurabi, who explained in detail exactly what part of you would be cut off if you misbehaved.

Many Mesopotamian gods have Sumerian and Akkadian variations. They're virtually identical, but with cunning changes of name. For example, **TAMMUZ** is the Akkadian equivalent of Dumuzi. (This can become confusing; is that one god or two? Do we treat them separately?) Things became a little easier when the two regions joined together to form Babylonia. At least until the Tower of Babel came along and confused it all again.

ME

The Tablets of Destiny and fundamental powers of the Universe. The most sought-after ultimate prize in prehistory, they have been nicked, stolen, chipped, dropped, snitched and snatched more often than you could imagine. And no wonder, as anyone who possesses the Tablets of Destiny becomes instantly omnipotent, omnipresent, omniscient and omniultrasupereverything. Not bad for a crumbling collection of clay lumps.

With Anzu and **INANNA** trying to grab them from **ENKI** and/or **ENLIL**, it's a wonder they ever remained in one piece. Fortunately **MARDUK**, who was worried about the stability of the Universe, came along eventually and superglued the Tablets of Destiny to his breast. Where they are now is more than you or I can know. And **ME** is not 'Me' – it is pronounced 'Mai'. In short, no-one has been able to keep tabs on the tablets. Fragments could even be the Ten Commandments lugged down from the mountain by Moses.

AKKADIA
ENLIL

Storm god. Doesn't care much for humans and snots with fury if disturbed. [Editor's note: I think that should be 'snorts with fury'. At least, I hope so.] **ENLIL** keeps the Tablets of Destiny (**ME**), which give him absolute power over everything and help ward off headaches.

NINURTA

Eagle god of war and irrigation – or could it be irritation? Son of **ENLIL** and Ninhursaga, he started off as an eagle and then asked his mum for a lion's head. But this made him aggressively unruly, so she left his wings and gave him a humanoid body. It didn't do any good. What he liked was playing with thunderbolts and shouting war cries and smashing and killing anything he felt like.

Realising he was out of control, his mother took to hurling rocks at him. These were living things at the time, but it was still no good. **NINURTA** pounded them into submission and his mother was so disappointed that she took life away from them. A few of the stones had refused to be used as missiles, so Ninurta turned them into precious stones and jewels just to highlight how mean he could be.

One eventful day, the incredibly precious **ME** Tablets of Destiny were stolen by Anzu the storm bird. He didn't know quite how to extract the knowledge and was trying to hatch them up in his mountaintop eyrie. The gods thought Ninurta's bully-boy tactics could at last be put to good use. Happily singing *Bring on the Clouds* at the top of his unmusical voice, he flew up to Anzu's domain firing off thunderbolts. This had no effect at all. Anzu had built the tablets into a protective shield around his nest, and apart from a slight chipping and scarring, the thunderbolts and storm lashings could not inflict any lasting damage. Baffled, Ninurta rushed back to dad for advice and was told for once in his life to try and use his brains and a bit of godly cunning. So Ninurta sat and thought until his brain hurt so much that even he didn't want any loud noises. And then he had an idea…

He crept up on Anzu and cast his thickest and darkest clouds over the nest. The mighty bird was baffled and couldn't see his beak in front of his face. As he peered helplessly into the gloom, Ninurta screamed with delight and stormed the storm bird. He hacked off its head and wings and felt himself again. Ninurta took the tablets safely back to **ENKI**. Then it entered his thick skull that he could have kept them for himself. He tried to steal them but at long last the silly old god had taken security precautions. The tablets were now kept in a trap containing a monster turtle, which Ninurta crashed straight into after an unexpected shove from Enki. The turtle pinned him down and Ninurta had to cry for his mum to come and save his life by pleading with Enki. He promised never to be naughty again.

TAMMUZ

God of vegetation. Every summer, when his powers are strongest, when the flowers are blooming and the harvests are looking great, he collapses from heat exhaustion and dies. His soul flees to the Underworld where it's nice and cool, leaving the world's vegetation to fend for itself. The resulting desolation causes much misery as plants decay and winter sets in. So his mourning wife **ISHTAR** nips down to the nether regions to rescue him. Which is such a complicated and arduous task that it always takes six months and by the time they reappear, spring is right on schedule. **TAMMUZ**, the son of **EA**, had many cults and festivals in his honour, and also spread himself around Mesopotamia under the names Dumuzi and Damu.

AKKADIA, HITTITE EMPIRE

KUMARBI

A god who created three new deities from deposed **ANU**. The only memorable one was Teshub who didn't feel obliged to have any affection for his father and couldn't wait to shoulder him out of the way. **KUMARBI** wasn't having his spitting image son taking over without a struggle and, enlisting the aid of his old supporters, he created a gigantic stone monster called Ullikummi that could only be carried by Upelluri – a Hittite **ATLAS** who complained bitterly as whatever it was he was now carrying seemed to be still growing.

Teshub had a go at it using his entire storm armoury – to no effect. He then did a quick abdication and ran to **EA**, who had a word with **ENLIL**, who popped down to have a word with Upelluri, who was moaning about the pain in his right shoulder. Enlil looked up and saw an enormous pair of stone feet. So he ran to the gods' workshop and selected the biggest stonemason's saw he could find and, rushing back, hacked through the giant's feet and toppled it. There the story ends. Although you can't tear the last page from a clay tablet, they do get dropped and mislaid.

AKKADIA, SUMER
GILGAMESH

Famous Sumerian and Akkadian hero who was two-thirds god, or was it one-third? His mum was **NINSUN**, a cow goddess, and his father (or fathers) was (or were) a demon (or demons) impersonating his father, who was the king of Uruk at the time.

Look, the Sumerians invented writing not mathematics, and it is the writing we are concerned with here – as **GILGAMESH** is the long-running epic superhero featured in the Akkadian Tablets. Get the full set – there are twelve of them. Not so much a case of 'couldn't put it down', but 'having immense difficulty in picking it up'. It's called the *Epic of Gilgamesh* and, no, it's not a murder mystery. In fact, it's a roller-coaster adventure with the gods, containing fantasy, love, bloodshed and allegorical insights into the human condition. It was first produced in clay tablet form – we had to wait several thousand years for the paperback edition.

There are also five Sumerian poems in case you've missed anything. These were all published in utmost antiquity but still top the mythological charts.

NINSUN

Cow goddess of wisdom and mother of **GILGAMESH**. She was very highly regarded by the Sumerians, being the embodiment of perfect cowness and bovinity. In fact, she was probably the cowiest cow in the world. Dissatisfied farmers would point to her effigy and harangue their livestock: 'Now that's what I call a cow. Why can't you be more like her?' **NINSUN** also has the power of divination and can reveal the secrets contained in dreams. Not bad for a cow girl.

AKKADIA, SUMER, BABYLON

ISHTAR

Being a love goddess, **ISHTAR** is beautiful, sexy and very popular. Her fame in ancient Asia was second to none and she's still going strong. Her lovers are legion – or, to put it another way, she can't keep her hands to herself. She even attempted to have a fling with **GILGAMESH** but he went all heroic on her.

Her official husband – at least in Akkadia – is **TAMMUZ**, the god of agriculture and rebirth. It's possible the strain is too much for him as he spends six months per year recovering in the Underworld. Ishtar seems also to have become the goddess of déjà vu as she shared almost the same life as **INANNA**. But considering that Inanna stole **ME**, the Tablets of Destiny, she may well have used them to both backdate and update herself – until she was everywhere and everyone from **ASTARTE** to **ISIS**. She may even have been born again as **APHRODITE**.

Ishtar's sister **ERESHKIGAL** is in charge of the Underworld, and when Ishtar pays her a visit, the results are usually very similar although there are a few script changes and updates. She is also goddess of the Evening Star and seems determined to stay in the ascendancy as long as a sex goddess is needed. Her symbol is an eight-pointed star, and she doesn't care if you think it's rude to point or look at her with naked eyes.

ASSYRIA
KINGU

Dragon-god consort of **TIAMAT**. As a token of her love Tiamat gave **KINGU** the Tablets of Destiny (**ME**) for safekeeping. He decided to wear them as a fashion accessory. They looked really cool and also gave him holy power, magnificence and top universal status – it was like having a Babylonian iPhone. Unfortunately for him, the boost he received from wearing the Me Tablets as a breastplate made a lot of people jealous, particularly since they'd been stolen in the first place. Kingu was killed by **ANU**, and his body recycled to form universal bonus tracks and extra bits. One of the extras was the human race, formed from his blood. Sometimes dragons have a really tough time.

BABYLON
ADAD

Storm god. He spends most of his time hurtling around in his chariot littering the skies with forked lightning. He is also a god of divination, manipulating entrails and rigging dice to convey future info to the wise.

    ADAD was one of seventy children and if, as some claim, his mother was **ASHERAH**, she must have taken a trip to the seaside because his father was some obscure sea deity with a name like 'Prince of the Sea' or 'Deep Sea Doohdah'. Adad destroyed him anyway with a total wipeout, so we shall never know. Adad is identified with the Sumerian Ishkur, and was also known as **HADAD** to the Canaanites.

EA

Creator, god of water and the father of **MARDUK**. He also created Adapa, the first human, out of wet mud.

    Adapa's story reveals a valuable lesson: it is not a good idea to tear the wings off a wind god. You may think you have reasonable cause if, while out for a day's sailing (your brand new hobby) on the River Euphrates, **SHUTU**, the aforesaid wind god, blows you all over the place and you come close to sinking. But honestly, it's not worth it. Adapa's display of river rage stopped Shutu's antics and he was very cross. Despite having the ability to grow new wings almost instantly, he brought charges and the case went to the Small Claims Court run by **ANU**, the god of many parts. When the summons came, Adapa went to his dad for advice. **EA** told him to dress sensibly and avoid any Heavenly food or drink. This was unfortunate advice, as the cuisine on offer came from the Kitchens of Immortality. If he had sneaked a doggy-bag of goodies back to Earth, humans could have avoided death.

Anyway, Adapa got off with a caution and a bout of community service. He was required to serve as a sage, teaching mortals how wise and wonderful the gods were, and also explaining to them how to conduct themselves as decent human beings. Which largely consisted of warnings not to go sailing when that prat Shutu was wafting about. The 'Entity Aquaticus', he's very very wet. In fact, he's half fish. But he knows absolutely everything and is more than happy to share the info.

KISHAR

Earth Mother goddess of the horizon. If you don't know what that means, we suggest you lie on the ground and stare at the horizon. You will then either glimpse a stunning insight, or else fall asleep. **KISHAR** is the consort of her brother **ANSHAR** and signifies all manner of female submissive horizontal things. We can also reveal that she is the mother of **ANU**, although there were no birth certificates at the time.

MARDUK

Top Babylonian deity, fertility god and chief of all the other gods. As the boss of Babylon and custodian of the Tablets of Destiny (see **ME**), **MARDUK** was definitely a force to be reckoned with, until he was stolen by the Assyrians – causing a lot of aggravation with failed harvests and war. We don't quite know how this theft was accomplished but when he went missing his worshippers were no longer able to offer him his two meals

a day plus musical performances. Rumours abound of a takeover bid by Ashur, but where is he now? Has anyone seen Marduk? Last seen with beard and very strange sort of Noddy hat.

SHUTU

God of winds and river breezes. Apparently he's as temperamental as most other wind gods and is likely to blow you off course if you don't treat him with respect. Adapa was so irritated by **SHUTU** whizzing around his head like an enormous windy fly that he pulled his wings off, which must have been somewhat embarrassing. Of course, being a god, Shutu grew them back almost instantly. And then instigated a lawsuit for damages.

BABYLON, AKKADIA
ANSHAR

Paternal god of the sky and the horizon. In those ancient times there was nothing much else to be the god of. His consort is the Earth mama and horizon goddess **KISHAR**, who also happens to be his sister. Together they opened new horizons by producing **ANU** and **EA**.

SHAMASH

All-seeing Sun god of the law. Keeps everyone under surveillance and judges accordingly. You can run but you can't hide, and don't even think of telling a fib. He slices truth from lies with a blade.

At one time he was known in Sumeria as Babbar. You can see why he fancied a change.

BABYLON, SAMARIA, SYRIA
ADRAMMELECH

Supreme god of the Sun, as featured in the Old Testament (2 Kings 17:31). Do you know where Sepharvaim was? Then I shouldn't bother. But for the record it was a city which, in Old Testament times, had a pretty decent library and was therefore in constant danger of being burnt to the ground. The consort of Anammelch, the moon goddess, **ADRAMMELECH** himself was very popular, offering warmth and protection for the very reasonable price of a few burnt infant sacrifices. We can't say what form his protection took, but as he was a Sun god it was probably sunstroke. When the

Sepharvites moved to Samaria, their gods went with them. The Sepharvites ended up as good Samaritans, but their gods were up against some pretty stiff competition. Consequently, Adrammelech appears to have burnt out long ago.

HITTITE EMPIRE

HANNAHANNA

Earth Mother goddess. She is a source of ineffable wisdom and may be connected in some oracular way with the Gulses, goddesses of fate and destiny. We expect there were three of them – there usually are. She is very opinionated – but did you ever meet an oracle who wasn't? She also seems a bit temperamental and may storm off in a terrible rage if things don't fit her point of view.

If this happens, the Earth gets very depressed; cows stop mooing, sheep burst into tears and small children are left to fend for themselves while their parents sulk. Luckily the Earth has a dark side and her anger slowly dissipates into it. Another thing: she has an amazing magic bee which buzzes around on her behalf. This comes in very handy for finding missing gods.

INARA

Protector of all wild animals. Except dragons, which she has a tendency to obliterate. In particular, she clobbered the dragon Illuyankas who, with his own family, was causing much aggravation. **INARA**, with the aid of her human lover Hupasiyas, laid on a dragon's feast. There was booze by the barrel-load and calories by the cartload. The dragons came early, ate everything in sight and drank themselves into a stupor. Then Hupasiyas roped them down and they were dispatched. Or perhaps not – this dragon pops up all over the place. Was this his last pop? Was he sequalised?

With the reward money, Inara built Hupasiyas a Heavenly penthouse, but she warned him he must never look out of the window. Of course, he just couldn't resist and saw his wife and children all alone and pining. So Inara, who had a very hard Hittite heart, just had to eliminate him and put the penthouse on the market. After consultation with **HANNAHANNA**, she found herself another lover and also some land to make love to him on, which sounds like the cue for a happy ending. Only she went missing and not even Hannahanna's magic bee probe could find her again.

TELEPINU

A rather incompetent god of farming and agriculture. Rather prone to temper tantrums. He once caused almost insurmountable problems by putting his boots on the wrong feet; this made him so cross that he flew off in a rage and all the crops withered. It was left to **HANNAHANNA** to locate him, which she accomplished with the aid of her magic bee – programmed for seek and sting operations. **TELEPINU** returned – with blisters on his hands and feet and a very glum expression.

SUMER

ENKI

Creator god and the first Sumerian god to discover sex – while he was in his bath. It was such a new discovery he tried it out with his wife Ninhursaga, and in no time at all he had a daughter. This was also something new. So in time he had sex with her too, because he didn't know any better – and there were no written rules as he hadn't gotten around to inventing writing yet.

When his daughter had a daughter he did it again. In between times he experimented with earth, rocks and streams. Being of a rare god group, sheep and cattle were generated. Soon he had three daughters: Ninsar, Ninkurra and Ninimma. But when a fourth came along Ninhursaga decided enough was enough and said 'not Utu!' She began to intervene when he started doing what he always did. Frustrated, he took to doing things with vegetables, but it all backfired when he started eating them and he became very ill.

Ninhursaga, who had been refusing to have any more to do with her husband, including cooking his meat and two veg, took pity and nursed him back to health. They went back to square one: she became his consort and had another eight gods. **ENKI** then took up another hobby: playing with dolls. Not the inflatable kind, but clay dolls which he could bring to life. Although no-one likes to mention it, his sexual appetites had not been entirely curbed. Several missing clay tablets later (and these are the only known narrative source), Ninhursaga had become Ninmah, and after a night on the beer, possibly another Enki discovery, they had a clay person-making contest. This produced some people with bits missing and handicaps, so they had another competition to see if they could find them skills rather than throw them away. Thus a blind man became a musician and a man without hands became an attendant on a king because he could not steal.

With the other eight gods perpetrating and breeding, and the populace swelling and new races being formed, god-swapping was a popular hobby. The Sumerians, Akkadians and Babylonians were well into the god-share business. There was plenty of power-sharing and a plethora of ministers, priests, and scribes to draw up laws on clay tablets as calligraphy took hold.

Enki is now taking a back seat happily engaged in his new capacity as chairman of a campaign for real ale, which involves much sampling of the wares from breweries.

ERESHKIGAL

The consort of **NERGAL**, and **ISHTAR**'s sister, she is a brooding, moody figure who is prone to fits of fury and spasms of tearful temper, particularly when she doesn't get her own way. If you see her lips turn black, you know things can only get worse.

She is known as 'Lady of the Great Place', which in this instance means the Underworld. 'Queen of the Great Below' doesn't have quite the same ring to it. In fact, the locals referred to her domain as 'The Land of Gloom' – and were not impressed by a menu offering a choice between mud and dust. **ERESHKIGAL**'s Underworld realm is guarded by seven judges and gatekeepers, who seem very zealous about keeping people out. Which, we feel, is hardly necessary.

INANNA

Goddess of words, language, syntax and meaning. The daughter of **ANU** (or possibly his son **ENLIL**), she has much in common with **ISHTAR**. She married a shepherd-type deity called Dumuzi and built him a city to rule called Uruk. She also has a sister (possibly a twin) called **ERESHKIGAL** who was ruler of the Underworld. One day **INANNA** said to her maid Ninshubar: 'Look after things for a day or two – I'm going down under to see how sis is getting on – we haven't seen each other for yonks.' Well, it was quite a lark. There were seven gates, and before she went through each one she had to do a bit of a striptease. This was a strip-search with a difference. By the time she got to the throne room she was starkers.

Unabashed, as she was not the bashful type, Inanna cried: 'Wheee – ain't we got fun! Wow – give us a kiss, move over and lemmee have a go on that fab throne!' The ministers and judges of the dead in attendance on Ereshkigal were appalled and gave Inanna the sort of looks that could kill. Sure enough, Inanna dropped dead and they hung the corpse on a butcher's hook. Ereshkigal did not seem very concerned as twinning had never been her thing.

Ninshubar was the one who became concerned when her mistress did not return. She prayed to the gods but there was much shaking of heads and shuffling from above and only **ENKI** came to her aid. He created two zombie-like beings and gave them a lunch box containing immortality snacks. Having no hearts or anything to prove they were alive they went through the seven gates without let or hindrance. In the throne room they just took Inanna off the hook and restored her to life. The judges' looks were of no use. Somewhat subdued, Inanna asked her sister if she could leave now. 'Well, I can let you off the hook for the time being,' said Ereshkigal, 'but you must send me a replacement, or you will have to come back.'

Doing a reverse strip on the way out, Inanna shot back to Uruk at top speed to find Dumuzi having the time of his life and sleeping with Geshtinanna, the goddess of wine and another sister of hers. She packed both of them off to the Underworld and they each had to do a six-month stint – Duz in summer, Gesh in winter. You would think all this sort of thing would have slowed Inanna down, but not a bit. She was always a headstrong girl and having heard that the **ME**, The Tablets of Destiny and Fundamental Powers of the Universe, having been left for safekeeping with Enki, she thought 'Me, Me, Me! They're going to be mine!'

She paid a visit to Enki, who now had a slight drink problem, and by using flattery, her considerable sexual charm and judicious application of

alcohol, she persuaded him to let her have a peek at one of the famous tablets. Then another one. And then could she hold one? By the end of the evening she not only held them, she loaded them onto her barge and pushed off rapidly for Uruk.

When Enki woke up with a hangover and found he had given the tablets away, he was not a happy god. He sent his minions in pursuit, but she outwitted them all, proclaiming that Enki had given them of his own free will. His being drunk at the time was not her problem – he should join Alcoholics Anonymous. (This of course was not really feasible because everyone knew who Enki was.) And that was that.

NERGAL

Underworld god. A bit of a bully in bull form, with lots of bellowing, roaring and raping. When the Sumerian gods were having a bit of a beano, they realised that **ERESHKIGAL** was stuck on duty down in the Underworld – the one ruling job that is reliant on you being in residence. You can't nip out for the merest moment without all Hell breaking loose.

So they invited her to send her minister Namtar up so they could give him a doggy bag full of delicacies for her. As a mark of respect all the gods paid homage to Namtar as the representative of Ereshkigal. All but one – **NERGAL** – who just snorted with derision. When Namtar reported back, Ereshkigal screamed: 'That son of a bitch is gonna die!' (or ancient Sumerian words to that effect). 'Go get him Namtar – drag him back here!'

But it didn't work out like that because Nergal hid in the gents or something and could not be found. This was not good enough for Ereshkigal who dashed off a very terse appeal to the gods on official Underworld clay tablet, worded in a fashion they would be wise not to ignore. At last Nergal panicked and asked his dad **EA** for help. Dad supplied him with seven pairs of demons to accompany him. The demons hustled him through the seven gateways, taking up the position of two demons per gate to persuade the minders that ritual humiliation attempts were not on the agenda.

This enabled Nergal to rush to the throne room and take Ereshkigal by surprise. He grabbed her by the hair and put a knife to her throat, whereby she immediately relinquished the throne. Then he repented and shared it with her because he decided that he loved her even more than violence. This is only one of many versions. Having invented writing, the Sumerian Tabloids took off in a big way. Every scribe and hack wanted to test their story-spinning skills to the utmost: 'Hey, hold the wet clay – I gotta new angle on this Nergal deadline!'

SUMER, AKKADIA, BABYLON
APSU

The primordial god of sweet waters and the Heavenly freshwater oceans of wisdom. In the beginning he encircled the Earth and filled it with optimistic goodness. However, the salty sea waters of Chaos produced by **TIAMAT**, a female dragon, were very bitter. So **APSU** merged with Tiamat and became her consort. The waters blended very nicely – he'd obviously allowed fermentation to cease before adding his extra sugar. As a result of their union, **ANU** and **EA** were born, along with all the other gods, who rapidly took control and started running things. Apsu was not too happy about this, so he declared war on them all but was slain by Ea and sent to a watery grave.

TIAMAT

Her side of the story.

She lived happily in the salt water below the mists of time, joined by **APSU**, the wettest water god ever. Their peace was disturbed eventually by a bubbling of silt, and up popped a couple of beings, who soon gave birth to a lot of noisy gods. When Apsu objected, **EA** kindly put him to sleep on a permanent basis. **TIAMAT**, left alone, became decidedly tetchy. She ripped up anything the gods tried to create and had them hiding and huddling in fear. Something had to be done. Ea eventually had a fine upstanding son called **MARDUK**, who was egged on to become their champion. 'You're young, handsome, and such a brave guy … You do this and you'll never have to buy another drink.' Flattery got them everywhere – after practising martial arts he was kitted out with the latest in advanced weaponry (a bow, a net and a mace) and set off in his storm chariot.

Meanwhile, Tiamat had met another dragon. His name was **KINGU**, and he was busy taking her mind off her woes with a little romance and as much monster production as he could get away with. However, Kingu was all talk and no fangs – and when he saw Marduk with all his fighting paraphernalia he fled in panic, leaving **TIAMAT** to go it alone. She rushed at Marduk jaws agape and he hurled his secret weapon into her mouth. This was a raging storm and she could not chomp. She was then transfixed by an arrow and enmeshed in a net before being whopped by a mace.

The junior dragons were all captured and Kingu surrendered the Tablets of Destiny, which Tiamat had given him for a wedding present in return for his life. Marduk chopped up Tiamat's corpse and used it to create all the bits of the World and Universe the gods hadn't managed to finish. Finally a gods' court decided that Kingu would have to go – but as a special concession his blood was used to create mankind. 'Don't think of it as being sentenced to death – think of it as being sentenced to life everlasting on a massive scale.' Marduk now took over and drew up plans for his very own kingdom of Babylon.

SUMER, BABYLON
ANU

Top Mesopotamian god of the sky, lord of Heaven and supreme manager of all the other gods. His parentage depends on whether you are Sumerian or Babylonian. It could be **APSU** and **TIAMAT** or **ANSHAR** and **KISHAR**. He himself had two sons, **EA** and **ENLIL**, and they all played dice to decide who did what. Ea won the sea, Enlil the land and **ANU** was left with the sky. Then they decided the Universe would make a good prize. This was a mistake as **MARDUK**, landlord of the Sun at that time, took objection and chopped Anu to bits. So Anu became a bit of a nonentity, and as no-one knew which bits to bribe, he was used as a god of judgement. Not that anyone took much notice. It was easier to roll dice.

THE GODS OF THE MIDDLE EAST

A massive melting pot of Near and Middle East, with the lands of the Old Testament, including almost everywhere that's not Egypt. Incredibly ancient places like Canaan, Israel and Persia. Think dust, donkeys and divine destruction. A mish-mash of creeds and cultures – Hittites, Phoenicians, Persians, Canaanites, Zorastrians, Philistines and Syrians.

The world's major monotheistic religions kicked off here, a place throbbing with differing cultures and competing gods. It was a classic environment for the process of Natural Selection: survival of the fittest ensured that only the very best gods evolved to prosper down the millennia. (If you can't cope with the idea that the existence of God proves Darwin's Theory of Evolution, you'll just have to put up with it.)

From here derived the three great monotheistic religions of Judaism, Christianity and Islam. But no doubt **SHAMASH** still shines and **BAAL** still batters the clouds with his club, even if calls for their services have dwindled to an all-time low.

CANAAN
ANATH

ANATH caused a lot of hassle by wishing to appropriate a very special bow belonging to a mortal called Aqhat. Being a bit of a bitch, she zapped him to the Underworld, but he wouldn't let go of the bow and it went with him.

This caused no end of problems as it was actually a sky bow which held up the Heavens. So the sky collapsed and Anath had to eat humble pie and ask **EL** to sort it all out – partly through embarrassment and partly because she was going bow-legged under the weight of the sky.

She then appears to have changed her name to Anat and become Mrs **BAAL**, if not his sister or even his mother, when he was having trouble with **MOT**. She was last heard of in Egypt claiming to be a daughter of **RA**.

BAAL

The cloud monster. From humble beginnings as the storm god **HADAD**, he grew to occupy top position in the Canaanite pantheon, taking charge of war and heroic action adventure. His consort is **ANATH** (later **ASTARTE**), the goddess of fertility and sexuality. She's also his sister, but gods don't worry about that kind of thing.

BAAL enjoyed top spot in the Middle East pantheon and was worshipped far and wide. But his reputation was irreversibly damaged when Jewish leaders took exception to his sneaky cult of sacred prostitution in Palestine. They littered the Bible with anti-**BAAL** messages and took to calling him **BEELZEBUB**. And so he became universally hated – such is the power of the religious press.

KUSOR

God of windows and technical support. He tried to build a skylight in **BAAL**'s temple, but The Powers That Be refused planning permission. Eventually they found a compromise when Baal promised never to cause a flood as long as the temple windows were kept shut. **KUSOR** went on to become a regulator of the seasons, dispenser of information, and inventor of many home improvement devices. Which leaves us with one question: was the god of windows employed by Microsoft? Note the similarity of Kusor to cursor. We know so little about the ancients that we'll never be sure what mysteries may have been revealed to them.

MOT

God of death. When **BAAL** paid him a visit he was humiliated and forced to eat mud and do ridiculous things to himself and then die. **ANATH**, the wife of Baal, was not having any of this; she stormed down to **MOT** and demanded a full restoration. Mot replied 'Over my dead body!' So she cut him into small pieces and then ground him into powder, which she sprinkled over Baal and he was back in business again.

CANAAN, PHOENICIA

ASHERAH

Known as 'She Who Walks Upon The Sea', **ASHERAH** is a mother goddess, the wife of **EL**, and the mother of seventy-seven gods – or was it eighty-

eight? She seems to have lost count. But no-one has heard of most of them, so it probably doesn't matter. Being an important mother goddess and also the wife of top god El, she was obviously held in very high esteem by her many worshippers. Wooden pillars erected in her honour were so numerous that even **YAHWEH** himself felt a little threatened. These so-called 'Asherah Poles' are mentioned several times in the Old Testament – usually accompanied by the words 'Thou shalt not'.

Despite her popularity, as usual with ancient Middle-Eastern deities, there is plenty of scope for confusion. The various spellings and regional changes of her name seem to lead everywhere and nowhere. And we still don't know why she walks on the sea.

EL

Self-styled 'Creator of All Created Things' and 'Father of Gods'. As Canaanite godfather he likes to remain aloof and inscrutable sitting high on his throne wearing his bull horn crown. The spot he picked to rule from was between two rivers – and this may have been the greenbelt area later selected for the Garden of Eden.

EL is a tricky god to pin down because at the time his name was basically the universal word for 'deity' in the Middle East. We're talking Arabic, Hebrew, Ugaritic, Phoenician and many more. So when some ancient text reveals that 'El did this' or 'El did that', you're never quite sure whether it's him or someone else they're talking about.

The Ugaritic tablets, discovered as late as 1929, are very fragmentary with pieces missing, so much is conjecture. There are Hebrew scholars who believe El to have been part of the Elohim, who fused himself into one identity to become Eloah, the singular version. This may have led to mono-god status and gotten him into the Old Testament under the name **YAHWEH**.

CANAAN, SYRIA

ASTARTE

Rampant goddess of fertility and sexual pleasure from Phoenicia. She is extremely horny – we're talking cow's horns, of course, as **ASTARTE** is a sexy cow – and ritual prostitution is always on offer. Astarte was very popular in Old Testament times and travelled far and wide, starting up in business all over the place with the help of her consort and brother **BAAL**. This kind of thing was always a cue for monotheistic fury and Biblical condemnation. She was also worshipped in Babylon under the name **ISHTAR** – and vice versa.

PERSIA

AHRIMAN

Zoroastrian devil, arch-enemy of **AHURA-MAZDA** and chief perpetrator of all the evil in the world. **AHRIMAN** was born dark and stinking

– and seems to have gotten steadily worse. He spawned the demonic world-threatening monster Azhi-Dahaka and sprinkles wickedness wherever he can. Like **SATAN**, his main goal is to fill the world with as much evil as he can so it will destroy itself. Current reports indicate that his policy so far has been highly effective. The good news is that supreme god Ahura-Mazda is his total opposite and has taken steps to ensure nice things happen – after the inevitable Apocalypse. So a round of applause for …

AHURA-MAZDA

The bright and beautiful Zoroastrian supreme god. He is so bright that a certain brand of electric light bulb is named in his honour. As the wise lord and god above all other gods, **AHURA-MAZDA** was – and still is – worshipped by Zoroastrians as the creator of the Universe and source of all good things. With the light bulb reference seeming so appropriate, we fondly imagine he created the Universe by flipping a cosmic light switch. 'Let there be light', in fact.

With the holy **AMESHA-SPENTAS** and also his sons **ATAR** and **MITHRA** providing back-up, Ahura-Mazda wages permanent war with **AHRIMAN**, a deity of unspeakable repulsiveness. Ahriman aims to devastate the Universe by filling it with pure evil. Much like God and **SATAN**, they've been battling it out for millennia, but Ahura-Mazda has a trump card tucked up his sleeve; **SAOSHYANT** will show up at the last minute and put everything to rights.

Zoroastrianism was founded by Zoroaster (also known as Zarathushtra) squillions of years ago, and flourished despite being such an awkward religion to spell. Its sacred scripture, the *Vesta*, unfortunately perished in the great fire at the Library of Alexandra, and only a remnant of this fascinating text remains. This is called the *Zenda Vesta*, which means 'Scrap of Vesta Which is Somewhat Charred but Still Jolly Good'.

With its monotheistic concept of God and ideas of good and evil spirituality, Zoroastrianism had a huge impact on subsequent religions such as Judaism and Christianity, which appear to have acquired many of its spiritual notions.

AMESHA-SPENTAS

The holy immortal attendants of **AHURA-MAZDA**. There are at least seven of them – that's how many it takes to change his light bulbs. These glorious Zoroastrian entities are half-god, half-angel, and act as intermediaries between humans and Heaven. Alternatively, they are also said to be aspects of Ahura-Mazda himself. You decide. The **AMESHA-SPENTAS** each have their allotted function. Their names and attributes are: Ameretat (immortality), Armaiti (devotion), Asha-Vahishta (truth), Haurvatat (wholeness), Khshathra-Vairya (perfect society), Sraosha (obedience), and Vohu-Manah (righteous thinking). **SAOSHYANT** is sometimes lumped in amongst them, but we're not entirely convinced.

ANAHITA

With all those dominating male gods strutting about the region, it's nice to come across a female deity, particularly one as benevolent as **ANAHITA**. She looks after the well-being of women, promotes fertility and safe childbirth, and generally makes female life a bit easier to cope with.

Perhaps as a symbol of purity, she is also involved in the water industry and loves to splish and splash in rivers and streams, preferably ones that are clean and crystal-clear. Her own-label pure spring water may well have been a best-seller in Scythia, Canaan and Phoenicia, as her popularity spread all over the place. She's still revered today, although her bottled spring water is no longer available in shops.

ATAR

God of fire and foiling evil. The son of **AHURA-MAZDA**, he was chosen to sort out **AHRIMAN**'s rampaging three-headed dragon Azhi-Dahaka. This had been created specifically to create anguish, cause pain, deal out death and finally destroy the Universe. After several million years, **ATAR** managed to corner the dragon and chain it to a mountain. It is still snarling, wrenching, and chewing up anything that ventures within reach. A horrible feeling prevails that the chains won't last for another million years. Has Atar taken early retirement?

MITHRA

Zoroastrian god of light, truth and judgement. The son of **AHURA-MAZDA**, he also wages war against the evil god **AHRIMAN** and helps keep the world safe from international terrorism. In his spare time, **MITHRA** also judges the souls of the dead, along with fellow goodies Rashnu and Sraosha. Always a popular god, he was around long before Zoroastrianism kicked off but seemed quite happy to endorse this new religion. Meanwhile, he was nicely integrated into the Vedic Hindu pantheon as Varuna's best buddy and partner in worldwide security. He outlasted most of his contemporaries, and cults devoted to him were still going strong in Roman times. Mithra has a thousand eyes and a thousand ears. So if you get the feeling you are under surveillance, you could be right.

SAOSHYANT

The Zoroastrian messiah. At the end of time there will be quite a lot of purging, but it will be well worth it. **SAOSHYANT** the saviour will be born of a virgin from the lineage of Zoroaster and put into motion for **AHURA-MAZDA**'s scorched-earth policy. The wicked followers of **AHRIMAN** will perish in a big bonfire with much screaming and wailing. But for the just and good, judgement day will be like a big party on Bonfire Night. Interestingly, Saoshyant's apocalyptic role has much in common with the Second Coming of **JESUS**. Except that Saoshyant had the idea first.

PHILISTIA

BEELZEBUB

Evil demon prince of Hell, lord of the flies and **SATAN**'s bastard-in-chief. Only for fly bastards and Philistines. He's the cause of more superstitious dread than Satan himself, which is odd, because he started out as a local variant of the perfectly respectable **BAAL**. He was a top god of the Middle East and had fan clubs everywhere. The Philistines worshipped him under the name Baal Zebub, meaning 'Lord of Flies', which seems like a strange thing to be lord of – until you realise that flies carry disease and plague. Anyone who can boss flies around just has to be respected.

PHOENICIA

AION

The Phoenician god of time. It is very wise to have an immortal for this sort of thing. His name gives us the word 'eon', in case you were wondering. And apparently he's also the god of discovering edible fruits, although it might take us an eon or two to figure out why.

WORLDWIDE MONOTHEISM

ALLAH

Islamic supreme being and the almighty god worshipped by Muslims. By all accounts **ALLAH** is merciful and just, but total commitment is required as he is considered to be the only true god, all others being false and fake. He has his own Holy Book of rules and regulations known as the Koran, or more correctly the Qur'an, which was dictated to his prophet Muhammed via an angel to the sound of bells sometime in the seventh century.

Now we have to confess we have a slight problem. The Qur'an advises: 'Reflect upon Allah's creation, but not upon his nature – or else you will perish.' This seems to indicate a deep need for privacy which we are reluctant to transgress. On the other hand, the Qur'an also says that the first thing Allah created was the intellect – and that 'a scholar is worth a thousand ignorant worshippers'. It's a tricky dilemma to grapple with.

Muslims believe that Allah is also the deity known as **YAHWEH** and/or **JEHOVAH** who are worshipped by Jews and Christians respectively. Jews and Christians reject this idea, claiming that their own scripture is inviolate and cannot lead to a sequel, no matter how much of a best-seller it might be. With these three religions it seems to us a case of 'so near and yet so far'. We throw our pens down in despair. If you have any queries, speak to the god of your choice, not us. We do not take sides in theological squabbles.

JEHOVAH

The one and only Lord God Almighty. Apart from a brief fling with **AHURA-MAZDA**, the first mono-god to make a lasting impression was **YAHWEH**, the god of his chosen people the Israelites. Then **JESUS** was born, and much to the distress of the Jewish high priests, Yahweh was given a holy makeover and became **JEHOVAH**, a somewhat more approachable, if more complicated, three-in-one deity comprising Father, Son and Holy Spirit.

In the chaos that followed, Christians, Jews, Romans and Greeks tussled and fought to defend their beliefs in a gigantic religious punch-up. Schisms and sects popped up all over the place and heresy lurked on every corner. This was bad for business. The Roman Emperor Constantine was a big fan of Jehovah but not of chaos. So in AD 325 the highest-ranking bishops assembled the famous Council of Nicea to define once and for all what they were supposed to believe in. This made Christianity the first and only religion ever to be decided by vote.

Christianity was a huge success – at least, for the Christians. Other cultures had a tendency to shrivel up and die when Jehovah arrived at the door. Like a sponge, Christianity absorbed pagan religions and stole all the best bits, for example, Easter (Saxon) and Christmas (Germanic and/or Roman). Local gods were demoted to the level of saints, angels or – in really difficult cases – demons.

After the rise of Christianity, Jehovah enjoyed top god status unchallenged for a while – until Muhammed came along with a whole new slant and explained that Yahweh and Jehovah were really just alternative versions of **ALLAH**, and Blessed Be His Name. Which was enough to drive the Christians into a fighting frenzy of holy war.

With so many different views of the One True God, it sometimes seems to us that all those schisms and sects are really a desperate yearning for the good old days of polytheism. The ultimate irony.

JESUS

The son of God, the second person in the Trinity of **JEHOVAH**, and the source of Christian belief. The strange thing about **JESUS** is that he didn't exist; if you had seen him in Nazareth and shouted 'Hey Jesus!', he would have taken no notice – because he was actually named Joshua. Blame this misunderstanding on the translation from Hebrew to Greek several years after the main event.

It must have been a terrible shock for Jesus when he found out God was his real father. How can one live up to such expectations? Goodness knows he tried, even though daddy never came near enough to give him a hug or take him out to the park. It must have put the family under a lot of strain when old ladies tickled his chin and said: 'Oooh, he looks just like his dad.'

By all accounts, Jesus was a precocious lad. But almost nothing is known of his early years, and Jesus the acne-ridden confused teenager is lost to history. Instead we next catch up with him as he starts his ministry, aged thirty-something. He soon became infamous for his outspoken attacks on the status quo and religious hypocrisy. By offering sympathetic counselling, free medical treatment, miraculous entertainment, and a highly popular course in moral philosophy, Jesus managed to upset almost everyone. There was that incident when the demons he'd exorcised from afflicted humans entered into a herd of swine. This was a blow from which the Gadarene pork industry never recovered. No-one has dared to touch a sausage since.

Finally The Powers That Be could stand it no longer and so he was crucified – a very nasty death indeed. His last agonised words were: 'Father, why have you forsaken me?' which we can't help feeling is a very good question, but one that takes us into the realm of theology. We've come across so many 'rational' explanations for the empty tomb that it's easier to believe Jesus was abducted by space penguins or the Flying Spaghetti Monster. But fear not: we've scrutinised every possible theory and have generously decided to believe all of them.

SATAN

The Devil – Mr All-round Evil Genius and the Adversary of God. A rebel angel, he was originally the team leader of the spiritual world, possessing great power and responsibility. But he turned nasty and tried to set himself up as a rival to God. As a punishment for his rebellious pride, he was cast out of Heaven, along with a rabble of other rebels. Now **SATAN** rules the infernal regions of Hell, with an army of demons to do his bidding. Out of pure malice and vengeance, he aims to overthrow the established order by turning humans against God. Using every trick in the book, he spreads evil whispers, plants the seeds of doubt, and tempts the unwary to fall from grace.

What does Satan look like? Answer: anything he likes. He can have the traditional horns, scales, a forked tail, the head of a goat, cloven feet – or turn up as a smooth dude in the latest Italian suit. But there's always more to him than meets the eye; his own eyes can glow like red-hot coals. As with most things in Christianity, older legends and rival religions had a strong influence on the concept of Satan. The Persian baddie **AHRIMAN** was sucked in – and popular gods such as **BAAL** were twisted into evil versions such as **BEELZEBUB**.

This also happened with **PAN**, a very popular god whose sexual antics horrified the early church so much that it labelled him the Devil. That is why Satan has goat's legs and horns; if Pan could sue for libel the pope wouldn't have a leg to stand on. Even the Roman Lucifer star got blamed. Because the Old Testament has little to say on the subject of Satan, the early Christians were free to speculate as they formulated their new theology. This was especially popular in medieval times, when cataloguing the attributes of demons and angels was virtually a career. You could almost get a government research grant for it.

Satan seems to inspire an eerie fascination and turns up in the most unlikely places. In his devilish guise he leaves bits of himself all over the landscape. Devil's Elbow, Devil's Footprints, Devil's Hollow, Devil's Chimney, Devil's Dyke… We think he just likes to be noticed.

YAHWEH

The one and only God of the Old Testament – the God of Abraham, Noah and Moses unto the nth generation. In the beginning, **YAHWEH** created the Heavens and the Earth. It only took him six days with no hired help. He also found the time to include incontrovertible evidence of a Big Bang, presumably to annoy future cosmologists.

Having created mankind in his own image, Yahweh soon discovered this was no guarantee of quality. Humans just wouldn't do as they were told. To keep order, his servant Moses was issued with the Ten Thousand Commandments. Of course rules such as 'Thou Shalt Not Clip Off the Edges of Your Beard' never made it into the Top Ten.

The Hebrew people didn't speak aloud the name of God. It was so holy that no mortal tongue dare utter it. The priests imagined what might happen if they burped while saying the name and shuddered with dread. Easier to tackle was the ritual slaughter and burning of animals, as there was nothing the Lord liked better than the aroma of barbecued goat.

The history of Yahweh and the Israelites is long and full of exciting adventures. David versus Goliath. Jonah versus the Whale. Ezekial versus the Flying Saucers. Read it all for yourself in the Old Testament. It's a great book, apart from the goat recipes.

THE NATIVE
AMERICAN GODS

Once upon a time there were Red Indians. Then along came the Palefaces… But before the White Man came trampling all over the land, the many native tribes of what was still to become America had all the space in their world. They made good use of it, living close to nature in what might seem like a glorious camping holiday with sing songs round the camp fire if there wasn't the constant threat of starvation and war.

There was much in the way of free-range food, but hunting wasn't as easy as getting up in the morning, taking a stroll and shooting a few passing bison with your bow. Even Plains societies who lived off the prolific buffalo fell under the threat of starvation at times. When herds were found, the people were grateful and thanked the gods profusely.

The Native Americans had a huge respect for nature. Animals had powerful spirits and it was necessary to thank them and placate them if you wanted to make a meal of them. When corn came by courtesy of the deities, it was also given its due measure of respect. Living so close to nature, you could see into the souls of the **BEAVER**, Badger and Buffaloes as they went about their business. You could feel the **THUNDER BIRD** fixing the weather, and revel in the rascality of **RAVEN**, **MANABOZHO** and **COYOTE** with their tantalising tricks.

ALGONQUIN, CREE, IROQUOIS AND SHAWNEE
GITCHE-MANITOU

The great creator spirit of the Algonquin people. He is the supreme being who created all and filled it with Manitou life force. According to the Algonquin-speaking peoples, Manitou is the primeval force which gives every animal and plant life. The word is usually translated as 'spirit' – but it seems to have more in common with The Force beloved by Jedi worshippers. He is therefore due a lot of respect. He also owns everything in the Universe, but seems happy enough to lend bits of it to humanity to play with.

In return for his benevolence, his Algonquin worshippers treat him with the utmost respect and make him ritual offerings of smoke. Why smoke? Because **GITCHE-MANITOU** is extremely fond of tobacco. But he is not a Cigarette Smoking Deity. With amazing generosity, he gave his entire tobacco supply to humanity a long long time ago. Having kicked the habit for the benefit of mankind, he remembers his worshippers fondly whenever they smoke a pipe in his direction.

According to one of our valued correspondents, the sacred pipe contains a herbal mix of red willow, bearberry and various other plants. The exact mixture is sacred and cannot be divulged. All we know is that, when smoked in the proper manner, the sacred smoke carries the prayers of worshippers up to the Heavens where Gitche-Manitou resides. Most definitely not passive smoking.

ALGONQUIN, LAKOTA, NORTHEAST, NORTHWEST, PLAINS
BEAVER

He abounds – he is bountiful. He beavers away everywhere. Damnation takes on a whole new meaning. Wherever there is a dam and it's near a Native American tribe, **BEAVER** is at work – with the emphasis mostly on work. You might say he's the god of storage, as he loves packing things away neatly ready for the winter months. But he's not averse to a bit of well-intentioned thievery. Among the Lakota he is known as Capa and surfaces all over the place into the mythology of many tribes.

ABENAKI, ALGONQUIN, NORTH, PENOBSCOT
MANABOZHO

A trickster god. He's the Great Rabbit, but don't you dare mock. Rabbit gods can be found all over the place in mythology – not surprisingly, as the breeding habits of rabbits are legendary. See the African Hare, for example. Not to mention Bugs Bunny, Roger the Rabbit and good old Flopsy. **MANABOZHO** is always ducking and diving and changing shape. He has a good line in creation, provisions and transformation, and is one of the most important critters in Native American mythology. The Algonquin's amalgamation with Asante slaves eventually produced the Brer Rabbit stories – and if you think you can outsmart Brer Rabbit you had better read the tales again. Read about his tussles with Ictinike, for example. His brother is the wolfish Chibiabos, and the two of them crop up in transmogrified form all over the place.

One of his tricks is to appear under other names such as **GLOOSKAP**, the hero god of ecology and nature, formed from the dust of the hand of **TABALDAK** the creator god. He's the good guy, with many tricks up his sleeve, while evil Malsumis does the dirty work like putting thorns on plants and stings in insects. Many legends abound: how Glooskap saved the world from an ocean-swallowing frog monster; how Glooskap corrected the climate by binding the wings of the Weather Bird; how Glooskap saved the world's hunted animals by stuffing them into a bag; how Glooskap saved the world's hunters by letting them all out again … He even negotiated the first environmental treaty to ensure that man and nature could live in harmony. That lasted until the white man came, and now Glooskap is very cross.

CHEROKEE
THE THUNDER TWINS

Enumclaw and Kapoonis, otherwise known as the **THUNDER TWINS**, are the twin sons of Grandmother Corn Selu. She created corn by rubbing her belly and having a rather extraordinary bowel motion. She was later killed by the twins, as they decided she must be a witch. A fair assumption. Who would want a mother that prepared breakfast by shitting cornflakes?

Having consulted with spirits, Enumclaw discovered the secret of making fire spears, while his brother Kapoonis mastered the somewhat easier art of hurling very large boulders. Together they caused all manner of mayhem on Earth. Not very amused, Father Sky grabbed both of them up into his domain and put them to use. Now Enumclaw makes lightning by casting his fire spears down to Earth, while his brother hurls thunderous boulders across the sky.

CHINOOKAND SALISH
IOI

Sister of Blue-Jay, the noisy screeching trickster god. She thought he would be more controllable if he picked a wife. She nagged him until he acquiesced. So who did he pick but the dead daughter of a chief. 'Don't worry,' he said as **LOI** shook her head in despair, 'I'll take her to the Land of Ghosts for a restorative makeover.' Which he did, but when he returned the chief demanded a dowry of Blue-Jay's hair. 'No way!' cried Blue-Jay, zooming off in a blue flash of bird mode without leaving as much as a feather.

His problems however are far from over and the wife dies again. So he sets off for the Land of Ghosts again, only to find the inhabitants have purchased Loi as a wife for themselves. They are all standing around in human form but when Blue-Jay does one of his famous screeches they all quiver and turn to bones in fear. Quickly Blue-Jay mixes up all the bones so when they re-form they will have the wrong arms, heads, legs etc. Then we can only presume Blue-Jay hightails it out of there taking his sister, but leaving the dead wife. There is no real ending as the fables and stories involving Blue-Jay are as mixed and shuffled as the bones of the ghosts.

HOPI, PUEBLO
KACHINAS

Spirits of Nature, ruled by Eototo. He controls every gust of wind, and has rather a shabby dull appearance for a Top Job. There's millions and billions of the little blighters, and between them they control everything, from rain, wind and animals to spirits of the dead. You have to admire their industry.

Every living thing has its own Kachina, and that includes non-living things, as everything is a living thing even if it's not living. Confused yet?

The top **KACHINAS** are known as the Wuya. Wooden Kachina dolls are very popular, and to show respect they're only made from dead trees. Which are also living things, but not quite so much.

Here are some of the favourites:

Ahea – grandmother of them all.

Aholi – spirit of spring. Wears a coat of many colours to symbolise bright fertile happiness.

Ahmeto-lela-okya – rainbow dancing girl.

Angak-chin-mana – long-haired girl. It's a beard, a bushy red one and she shakes it around when she dances as it is full of pollen.

Bototo – in charge of departure ceremonies.

Karwan – food production. Takes part in the sprouting bean ceremony.

Koyemsi – a holy clown known as 'mudhead' who performs strange antics wearing a strange head made of baked clay.

Kwikwilyaqa – spirit of mockery who pokes fun at passers by.

Mana – assistant of Karwan.

Momo – bee dancer who buzzes around with a tiny bow firing blunt arrows at everyone. If he makes any children cry he squirts water on the simulated sting until they laugh again.

Nataska – the ugly maid ogress.

Palhik-mana – butterfly spirit of grinding corn. They must be joking yet again.

HOPI, WINNEBAGO, ZUNI
KOKOPELLI

God of dating and mating. He's a jolly hunchback soul who skips around playing the flute and inspiring the fruits of love to blossom. Rather like the horny old **PAN**, he is a primitive god of carefree lust and consequently very popular. His most important organ is uncommonly large – and also detachable. Forget Cupid's arrow; if you're a young maiden taking a quick dip, you could find **KOKOPELLI**'s weapon being fired at you. And while you may enjoy the experience, the patter of tiny feet is sure to follow. Kokopelli also takes part in corn-grinding rituals as he loves a good gyration, and can even cause a quick downpour to cool things off afterwards. Life is never dull with Koko the clown…

INUIT
ALEUT

Wife of the Moon. She worshipped the Man in the Moon and he took her to be his Moon Wife. Imagine her disappointment when she found he did not live in the moon at all but in a very ordinary hut somewhere in the sky. This is what happens when you wish for the Moon.

EEYEEKALDUK

Eskimo healing godlet. He is tiny and lives inside a pebble. He has healing ray eyes which can draw sickness from you if you make eye contact. But you must not look at him if you are healthy or it works in reverse. You will already know all this if you are an Eskimo.

ISITOQ

God of surveillance and stern
warnings. He is a gigantic eyeball
who flies around keeping tabs
on everyone. He's the holy
Big Brother and he's got his
eye on you. Should a bad
word escape your lips or
a naughty deed be done,
ISITOQ will find you out
and give you a stern ticking-
off. Much more efficient than
a security camera.

SEDNA

The Inuit goddess of the sea and queen
of the Eskimo Underworld (Adlivun). She's
a sinister hag with one eye, no fingers, and a giant bloated body. She is
sometimes depicted as a walrus. This is a far cry from the good old days
when she was a beautiful maiden. That's what being sacrificed to the sea
does to you.

One legend tells how she made a vow to remain single in order to look
after her poor old father. All suitors were spurned and offers of marriage
refused. Then one day a mysterious but utterly charming fellow turned
up in his kayak. He was a handsome foreigner; intelligent, exotic and
very alluring. Not only that, he was rich! **SEDNA** was offered blubber in
abundance. Luxuriant furs to sleep on. All the fish oil she could possibly
make use of. This was too much for a young girl to cope with and she
allowed herself to be lured into his canoe.

The marriage was not a happy one. Although he adored her, she soon
came to find him repellent. 'You're not the man I married,' she often
said. With some justification it turned out as he was really a spooky
bird spirit. Meanwhile Sedna's father was tearing his furs in anguish.
Deciding to pay a visit to his lost daughter, he sailed to the Land of Birds
and found her in a state of distress. That evening, her husband returned
home from work and found her gone. In a screaming rage, the bird spirit
climbed into his kayak and paddled in pursuit at full speed. (He did an
awful lot of paddling for a bird spirit.)

As he approached, Sedna tried to hide under some furs, but her husband became so angry that the skies turned black and the ocean began to seethe. That was enough to terrify anyone, and Sedna's father, fearing the very world was coming to an end, chucked her overboard.

Poor Sedna clutched at the side of the kayak, but her grim father chopped her fingers off and down she went. At once the skies cleared, the bird spirit flapped off and peace descended. Sedna's fingers wriggled onto an ice floe and became the first sea creatures, and Sedna herself floated to the very bottom of the sea and stayed there.

Many years have passed since then. Now she rules all Arctic Sea life, deciding the fate of all ocean creatures – and the people who hunt them. If you haven't said a prayer to Sedna, you might as well pack up your harpoon and go home. As Queen of the Dead, Sedna rules over the Adlivun Underworld from her eternally unreachable ice palace on the outer reaches of deathsville. She has also given her name to the so-called tenth planet, a remote object lurking in the nether regions of the solar system. Located way beyond **PLUTO**, this object is small, remote and extremely chilly. Like Adlivun, it's the kind of place most people would happily pass up the chance to visit.

LAKOTA
WHITE-SHE-BUFFALO

She first appeared as a beautiful stranger. She stirred up desire, but refused to appear in the buff. In fact, she implied that if she was treated like a queen as she deserved, then she would return with some goodies.

A queenly lodge was built for her, and she did indeed return with a pipe and tobacco. Also some milk which, when planted, could produce corn. She taught mankind how to smoke and revealed some of life's mysteries. Then mysteriously she turned into an old buffalo cow with skin of the purest white… and vanished. We wonder if it was really tobacco they were smoking.

MORE OR LESS EVERYWHERE
COYOTE

The wily, tricky, sneaky, pesky, cheaty god of the Wild West. He's the ubiquitous trickster god and cultural hero of Native American mythology, the original Marx Brother and thorn in **RAVEN**'s side. Responsible for many things, including the Milky Way and the diversity of mankind, there are more stories about him than stars in the sky.

For example, did you hear the one about the spying Moon? It seems that someone had pinched the moon, and **COYOTE** offered to stand in as replacement. Everyone agreed that he made a fine moon, but from his elevated position Coyote could see everything that was going on. Being of an irritating disposition, he couldn't resist blowing the whistle on friends and enemies alike. 'Hey, look what Badger is doing behind his tepee!' Pretty soon everyone was sick of his snooping and voted him out of the sky.

Another tale: Sanopi was the stuck-up sticky god of tar, glue and pitch, an amorphous black blob who once taunted Coyote and got into a fight. The enraged Coyote tried to bite him, but his paws got stuck in the black gooey mess. Sanopi wouldn't let go, and pretty soon Coyote was stuck fast. Several years passed. Coyote slowly starved to death. Only then did Sanopi let him go. But not without an apology.

But nothing can keep Coyote down for long. Being a boastful old show-off, he loves to impress the girls by juggling his eyeballs. One day he threw one so high it got stuck in the sky and became the star Arcturus. So even now he's keeping an eye on us all.

EVERYONE EVERYWHERE
RAVEN

Famous Native American creative trickster god, known by many tribes under many names. There is more to **RAVEN** than meets the eye. And how many of you have met the eye of a raven? They've always been associated with godliness. Few people know that the first bird out of Noah's ark was a raven. It just didn't return. It didn't feel the need. Edgar Allan Poe's raven shrieked 'Nevermore' but what that has to do with anything only Poe knows.

In the beginning, Raven was first and foremost a creator and trickster god -- especially of the Haida tribe, who claim he discovered the first humans hiding in a clam shell and brought them berries and salmon.

A bit of a tricky God himself, he's also the long-suffering victim of arch-rival in trickery, **COYOTE**. His brother Logobola is also a bit of a tricky customer, being a very mean sibling, always teasing and sniping and playing tricks. He hid the water when Raven was thirsty, argued annoyingly over who was best at target practice, and even left his brother lost and terrified in a dense misty fog before returning to scoop it all up with his hat. And now here's a funny thing. Due to a typing error, one online version of the legend insists that Raven got lost in a large frog. And this simple mistake has trickled through the web to such an extent that Raven and

Logobola now make guest appearances on websites devoted entirely to frogs.

Stories about Raven abound. Here's one handed down by the Tsimshian tribe…

Once upon a time, the only light in the world was hoarded by a mean old chief who was not disposed to share it. Raven, bored of fluttering around in the dark, decided this would not do. So he turned himself into a cedar leaf and sneakily fluttered into the chief's dwelling.

The chief's daughter was sipping a drink and Raven fluttered into the cup as she raised it to her lips. Swallowing him down, she immediately became pregnant and gave birth. Which caused no end of confusion. The baby had raven-black hair, dark glowing eyes, and was very temperamental. Whenever it was bored, it shrieked. The chief, trying to be a doting grandad, said: 'Give the baby what it wants'. So they gave the baby a bag of shining stars. It played merrily with these, until one day in gurgling excitement it threw them through the smoke hole in the ceiling and they scattered up into the sky.

Oh dear. The baby is bored again. It's bawling. It wants another bag. It's driving the household crazy. It must be pacified. So they give it a bag containing the Moon and soon the baby is happy again, bouncing the Moon all over the place. You'll never guess what happens next. *Whoooosh!* – up through the smoke hole goes the Moon. (Pause for gasp of astonishment from the audience.)

Deprived of another toy, the baby becomes *really* disruptive. The chief is tearing his hair out. The whole household is muttering. Find something, anything, to keep the baby quiet! The baby rejects all homemade playthings and points to the last bag. Uh-oh. They give it to the baby but with dire warnings. 'Don't untie it because it contains Light – and that leaks like nobody's business.'

Now you think you know what's going to happen. But you don't. What happened is that the baby turned back into Raven, cried 'Ka very much' and flew through the smoke hole carrying the bag in his beak. He'd stolen the Sun. Raven spread light throughout the world and so the chief's daylight saving scheme came to an end. He was very disgruntled. His recorded comments contain very strong language in the Tsimshian dialect.

WAUKHEON

The Thunder Bird. He's a nature spirit of great importance. The flapping of **WAUKHEON** on his way to war makes the sky shake with thunder – and when he glances down to Earth, lightning hits the ground. Waukheon constantly battles with Untunktahe the water god. Will they ever settle for a draw? Images of Waukheon are famously found sitting on the top of totem-poles. As powerful symbols of nature, war, strength and victory, it's no wonder every tribe has a Thunder Bird to look over them. Thunder gods are go!

NAVAJO
BEGOCIDI

Trickster god known as 'The One who Grabs Breasts'. So you know what type of deity to expect here. Or do you? He may be a transvestite and there is no telling what other things he may be tempted to grab. Females beware – if your lady glands are groped, a monster child may result.

He is believed to be a child of the Sun, but harder to believe he is also into creative pottery.

BLACK-GOD

Space god of night sky nothingness. In the beginning he was mostly a shapeless mass of black space. But despite the lack of body, he did own a belt. (He must have worn it somewhere. A waist of space?) Anyway, from this belt dangled a pouch containing shiny twinkling crystals. In an effort to define himself, he took to sticking them all over his body – join-the-dots fashion. And there he is to this day, his outline picked out in all the most important stars. If you know where to look.

The dog star Sirius was an afterthought, put there by the meddling **COYOTE** in a fit of cosmological hindrance. The **BLACK-GOD** wouldn't let him touch the pouch but Coyote snatched it anyway. He sampled the crystals inside, didn't like the taste and spat them into the face of the Black-God, who snatched the pouch back. But there was nothing left but dust, which he shook out, forming the Milky Way.

PUEBLO
IYATIKU

Underground corn goddess. Everything has to be ship-shape in her Underground domain. She runs it very much on the principle of the London Tube, but without the buskers and not quite so many delays. Life is like the Circle Line. There is an exit, where babies emerge screaming through the ticket barrier. Your lifetime is spent wandering around the confusing capital, shopping for goodies, trying to find a decent cup of coffee and dodging taxis. When you die you descend back into the Underground … to emerge at some later date very small and helpless as a baby again. What it's like inside is not known, but it must be crowded, badly lit, confused and smelly, with conveyor belts, tracks and warning lights. Visit the London Underground to get a taste.

SKAGIT
DOQUEBUTH

A sort of low-budget Noah. He only had a canoe. As his world was situated in what is now the Northwest of the States we can understand why there are no elephants, giraffes or other tropical animals there. Clearly they all drowned in the flood.

SNOHOMISH
DOHKWIBUHCH

As a creator god he made a terrible glitch. He built the sky too low. It wasn't long before most of the human race was suffering from concussion. It was just like walking into double glazing. Fed up with no answers to planning applications, Earthlings decided to take matters into their own hands and rounded up every living creature for the Big Push. 'All together now, everyone and everything. One… Two … Three … Shove!' It was all a great success. Only a few creatures forgot to let go and had to develop wings.

TONGVA TRIBE OF SOUTHERN CALIFORNIA
QUAOAR

In the beginning was chaos. Then along came **QUAOAR** with a spring in his step and a song in his heart. He danced and whirled and sang the Song of Creation, and thus the Universe began. First to be created was Weywot, god of the sky. He joined in the dance routine and helped to create Chehooit, goddess of the Earth. With complicated three-part harmonies now possible, the song grew ever more creative – so Tamit the Sun and Moar the Moon soon popped into existence.

For a grand finale, the quintet sang into being plants, animals, people, stars, paperclips, clouds, agrophobia, comets and everything else that exists. Not forgetting further deities Manisar, Manit, Pamit, Tolmalok and Tukupar-Itar. And the audience roared. His work done, Quaoar settled back for a well-earned rest. They don't write songs like that anymore.

THE NORSE GODS OF SCANDINAVIA

The red-blooded, rip-roaring, gung-ho gods beloved of the Vikings. We could have listed them as Nordic, but 'Norse' sounds like the snorting of a giant battle stallion so we went for that.

So welcome to the Norse pantheon of Norway, Denmark and Sweden. The Swedes travelled mostly eastwards, and the Danes and Norwegians travelled mostly westwards. (The Swedes also ventured into Finland, which was not too impressed and mostly preferred its own gods.) Iceland came into the equation and did its own Viking things from AD 800. Something which helped enormously was that all these people spoke the same Norse language, and would have known their own kingdoms under the names of Danmark, Vastergotland, Ostergotland and Svealand. Even now days of the week and also the sun are named for Norse gods.

Thanks to the richness of its legends, as told in the Eddas and a host of poetic sagas, Norse mythology is as popular as ever. JRR Tolkien's Middle Earth saga is stuffed with Norse inspiration and takes the whole thing to a whole new dimension. Which is more than you can say for Wagner.

THE NINE WORLDS

The Nordics liked nines. So they have nine worlds. Yggdrasil, the Tree of Life, has nine roots which feed or lead to different realms. Starting from the bottom up are:

1. Helheim, **HEL**'s domain of the dead
2. Niflheim, the frosty underground realm of ice where the **FROST GIANTS** kick-started everything. The **NIBELUNGS** also live here. Watch out for the gap: it's called Ginnungagap and it is a cosmic void which separates the cold world from Muspell, a land of fire and desolation. This is a no-man's-land ruled by Surt the fire giant.
3. Jotunheim, land of giants

4. Nidavellir, land of dwarfs
5. Svartalfheim, domain of the dark elves
6. Midgard, Middle Earth, the realm of mankind. Our bit
7. Alfheim, the land of the light elves
8. Vanaheim, the world of the Vanir – rival gods to the Aesir, they were very much second division
9. Asgard, the world of the Aesir. This is Norse god HQ, where the top gods live and rule under **ODIN**

Asgard lies at the far side of Bifrost, the rainbow bridge, and security is very tight. You won't get in unless you're a dead hero on the way to Valhalla via the tradesman's entrance. The halls of Asgard have been built to withstand the onslaught of giants, and for extra security the exact geography of the place is a closely guarded secret. Although brochures of the warrior's paradise Valhalla are readily available, what goes on in Thrudheim and the remaining halls is out of bounds. The gods seem to do most of their carousing at their local club, a banqueting hall called Gladsheim. They are often to be found hanging out at the Well of Urd to catch up on the latest gossip from the three **NORNS**.

Also fitting somehow into the picture are Muspell, a sort of no-man's-land of Fire ruled over by Surt (Mr. Sooty), and Ginnungagap, the ancient void of chaos. And don't forget Yggdrasil itself, the giant ash tree which supports the **NINE WORLDS** and is the hub of the Universe.

Its roots run riot, some starting from the Well of Knowledge where **MIMIR** lurks. It is home to Nidgogg the dragon even though he is a parasite. And the Norns reside under it. At the top is Vithofnir the rooster, whose crowing will announce the awful terrible catastophic **RAGNAROK**, thus ending the world. There's also an eagle and Ratatosk the messenger squirrel and who knows what abundance of wildlife. Dew from the Yggdrasil supplies mead for Valhalla, and when the world ends in almost total devastation this tree will still be there, containing seeds for the next crop of beings. Hopefully humans, but most likely more bloody ash trees. I swear one is coming up at the end of my garden where I have a constant battle to keep it at bay.

AEGIR

God of the sea. As with all sea gods, he is worshipped and feared by sailors. It always pays to respect watery gods, especially **AEGIR** as he has a fondness for dragging ships and men down to his halls. But as he is well-known for his wonderful parties, it could just be his way of avoiding gatecrashers. He is married to sea goddess **RAN**, and sea froth is caused by his Underwater brewery. See also **HYMIR**.

ANDHRIMNIR

God of cooking. He's an Aesir celebrity chef with a very limited menu. He takes the cosmic boar, kills it and cooks it for the gods to eat. It returns to life in the night ready for use in the next set meal. It's a real pig of a life for the boar. A little variety in the kitchen would work wonders.

ANDVARI

The dwarf who created a magic ring and became master of all the gold in the Universe. But he hadn't reckoned with **LOKI**, who seized it along with a great deal of treasure as pay-off for a murder he'd committed. **ANDVARI** just had time to curse the ring so it would bring death to all who owned it.

Loki, being much too wily to be caught by a trick like that, didn't touch it, and the ring went straight to Regin and **FAFNIR** as ransom for the death of their brother Otr. There's more than a passing reference to Andvari in *Lord of the Rings*, but Wagner completely cribbed him for 'Ring of the Nibelungs' where he was forced to sing lustily under the name of Alberich with lots of Rhenish maidens.

AUDHUMBLA & CO.

The first life to emerge from the icy wastes of Niflheim (see **NINE WORLDS**) was a giant cow. 'Did the Earth moo for you?' would have been the first question if there had been anyone to ask it. In a way – yes. As she licked at the ice-lolly surface Buri, the first producer god, emerged and he produced Bor. Don't ask how the cow got there – to ensure milk supplies we suppose. Amidst the meltings: Ymir, a frost giant. Then fire from the adjoining wastelands of Muspell hastened thawing and a man and a woman appeared from the sweat from Ymir's armpits. So it all kicked off with frozen milkshakes and kept going with more frost giants including **BESTLA**, a female one who flung herself at Bor and he was the father of **ODIN**, Vili and Ve, and Earthy **HERTHA**.

BALDUR

ODIN's son **BALDUR** is the Scandinavian god of peace. A champion of goodness, innocence and forgiveness, he was loved by everybody, especially his wife Nanna. But news has just reached us that he was killed by **LOKI**. The good news is that, due to extensive mourning by all earthly things, he may be brought back to life.

No. It's failed – one old hag called Thokk has refused to weep, saying he never done nuffin for her. How did he die? Every thing in existence had promised never to harm him, thus making him completely indestructable. In fact, he was so impervious to injury that at banquets guests used to amuse themselves by hurling things at him. So how did Loki kill him? (It's more convoluted than Agatha Christie but bear with us.)

Ah: when all the world was promising not to hurt Baldur, there was an abstainer. Mistletoe. Yes, mistletoe. When Loki found this out, he made a dart of sharpened mistletoe and gave it to a blind god called **HOD**. In the middle of a banquet, Hod with sharp ears and sharp mistletoe hit the target. Zap! But that's not the end of it. The old hag Thokk turns out to have been arch-villain Loki in one of his many disguises. When confronted he tried to escape by turning into a salmon. But he was not slippery enough to escape the net and now faces perpetual punishment.

There's more! Hod turns out to be Baldur's unsuspecting twin brother. But was he full of hidden hatred? Will Baldur return? Can **HERMOTH** save him from the Underworld? Tune in soon for the next instalment.

FAFNIR

He was the son of Hreidmar the wizard, together with two brothers, Otr and Regin: shape-changers all. When Otr was in otter form, **LOKI**, who fancied a nice bit of otter to go with his fish, killed him by mistake. This was a big mistake since he turned up at Hreidmar's house in the company of **HONIR** and **ODIN** bearing a strangely familiar otter skin. The wizard family thought Loki was a rotter. Now Loki, Honir and Odin were in deep trouble.

Loki, using all his considerable cunning, suggested a hefty ransom fee to repay his debt. This was agreed and the other two gods were taken hostage until his return. Knowing where **ANDVARI** the dwarf king kept his treasure, Loki forced the dwarf to hand it all over, even down to a special gold ring he'd just forged. Andvari just had time to curse the ring so it would bring doom to whoever owned it.

Loki never got to own it – in fear of his life and those of his compatriots he took it straight to the wizards, who released the gods after a quick gloat. **FAFNIR** gloated the most and was so inflamed with greed he turned himself into a dragon and stole the hoard, hiding it in a mountain lair where he could carry on gloating. He killed his father and exiled his brother Regin, who by chance ran into the hero Sigurd. The curse was now working overtime. Sigurd ambushed and killed Fafnir, taking the treasure and pocketing the ring to use for a planned engagement to Brynhild. Untimely ends followed shortly. If you see this ring don't faf about – get in touch with Andvari and see if there is any reward money for its return.

FENRIR

The wolf monster son of **LOKI** and evil giantess Angrboda. He turned rather nasty and had to be bound over to keep the peace with a magic chain. Even then he managed to bite off Tyr's hand.

One adventurous day **ODIN** chanced upon the rest of Loki's monstrous brood via Angrboda. He cast **HEL** into Helheim, and slung **JORMUNGAND** into the sea, but brought **FENRIR** the puppy back to Asgard where an eye could be kept on him. After all, he might prove useful as a guard dog. Tyr, a right-hand man of Odin, was given the job of kennel master but as Fenrir grew at an alarming rate and became ferociously menacing it became apparent he could not be taken for walkies much longer.

It was decided Fenrir should be restrained. After twice snapping the chains with which he was entwined with a sneer, Fenrir caused great alarm. So the gods called in the technical experts known as dwarves. Instead of a heavy-duty macho chain, they forged a very slender little ribbon which hardly seemed up to the job. It was fashioned from magical ingredients: the sound of a prowling cat, the beard of a woman, the roots of a mountain, the sinews of a bear, the breath of a fish and the spittle of a bird. But strangely enough this innocent little ribbon was infinitely tough and more than enough to keep Fenrir restrained.

Fenrir, however, declined to be trussed until Tyr placed a hand in the

wolfish mouth as a gesture of trust. The creature was bound over and now has to keep the peace. He also kept Tyr's hand which he bit off. Tyr was now Odin's left-hand man. When **RAGNAROK** comes, Fenrir will finally manage to break his bonds and join the giants in their final battle against the gods. Odin will go the way of Tyr's hand and be swallowed alive before Fenrir is finally dispatched by **VIDAR**'s avenging sword.

FREYA

Goddess of love, fertility and sexual desire. She's also a feisty warrior and queen of the **VALKYRIES**. The daughter of **NJORD**, and the beautiful twin sister of **FREYR**, she is – to put it in modern vernacular – a bit of a goer. She did marry a god called Od, causing much confusion amongst academics and historians who have confused him with **ODIN** leading to further confusion by confusing her with **FRIGG**. (This is why you need Godchecker.) But Od was a bit of a goer himself and nipped out one day for pastures new.

This caused much weeping of golden tears, but as usual **FREYA** made the best of a bad job and really went off the rails. She ran wild with gods, mortals, giants and dwarves. The stories and allegations of how she gained possession of Brisingamen, the golden amber necklace of desire, are scandalous, especially the one about her bedding four dwarves in turn before they would give it to her. But this sort of thing is just titillation. In any case, the necklace was stolen by **LOKI** and – although it was rescued by **HEIMDALL** – we don't think she got it back.

Being a strong-willed warrior maiden, she joined and then led the Valkyries – so that she could have first pick of the slain battlefield warriors. Most of the slain go to Valhalla, but the good-looking heroes go straight to her palace for rest and recuperation. But Freya does have a softer side – she loves romantic music and bunches of flowers. Her daughters are the beautiful Hnoss and the equally beautiful Gersemi.

FREYR

God of plenty, son of **NJORD**, and **FREYA**'s twin brother. He's in charge of Sun, rain, harvests, peace and prosperity. Very popular and very handsome, Freyr's got a wonderful sword and he loves to flaunt it – he's always present and erect. If you're having marital problems of a physical nature, a prayer to him should sort you out. He's married to the giantess Gerd, thanks to his resourceful servant Skirnir. He also has an amazing magic ship that always sails in the right direction. It never sinks, but it does shrink. Freyr keeps it in his pocket.

FRIGG

Top Norse goddess of marriage and motherhood. She's a goddess of much confusion; is she the wife or daughter of **ODIN**? Was she **BALDUR**'s mum? Is Friday really **FRIGG**'s day? Even Godchecker is more baffled than usual over this one and may have to visit the Well of Urd for some answers. However, our tireless research has come up with the following facts: Frigg is Odin's wife and mother of Baldur, who she tried her best to save from a gruesome mistletoe-based death. As queen of Asgard, she seems quite a sassy lady, keeps Odin in check and usually gets her way (unless mistletoe is involved).

Frigg knows everybody's destiny, but will never reveal it. She is also in charge of housekeeping on a big scale. She rides a broom and sweeps away clouds when they pile up – sort of air traffic control for the gods. Or could it be something to do with witchcraft? And because she was best mates with **VENUS**, the Nords decided to borrow Venus's day and turn it into Frigg's day. So thank Frigg it's Friday.

FROST GIANTS

A race of monstrous creatures who started out as icicles in the time of **AUDHUMBLA** and became a dominant Norse force. **ODIN** never took to them and recycled Ymir very early on.

GEIRROD

One of the **FROST GIANTS**, with two gruesome daughters, Gjalp and Greip.
He captured **LOKI** and used him to lure **THOR** to his dwelling with the intent of killing him. The two-faced Loki, pretending friendship, invited Thor to a slap-up feast at **GEIRROD** Hall. Casual dress, all the boar you can eat, and absolutely no need to bring any weapons – honest.

The innocent Thor left his battling gear at home, but it was a long journey, and he opted for an overnight stay at Grid's. She was a giantess and long-standing old flame of his. When Loki was asleep, Grid warned Thor that she had heard on the giant grapevine that Geirrod was up to no good and was on no account to be trusted. She was so concerned that she lent him her magic belt, iron gloves and unbreakable iron staff.

On arrival at Geirrod Castle, Thor used Grid's gifts to great effect. The host was not there when they arrived, and Thor, still tired after a sleepless night, dozed off in a larger chair. The gruesome twosome daughters crept under the chair and heaved upwards to crush Thor against the ceiling. Thor snapped awake just in time to wedge the staff between him and the ceiling. Then he too became pushy. Pushing down beat pushing up and Thor broke their backs and crushed them to death.

Geirrod didn't appear until breakfast next day, when he acted as if nothing had happened. Then with no warning he seized a lump of red-hot iron from a brazier and hurled it at Thor who, on the alert, caught it in the iron gloves and returned the favour with interest, bringing down a pillar supporting the roof before rebounding through Geirrod's midriff with fatal results. Just before the whole building collapsed Thor zapped the quaking castle staff with the iron staff, grabbed Loki, and was out of there.

GROA

Here we are left trying to come to grips with why **THOR** should hurl the toe of some unfortunate minor god called Aurvandhil into the sky to become a star. It is true that Thor had been hit on the head after a battle with the giant Hrungnir and had fragments of whetstone embedded therein. This is where **GROA** becomes involved.

As a seeress with healing powers she had been summoned to charm the fragments from Thor's head. Also she had been the wife of Aurvandhil. We are now no longer at a total loss. According to a report by an onlooker at the time, Thor was telling Groa how he knew her old man, and once when they were stranded in the kingdom of the **FROST GIANTS** he had to carry poor old Aurvandhil home in a basket because he had frostbite in his toes. Sadly the toes had to be amputated, and to cheer up his old mate, Thor hurled them into the sky to become stars.

Groa, who had never heard this story, was so excited and enthralled she stopped her incantations, and then could not remember the spells, so some fragments remained forever in Thor's head. Which all goes to prove she was a pretty useless seeress – why hadn't she consulted hubby or an oracle? She was not much good as a nurse either.

HEIMDALL

God of light, security and surveillance. The watchman of the gods, **HEIMDALL** is the strong silent type and guards Bifrost, the gateway to

Asgard. He can see for a hundred leagues night or day, and can hear the grass growing.

Apart from guard duty, Heimdall is the ever-watchful sentinel who waits with his horn to announce the end of the world. His horn is called Gjail or Gjallar. When **RAGNAROK** arrives, he'll blow the most amazing note and the last battle will commence. Listen out for further announcements. Although he seems to be the most placid and stationary god, Heimdall has been known to sneak off duty under the name Rig and have exciting adventures.

He also rescued **FREYA**'s precious necklace after it was stolen by **LOKI**. Apparently there were two seals sitting on a rock, looking at a bright shiny thing by their feet. They nodded a cursory 'Good morning' to each other and continued to gaze down at what was actually the infinitely precious Brisingamen. One of these seals was Loki. He'd stolen the necklace and retreated to the safety of an obscure sea-bound rock in the guise of a seal. Blending in with the seal population was proving somewhat difficult, but it was his best chance to avoid detection.

The other seal, having sat quietly on the rock for several hours with hardly a glance in his direction, hauled itself up, brushed itself down and unexpectedly punched Loki in the face. It was Heimdall, come to rescue the necklace. He'd disguised himself as a seal, positioned himself on the rock first and lulled Loki into the most embarrassingly false sense of security. The Brisingamen was returned to Asgard for safekeeping, but we understand Freya wasn't let near it ever again.

HEL

Goddess of the inglorious dead and queen of Helheim, the Norse Underworld. The daughter of **LOKI** and Angrboda, she's an ugly half-dead hag with gangrenous legs and a hideous face. Which just shows that sometimes you *can* judge by appearances.

Having been banished to the Underworld by order of **ODIN** – merely for being the ugly evil daughter of Loki – she made the place her own and became **HEL** of the Helheim Hell Hall, which tends to become Hellishly confusing. Yes, her name gives us the word 'Hell', but her domain is almost the complete opposite of **SATAN**'s abode: it's cold, damp, and populated by the kind of apathetic souls most devils would hardly feel worth the trouble of roasting. In fact, most souls go to Helheim because they've spent their lives sitting on their arses instead of killing, pillaging and then singing rude songs about it. It's a melancholy and depressing place filled with gloomy pessimistic spirits, which is why **HEL** is also goddess of the blues. Half her body is blue and the words associated with her say it all: dank, clouds, hunger, tardy feet, splendid misery...

With marrow-clenching cold and no heating facilities, there is nothing for the punished soul to do in Helheim except shiver out their miserable stint in eternity. If you ever get haunted by a spectre, you can easily tell if it's come from Helheim – the ghost will be shivering and covered with goosebumps instead of you.

The place appears to be a frozen subsidiary of Niflheim of the **NINE WORLDS**, the vast underground realm of ice. But Helheim is at the dead centre of operations. It's Hel in there.

HERMOTH

Nimble-footed messenger of the gods and brother of the unfortunate **BALDUR**. He risked life and limb by racing **ODIN**'s eight-legged steed all the way to Hell to plead for his brother's return. This was granted on condition that everything in the entire Universe weep for him. Unfortunately the 'Shed a Tear for Baldur' campaign didn't make much impact on the man in the street and Baldur stayed firmly dead. In token of his heroic attempt, Hermoth became the landlord of Valhalla. He's your host if you wish to die bravely in battle.

HOD

Son of **ODIN**, he's the blind god of darkness and winter. He's also **BALDUR**'s twin brother. Most twin gods come in goodie/baddie editions, and as he killed his beautiful brother you'd be forgiven for thinking that **HOD** was a nasty sort. But actually he was tricked into it by **LOKI**. Read all about it in Baldur's entry. The gods were most upset, and Hod was killed by **VALI** in revenge. That might seem unfair, but then he shouldn't have been chucking mistletoe about, should he?

HOLLE

Trinity goddess representing the stages of womanhood. She's the teen, the mother and the granny mixed into one, which means she can rebel against herself, scold herself and sympathise with herself all at the same time. As the teen goddess, her face is covered in soot, which is either a reference to Cinderella or the latest fashion trend. She's just as messy in granny mode (when she's known as Holda), shaking out her feather bedding to make it snow. A bit on the witchy side.

HONIR

God of indecision and avoidance. Or was he? You can never get a straight answer out of him. The Aesir sent him as a knowledgable and valuable hostage during their truce with the Vanir, but it soon became clear that he was cribbing his speeches from **MIMIR**. When Mimir wasn't around, **HONIR** became a gibbering imbecile. The Vanir took their revenge by cutting Mimir's head off and sending Honir back with it. Also known as the Silent One, sometimes he might not be there at all as he has very long legs and can vanish from sight very rapidly.

HYMIR

THOR does have trouble with giants. This one owned the world's largest cooking pot, which Thor wanted to borrow for **AEGIR**'s underwater brewery. It was all best buddies to begin with and how about a day's fishing? So out at sea, Hymir hooked two whales, and then he found that Thor had chopped off the head of his prize bull for bait. Thor then managed to hook **JORMUNGAND** the mighty serpent, and had to cut it loose before they were both pulled under and drowned. The best-buddy mood was beginning to sour.

Back on land it got even more out of hand, with drink playing no small part. Thor tried to shatter Hymir's special drinking cup which proved impossible. Hymir howled with laughter at his futile efforts until Thor dashed the cup on Hymir's head, the only thing hard enough to crack it. After that all Hell broke loose, and as usual Thor left a trail of dead giants in his wake. Thor always claims the fishing story was greatly exaggerated, and Hymir just fell overboard in fear when he hooked Jormungand. We have a feeling that Aegir got the cauldron though. You can still see the froth from his beer on every coast – that's what sea foam is.

IDUN

Nordic goddess of spring, youth and immortality. She's always fending off muggers as she carries the basket containing the golden apples of immortality. When the gods are feeling a bit past it, one nibble is all it takes to put a spring in their step. Her abduction by Thiassi the storm giant led to all the gods growing incredibly old until she was rescued by a wrinkly **LOKI** in the guise of a falcon.

JORMUNGAND

The world serpent. He's the monstrous evil offspring of **LOKI** and Angrboda. He lies coiled around the world with his tail in his mouth, waiting for **RAGNAROK**…

KVASIR

God of inspiration, knowledge and beet juice. After the war between the Aesir and Vanir, all the gods made a truce by spitting into a bowl. They stirred up the mixture and created a new god of knowledge out of the potent mess. His name was **KVASIR** and he was made the most amazing diplomat to prevent further disagreements. Sadly he didn't last long as he was slaughtered by treacherous dwarves, who drained his blood, mixed it with honey and fermented it into a highly potent mead. This became known as Kvas, the mead of inspiration, a fiery brew the colour of beetroot. Drinking it was a highly enlightening experience. The entire supply of Kvas was then taken from the dwarves by the giant Suttung in payment for a family feud, and hidden in the mountains with his sister Gunnlod guarding it.

ODIN, who desperately wanted a taste of the infamous brew, used every subterfuge in his extensive repertoire to gain access. Eventually he appeared in front of the buxom barmaid Gunnlod and begged for three tiny sips. After a little friendly persuasion, she granted his request and watched in horror as he drained all three jars to the dregs. He then changed himself into an eagle and flew off, somewhat unsteadily.

This looked like the end of the mead of inspiration, until it was discovered that fermented beetroot juice produced much the same effect. We have a theory that the blood of Kvasir was such a beautiful godly red that the leftover dregs were thrown onto a field of beetroots to inspire growth. This is so far unsubstantiated, but you have to start somewhere and stranger things have happened.

Soon everyone was making Kvas. So the Kvasir Beetroot Brewery is more than likely the cause for the proliferation of drunken poets which permeate society in every century. It also happens that once upon a time the Chief Godchecker, in a previous spiritual existence, made some Beetroot Wine. It was indeed a rich and inviting red in the first stages, but as fermentation ceased, the colour slowly faded to a pale tawny rust, or washed-out bloodstain. It was left to mature for a year or two, when upon sampling it did indeed prove to be very inspirational...

LOKI

God of hokey pokey and one of the world's major trickster gods. In his early days **LOKI** was a rascal; crafty, sneaky, silly and malicious – a Loki the lad. The son of two giants, he was so outrageously mischievous that he even sneaked his way into becoming a god. He was the first anti-hero, quick-witting his way out of the tight corners and confrontations caused by his misdeeds. But as time wore on he became increasingly nasty.

His first escapade was a very rampant romp. When the gods were struggling to build Asgard, they found they'd run out of funds. Which is not surprising as money and banks hadn't been invented yet. All the basic construction had been completed but they needed a large protective wall to keep the riff-raff out.

Loki came up with the plan of contracting a giant to do the job. As payment, the giant asked for the Sun and Moon and also the goddess **FREYA** if the work was completed to schedule. The gods were not too sure. 'Don't worry,' advised Loki. 'He'll never manage it on his own, even if he works night and day – and the deal will be off. We'll let him keep the wheelbarrow or something.' Alas, the giant was not alone. He had a huge stallion called Svadilfari, which could haul boulders like there was no tomorrow. With three days to go, Freya was in distress and the gods aghast.

Now Loki, like fire and smoke, was a shape-changer from the word go, a talent he'd developed to make him the shiftiest transmogrifier of all time – from flea to fish to fast-flying feathers in 0.3 seconds. So he changed himself into a mare and seduced the giant's stallion. By whinnying and prancing off into the woods, Svadilfari was led far away from the stone pile.

With his horse missing, the giant didn't quite make the schedule. Seething with rage, he tried to take Freya by force – until **THOR** cracked his skull with his hammer. Meanwhile Loki was having a fine old time frolicking in the fields. In fact, he became pregnant, and decided to sample the joys of motherhood. He gave birth to a fine baby boy stallion with eight legs. He gave this as a gift to **ODIN** and it was called Sleipnir.

Loki was now well in with top god Odin and his son Thor, with whom he shared numerous adventures. Thor, the perfect fall guy, was persuaded to appear in drag as the prospective bride of a giant and other embarrassments. Thor could always be relied on to supply the muscle

when corners became too tight for trickery. Loki never missed an opportunity to take advantage of any goddess, despite already having had three wives. The first not many folk know about, and it is only by assiduous research we have discovered Glut, who bore him two daughters. Next was Angrboda, a giantess who spawned **FENRIR** the giant wolf, **JORMUNGAND** the Earth-encircling serpent, and **HEL** the Underworld goddess. Finally there was his wife **SIGYN**, who produced their ill-fated sons Narvi and Vali. Loki's adventures are abundant, and you will find his name popping up frequently under other entries.

As the most scandalous god of all time, Loki was seldom out of the *Nordic News* or the *Sunday Runes*. But his tricks came to an end after causing the death of **BALDUR**. Now he's trapped in eternal punishment until **RAGNAROK** rolls around.

MAGNI

God of strength. He's the son of **THOR** and Jarnsaxa, which easily explains that one. In fact he's even stronger than Thor himself. Thor was lying trapped under the colossal leg of the stone giant Hrungnir, whom he'd just demolished. The gods couldn't release him. Sadly they sent for his young son **MAGNI** to make his fond farewells. 'Good god dad', said the lad. 'What are you doin' under that leg? I'll have you out in a jiffy. Cor look at it. It's big, where is the rest of it. I see you gave it a hammerin'. I could have punched its lights out with my bare fists. Pity you didn't send for me sooner.' Magni was three years old at the time. Thor didn't know whether to kiss him or give him a clout round the ear.

MANI

The Moon god, and brother of **SOL** the Sun. Flies through the night sky in his horse-driven chariot, chased by a hateful wolf. Whenever the wolf gets too close, a lunar eclipse takes place. Here's a cute thing: **MANI** was pestered by a little girl called Bil and her brother Hjuki, who were messing about with his reflected image in a well. So he whisked them away and now keeps them busy putting spots on the moon and helping to roll it around. (Is it being used for some great celestial game of soccer?) The tale of Hjuki and Bil is said to be the origin of the nursery rhyme Jack and Jill.

MIMIR

Giant god of wisdom and knowledge. His head was hacked off by the Vanir but **ODIN** applied herbal therapy and restored it to life. **MIMIR** then became the Talking Head at the Spring of Knowledge by the Yggdrasil Tree. He knows the secrets of the Universe and has one of Odin's eyes, which forms part of his very own neighbourhead watch. If we knew where he could be found it would make things a lot easier. A map might be useful.

MYSTERIOUS THREE

Three strange sages who sit on thrones above a rainbow in Asgard and answer frequently asked questions. If you're ever passing that way and have a nagging question to get off your chest, by all means pop in for a shot of mead and wisdom. When Gylfi, the king of Sweden, tried his luck they gave him the complete history of the Universe in spoken word form without even pausing for breath. Naturally he rushed home afterwards and scribbled it all down for the benefit of future generations.

NIBELUNGS

Despite having four epic Wagner operas devoted to them, with all the trappings of hardcore mythology at work, details of the underground-dwelling **NIBELUNGS** is pretty scarce. Our main source of information is the *Nibelungenlied*, a thirteenth-century work written in Low, Medium and High German.

The Nibelungs are revealed to be a race of tough but valiant dwarves living in the realm of Niflheim. But they guard a most precious treasure, which is of course the cue for an exciting tale or two. However, can we interest you in a Nebelung? Nebelungs are a breed of cute fluffy kittens which make affectionate, devoted companions. Rumour has it that Wagner was inspired by them for his opera *Der Ring Des Nebelungen* (The Ring of the Cute Fluffy Kittens).

NJORD

Nordic and nautical. The original old man of the oceans, in charge of fire, wind and sea. After being chosen by the goddess **SKADI** in a footsie contest, things didn't work out, and he found Nerthus much more compatible. With his sister he produced a whole boatload of deities, including **FREYA** and **FREYR**.

NORNS

These three fatalists can be found tending the ash tree Yggdrasil in Doomstead. They are Past, Present and Future, spinning your destiny at this very moment. Urd does Fate, Verdandi does Present and Skuld the Future. They are engaged in tapestry work of such complexity that nothing ever gets finished. Until one of their destiny tapestries is completed, confusion and uncertainty will be the **NORN**. Skuld, who is the youngest and most beautiful, also takes time off to serve with the **VALKYRIES** on a voluntary basis.

ODIN

Father of the gods, king of Asgard, ruler of the Aesir and the lord of war, death and knowledge. To travel the world without being recognised, he wears a huge wide-brimmed hat. He also – thanks to **LOKI** – rides an eight-legged horse named Sleipnir into battle. All he needs is a six-shooter and a sheriff's badge to be able to stand in for John Wayne in *True Grit*. His biggest fans include the Berserkers, which should give you some idea.

He's also very hot on knowledge and military intelligence, having two ravens, Huginn and Muninn, who fly around the world every day bringing up-to-date reports. **ODIN** himself has only one eye, having traded the other one for a sip from **MIMIR**'s Well of Wisdom during his visit to the great World Tree Yggdrasil. Consequently he's full of knowledge, while his missing eye is hidden in an unknown location care of Mimir the talking head. The eye enabled Mimir to focus on far-distant events, allowing Odin the ability to always see far ahead.

To become the top wise guy, Odin put himself through some incredibly rigorous ordeals. The Well of Wisdom lies under the second root of Yggdrasil, which allows the Dew of Knowledge to seep into it. So Odin stabbed himself with his own spear and hung himself on the tree for nine days and nights. He was then allowed a peep, and saw magic runes appear on rocks beneath him.

With a superhuman effort he struggled to lift them, which must have been quite an acrobatic feat. Running his eye over the mystic symbols, he was instantly freed of all encumbrances; restored and rejuvenated with everlasting vigour enabling him to drop lightly to the ground. His ordeal accomplished, Odin was at last able to take a well-deserved swig from Mimir's well, making him well-wise as well as wise. It was even tastier than his usual tipple Kvas, the mead of inspiration, a special brew made from the blood of **KVASIR**.

If you think a wise one-eyed Norse cowboy on an eight-legged horse would be easy to recognise, this ain't necessarily so for Odin is a shape-changer, and his range of disguises makes Sherlock Holmes look like Miss Marple. He also travels incognito under a variety of false names. Sharing primeval god status with brothers Ve and Vili, the great Odin helped bring the world as we know it into being, so we can forgive his little foibles. The legend tells that in the ice-laden wastes of Niflheim, he got into a rather catastrophic snowball fight with Ymir, the king of the **FROST GIANTS**. The abominable snowgiant was slashed into pieces and Odin made the world from all the bits. He even found a use for the eyebrows.

Here's a genuine extract from the *Havamal*, Odin's own autobiography, showing his wit and wisdom:

Reasons To Be Cheerful, Part 3
Praise day in the evening,
A wife, when dead,
A weapon when tried,
A maid, when married,
Ice, when it's crossed,
Ale, when it's drunk.

Although the exact authorship, date and publisher of the *Havamal* is unknown, we can tell you that it forms part of the *Poetic Edda* (circa AD 850) and was voted Book of the Year by the *Runic Chronicle*.

RAGNAROK

The end of the world and doom of the gods, literally 'Destruction of the Powers'. After three terrible winters of bitterness and conflict, Skoll the wolf will eat the sun he has been chasing all his life, just managing to get in the odd bite that causes an eclipse, and his brother Hati will scoff the moon. Three cocks will crow (or is that three crows will cock?) and **HEIMDALL** will finally blow his awesome horn, bringing the gods to the final battle.

All Hell will be let loose. The Earth will tremble, **FENRIR**'s bonds will be shaken loose, and **JORMUNGAND** will emerge causing awful devastation with every twist of his serpent body. Everybody who's anybody will be beating the living daylights out of their enemies in a final glorious slaughter of gods, giants, monsters and dwarves. Even the dead will join in with **LOKI** as their captain. And nobody will win. The gods will defeat their enemies but be defeated themselves, and everyone and everything will perish utterly. Only two people will survive: Lif and Lifthrasir, two humans hiding in a secret forest, will awaken to find a lush and empty new world waiting for them…

RAN

She's the wife of **AEGIR** but is terribly randy and fancies mortals. The snag is she lives at the bottom of the sea, so has to snatch suitors from the surface in a net. She doesn't have a lot of luck with her infidelities as drowning seems to render the poor chaps incapable.

RIG

This is an alias of **HEIMDALL** when he's off having adventures with mortals. He created the first serf after sleeping with a farmer's wife. The farmer was very disgruntled – at least until he realised he could put the son to work. They called him Thrall and that's exactly what he was. All serfs and slaves derive from him. Having had a go at the lower orders, **RIG** carried on with his secret mingling and produced Karl, or Churl, to start the pleasant peasant class, followed by Jarl or Earl, progenitor of the upper-crust top-notch types. Heimdall aka Rig was therefore responsible for creating the first social class system. He's got a lot to answer for, wethinks.

SIF

Mrs **THOR**. Nordic corn goddess with hair like a golden harvest. She suffered terrible embarrassment at the hands of **LOKI**, who sneaked into her bedroom and cut all her hair off. Thor was furious. Luckily Loki managed to persuade some clever dwarf hairstylists to make **SIF** a wig out of finely spun gold.

SIGYN

Wife of **LOKI** and the mother of Vali and Narvi. She remained faithful to Loki – even after he committed adultery, stayed out all night and killed **BALDUR**. As punishment for that, he was bound with the entrails of his own son under three flat stones with a snake dripping poison. Now **SIGYN** has the thankless task of catching every drop in a bowl before it falls on him. Every so often she has to nip off to empty the bowl – and he gets it right in the face.

SKADI

Giant goddess of skiing and winter. She's known as the snow-shoe goddess after being forced to choose a husband from among the gods, who would only let her see their shoes. Unfortunately, the fairest footwear belonged to the ugly **NJORD** and not the handsome **BALDUR** she was hoping for. Needless to say, the marriage was a disaster and they never became sole-mates. Eventually she ran off with Ull, presumably because he's good at skiing.

SOL

Sun goddess. Like her brother **MANI**, she rides through the sky in a horse-drawn chariot. And also like her brother, she is chased by a wolf. Occasionally Skoll, the wolf in question, gets close enough to risk a bite and we get an eclipse. But he'll never catch her properly until **RAGNAROK**. By extraordinary coincidence, there's also a Roman Sun god with the same name.

THOR

God of thunder. Son of **ODIN** and Jord, he's the famous Scandinavian god with the hammer, the burly red-bearded lord of thunderstorms. He rides through the storm clouds in a chariot pulled by goats and throws his hammer, Mjollnir, all over the place to create lightning.

As perhaps you might expect, he's not terribly bright and **LOKI** was always leading him astray. But they were firm friends and **THOR** was always ready to bash his enemies with the business end of his hammer.

Married to **SIF**, he's also been known to have a fling with the giantess Jarnsaxa, with whom he produced the equally fearsome Magni and Modi. His daughter is Thrud, and that's not an insult, it's her name. It actually means 'Power', but it still sounds ugly whatever language you say it in. She was betrothed to a dwarf called Alvis, but Thor was not happy and tricked the dwarf into staying up all night. As the morning dawned, Alvis got caught by the sunrise. This is not good for dwarves as they turn to stone. Wedding off. After this unfortunate enforced jilt, Thrud seems to have taken a vow of chastity and become one of the **VALKYRIES**. Thursday is Thorsday.

VALI

Son of **ODIN** and Grid, he was born for the sole purpose of avenging the death of **BALDUR**, which meant shafting **HOD** in no uncertain terms. Mere hours after he was born, **VALI** grew to an enormous godly size and ran off to play hatchets and victims.

VALKYRIES

Choosers of the slain. They are a team of warrior maidens led by feisty **FREYA**. If you are a handsome warrior strutting your stuff on the battlefield, watch out for forty raving beauties on flying horses descending upon the pitch. They can grab any warrior they fancy, and take him away. There is only one rule: the bewildered chump must be dead first. So fight for your life, because if you fail you could be scooped up and borne off to Valhalla, the heroes' Heaven. There you will be forced to feast, guzzle gallons of mead, and fornicate madly all night. Then fight exciting battles all day. If you get wounded, you'll be miraculously restored in time for the next round of fun and frolics. Could you cope with all this?

VIDAR

God of silence and revenge. If you want to put the boot in, **VIDAR** is the god for you. He has an enormous iron shoe with which he can trample anything to death. Just what you'd expect with **ODIN** as a father and Grid as a mother. To complete the happy family, his brother is **THOR**. It is his duty to kill **FENRIR** the wolf after it has chewed up his father. This may have already happened as there is some confusion as to whether **RAGNAROK** has been and gone or is still to come. Being the strong silent type, Vidar hasn't said.

VALI

Son of **LOKI** and **SIGYN** and used by the gods to extract a terrible revenge for the death of **BALDUR**. By some kind of fenririsation, he was turned into a wolf, encouraged to attack his brother **NARVI** and tear his throat out. The entrails of Narvi were used to bind Loki to rocks. They seemed a bit stretchy so the gods turned them into iron and then **SKADI** came up with the idea of the venom-dripping snake. We don't know what happened to **VALI** after this. He probably ran off into the woods to become a run-of-the-mill werewolf.

WODEN

God of Wednesday. He's the Germanic version of **ODIN**, so it should really be called Odinesday. There is more. The Persians called it Red Letter Day as that was the day the Moon was created. The last Wednesday in November is called Black Wednesday but don't ask me why.

WAVE-MAIDENS

The nine white-robed billowy daughters of **AEGIR** the undersea brewer and **RAN**. Their names include Bylgia, Dafn and Jarnsaxa. They can often be seen waving from the waves and one day they waved at **ODIN** causing him to have salacious thoughts. He wondered what it would be like to have his wicked way with all nine of them simultaneously – and the naughty thought alone was potent enough to make them the joint mother of **HEIMDALL**. All nine of them had to share a single family allowance.

THE GODS OF OCEANIA

The trouble with Oceanic legends is that there are more islands and peoples than fishes in the sea. And every culture has its own twist on the legendary themes. Gods from one island pop up in another. They change their names. They hide and sneak about. They impersonate one another. It's a nightmare for dedicated Godcheckers. Every time we see waving palms we shall wave back and examine the coconuts. Maps are being flapped and boundaries are being pushed and lots of skirting and scouting has been invoked.

Once upon a time it was just the South Seas and a setting for ripping yarns involving pearls, buried treasure, typhoons, a thrilling battle with a giant octopus and escape from sacrifice and the cannibal cooking pot as a volcano erupted. Not much has changed.

BANKS ISLAND
QAT

Creator god. He had a nasty surprise when he found his brother's bones in the lair of a cannibal monster called Qasavara which he rapidly slew. He then needed to know he had the right ones before restoration so he made them laugh by blowing through a reed. Then after sorting out this part of the world **QAT** paddled off in his canoe towards the setting sun. His return is awaited. But what does he look like? Captain Cook was one instance of mistaken identity. If it's the captain look, could he resemble Captain Hook, Captain Pugwash, Captain Birdseye, or even a captain of industry?

CAROLINE ISLANDS
GORA-DAILENG

A purging god of punishment. He burns the wicked after death and flushes their charred remains into the Underground River of Oblivion. This river is infinitely long and thus carries the burnt souls away on a dismal journey that never ends. Unfortunately for them, they remain conscious.

FIJI
ADI-MAILAGU

Goddess who came down to Earth in the guise of a grey rat, but had the ability to change into a beautiful woman or a hag with a tongue a yard long. If she visited a man at night in her beauty mode he would be sure to die. What a tease. She also ran an oracle service for priests, offering hot tips for future success in exchange for a little sacrifice. But word got out that she spent most of her time in a tree as a grey rodent – someone must have ratted on her. One night, a person or persons unknown cut down the tree. She must have realised she had outstayed her welcome, as she was never seen again.

DEGEI

The great she-serpent. She lived alone in the sky, although she shared flying space with Turukawa, a female hawk. One day the hawk made a nest and laid two eggs, so goodness knows where she had been skylarking. Intrigued, **DEGEI** offered to baby-sit and was astounded when the eggs hatched and out popped a baby girl and boy. Turukawa seems to have shrugged her feathers and flown off, so Degei became a foster mum. She taught her adopted children everything and made them wise enough to start the human race. Some time later, a group of first-generation brothers on hunting practice shot down a hawk. This hawk turned out to be Turukawa. Degei decided to punish them with a flood, but she was too kind-hearted to let them drown. Instead she sent down a shaddock fruit for them to use as a life raft – and as a snack for when the flood subsided.

LINGADUA

God of the drum. Strangely he has only one arm, so single stroke rolls could have been his idea. He supervises the royal drums of the kings. He can take their voices away if the sacrifices to him are not up to scratch.

NDAUTHINA

God of lighthouses. When he was a child his mum fastened a burning taper to his head so he could be seen after lighting-up time. His torch-bearing activities extended to becoming a navigational aid to sailors who praised him to godliness.

NDENGI

God of night who has a bit of trouble with his timing. When he sleeps, it becomes night and nothing can happen. Unfortunately he does tend to oversleep because some nephews stole the black dove he used as an alarm clock. His clock was taken because he mostly used it to tell him it was bedtime whenever he felt like a snooze – which was most of the time. He is now very confused and stays awake all day worrying, which has resulted in a lot of daylight saving.

RATU-MAI-BULU

Creative geographical god married to Raivuki, who puts the seasoning in seasons. She is mostly hot and sunny or wet and windy. He started from the bottom pushing the ocean floor above sea level to turn Viwa from an atoll into an island. He then did all the growth and fertility things for the area known as the Yasawa Islands: coconuts, fresh water etc. You will know if you have upset him because your home will be crawling with snakes that will eat all your food. He many even appear in serpent form himself.

GILBERT ISLANDS

TABURIMAI

From sea to tree deity. Somehow he has arms and legs even though all his siblings were fish. In fact, his brother Teanoi is a hammerhead shark. His dad Bakoa, also on the aquatic side, was worried when he heard his finny kids plotting to do away with Tab. Teanoi, the only level-headed one, was given the job of whisking Tab off to safety, for which he was rewarded by having the chance to become a big star in the sky. Now safe on an island and able to run around, **TABURIMAI** met and fell in love with Te-Reere, the sacred tree goddess. It wasn't long before new branches of humanity came into being and fish were history's supper.

HAWAII

HIIAKA

Younger sister of **PELE** the volcano goddess. She started life as an egg carried under her sister's arm until finally she hatched. **HIIAKA** used to run errands for her big sister and one day was sent off to fetch a handsome prince for matrimonial purposes. The prince seemed willing enough to accompany her, but on the journey back they came under deadly demon attack. The prince, being mortal, kept being killed and had to be reconstituted after each affray, with Hiiaka having to run around and catch his soul which kept turning into a butterfly, or smoke, or perfume. It was a very versatile soul and made the most of its freedom.

Meanwhile Pele fretted with impatience, and then jealousy, which finally erupted when the wayward couple appeared. She swamped them with volcanic lava which proved fatal to the prince. Hiiaka reconstituted him for the last time, and decided they could not go on meeting like this. The prince, having experienced Pele in action, agreed. So they did a runner because they realised love was just around the corner. Or maybe a bit further, because Pele never found them.

KANE

Part of the Hawaiian creator trinity. With **KU** and **LONGO**, he's the god of procreation and the sea. Having made the world and created humans, he dwelt among them for a while but got bored and ascended to a Heaven which he'd just made. **KANE** is associated with the Polynesian **TANE**, although we're not sure why, apart from the similarity in spelling. It must be a conspiracy by Oceanic rhyming poets.

KU

War god. He looks the part too – he's ferociously ugly. **KU** is head of the Hawaiian creator trinity, along with the far nicer **KANE** and **LONGO**. It's always a little disturbing when the military are in charge of things.

KAMAPUAA

A hog of a god. He must have started at the bottom of the sea as his mighty snout pushed up enough silt to form piles of land. He settled on the land and wielded a mighty mace (his trotters weren't just for trotting) so it was best to stay on the right side of him. He could also dig wells for fresh water. He fancied **PELE** and snuffled after her, but she thought he had the manners of a pig. When he started extinguishing her lovely volcanic fires with mud she was forced to think again: 'I still think he's a pig but perhaps I had better marry him before he puts me out of business.'

LOAU

God of kava. He came down to Earth to see how humans were coping but everywhere he went he was thought to be a king at the very least. He was feted and feasted using the very best turtle shell tureens, but the booze was pretty rough. Trying to use a humbler approach he eventually came to a poor couple living in a shack. It was no use – he was a visitor and had to be given the best. But in this case was there was no best. Just a vegetable patch.

So they cooked a small daughter after burying her cut-off head, hoping they could pass her off as chicken or something. **LOAU** was most upset and didn't take a bite; pointing out the error of their ways and insisting the poor little corpse must be properly buried. He now needed a strong drink to help cope with the shock but there wasn't any. This caused even more shock, and realising he was a god and ought to remedy the situation, Loau blessed the little corpse and from it sprang the kava plant. This is a kind of pepper, the fermented roots of which make the kava drink, which became known and loved throughout Oceania.

LONGO

God of peace and food. Part of the Hawaiian creator trinity, along with **KU** and **KANE**, he makes the crops grow and the rains bow. **LONGO** loves a good feast and is particularly partial to sweet potato. If you need some rainfall, better give him a large portion.

PELE

Volcano deity. A goddess of fire, she makes her home in the crater Halemaumau on the summit of Kilauea, which is probably a place to be avoided unless you're into lava in a big way. Her younger sister is **HIIAKA**, who was definitely not into the whole lava deal as it interfered with her amorous intentions…

She has another sister, Pu-Uhele, but we have no idea how they get on. And **PELE** had to submit to the advances of **KAMAPUAA** the hog god. Are they still together?

TAGARO

Creator god. He once played a lengthy game of skittles with himself. Well – not entirely. That would be rather painful we would imagine, not that we should let our imaginations dwell on such matters. What he did was make ten little clay effigies of himself and roll a coconut or something at them. When one got a little appendage knocked off it turned into a living doll – the first female. The rest, as they say, is history.

TANGALOA

Another creator god. We get in a bit of a tangle with Oceanic gods, particularly when it comes to sorting out the **TAGARO**s from the **TANGAROA**s. But **TANGALOA** is definitely the one with the grubs. After making himself a wife out of stone, he planted a special vine. The grubs that rooted around in the roots were re-routed to Earth to become mankind. So there you are. Tangaloa also sent a messenger bird, Tuli, to provide shelter.

MAORI PEOPLE OF NEW ZEALAND

HINA-IKA

Lady of the fish and fine hair. Her brother Maui used it to make a net to pull the sun to where he wanted it. Her husband Ira-Waru, a merman, used her hair for his fishing nets. Being so fine and silvery, her hair also supplies the threads for moon rays.

HINE-KEHA

A full moon goddess. Known as 'Lady of the Ocean Waves'. She was washed ashore covered in seaweed and flotsam, and was discovered inside the tangle by a mortal who fell in love with her. Accounts are variable from then on.

He was everything from a humble beachcomber to a handsome prince. They gave birth to a son who as far as we can ascertain was called Tuhuruhuru. She was then entitled to become a goddess of childbirth. They took on a pet dog and should have been married happily ever after, but it seems the mortal was already married. She still lives by the seaside but may go off for long swims.

HINETITAMA

Goddess of dawn. Being married to Tane-Mahuta, the god of forests, was wonderful. Until a little bird told her that he was also her father. **HINETITAMA** was so shocked that she ran all the way to the Underworld, locked herself in and refused to come out.

Eventually a saddened Tane-Mahuta decreed that from now on she would be known as Hinenuitepo, the goddess of death and darkness. So now she takes care of the dead and waits for the souls of her departed children, grandchildren, and great-great-great-great-great-great-great-grandchildren. She was also responsible for the death of Maui the trickster god, known throughout Polynesia.

NGARARA

Goddess with a long tail. Her disposition was a little on the snaky side and took a fancy to young Ruru who landed on her island estate in search of fire and water. She wound her tail around his neck and invited him to a meal. He knew it would not be a good idea to eat anything if he wished to avoid growing scales.

He managed to escape and contact his brothers waiting anxiously offshore. They made a hasty statue to resemble Ruru and put it inside a rapidly assembled reed hut. **NGARARA**, hot on the trail, was fooled by the effigy and wound her tail round its neck, whispering sweet everythings into its ears in the gloom. The gloom was rapidly dispelled as the brothers set fire to the hut. Whoosh! Ngarara managed to escape by leaving her tail behind, and was purified by the flames which made her as nice as pie afterwards.

TANGAROA

God of the sea. He also seems to be the god of fishermen. Married to fertility goddess **FAUMEA**, **TANGAROA** is often depicted with only three fingers on each hand. Does this ensure good bites, or has he succumbed to Walt Disneyfication? Maybe we've got our lines tangled as other accounts make him responsible for everything coloured red. But he may also be **TAGARO** or **TANGALOA**, or not, and one of these may be responsible for redness. Surely the Demas and **DARVI** brought redness to the land?

His grandson is Ika-Tere-Maeri who keeps things in the swim by being known as 'Father of Fish'.

RANGI

God of the sky. In the passion of their embrace, the Earth and the sky were so tightly cuddled together that there was no room to move. This was somewhat embarrassing when their children Rongo, **TANE** and Tu were born. Faced with a lifetime of stunted growth and intense parental pressure, the kids decided that something had to be done. So Tane tried to force his parents apart. He pushed and pushed for days, weeks and years until Papa and **RANGI** slowly parted company. Light entered the world for the first time and plants began to grow. Papa and Rangi were terribly upset at their separation. Rangi's tears covered the world in ocean, and Papa's wistful sighs became mists and clouds. Youngest son Ruaumoko never got a chance to climb the godly ladder – he stayed in the womb of Papa and causes volcanoes when he moves around. That must be even more painful.

TAWHIRI

Wind and storm god son of **RANGI** and Papa. Quite when and how is difficult to know – and we don't. He has thirteen cloud children, all born to confound and confuse weather forecasters. They're known collectively as the Ao. We have scant details for most of them; we think the others may have been blown away. So we have one for fluffy clouds, one for scruffy clouds, one for thundery, one for overcast etc. A sort of godly weather forecaster.

WHAITIRI

Goddess who married a mortal chief but she soon found he was not fond of her cooking. He never touched his nice juicy portions of roasted human flesh. Then he complained about children's poo left lying around and she had to invent the Earth closet to keep him quiet. Being called the Dinner and Poo Lady was more than she could bear so she returned to her old home in the sky. Now she can send for a tasty flesh takeaway, and there are no lavatorial problems. Just use the Heavenly thunderbox and empty it on Earth when full.

MARQUESAS, TUAMOTU
ATEA & ATANUA

Creator god. According to Marquesa legend he popped up out of chaos one day, married **ATANUA** and spawned the first humans. Meanwhile, Tuamotu mythology claims he's a sky god with an embarrassing lack of knowledge about female anatomy. Having created a nice lady god called Fa-Ahotu to be his wife, it didn't occur to him that he'd missed out two important bits until their baby sons almost died of malnutrition. Fa-Ahotu had no breasts.

   ATEA had to suckle them himself, but despite this little mistake and even without powdered milk Tahu, Ro-o and **TANE** survived and thrived. In fact, Tane went on to be top god after hitting his dad with a thunderbolt to cause early retirement. As for Atanua, a dawn goddess, she had her own problems with things that hadn't dawned yet and created things with amniotic fluid. Don't ask us – ask her.

MELANESIA, NEW GUINEA
ABEGUWO

Rain goddess. The world is her lavatory. **ABEGUWO** lives in the sky, and whenever she needs to relieve herself she has no inhibitions about letting loose all over the planet. She really should be called Abiguwee. When she takes a pee it's time to get out your umbrella; this might sound a little unsavoury, but if you think about it, it could be a lot worse. Better be nice to her or she'll rain on your parade. And don't even think of challenging her to a pissing contest.

MICRONESIA GILBERT ISLANDS

NA-KAA

When **NA-KAA** had a hand in creation he was very fond of his beautiful garden and his two magnificent trees. When it came to humans he decided to keep them segregated to avoid all the normal human hassle. So each sex (there were only two at the time) was allocated their own tree to sit under, not knowing there was another tree occupied by the opposite sex.

About to set off on an urgent business trip, Na-Kaa foolishly called them all together to give them gardening instructions whilst he was away. The final words were 'Back to your own trees. Do not mix or mingle. Do not look back. Stay with your own tree. Ladies to the left. Gentlemen to the right. Off you go – quick march – no dawdling.' Well – they had seen each other. Mad with excitement and curiosity they all ran under the same tree the moment the boss was out of sight. It would have been the nearest one. It was the wrong choice.

When Na returned he coldly informed them they had made a bad choice. They had chosen the Tree of Death, and they would all eventually die, whereas the other tree was the Tree of Life but it was too late now. We think he was just making this up because he was riled, as it has never been made clear which sex was fobbed off with the Death Tree in the first place. Typical of gods; they just can't stand the idea of humans competing in the immortality stakes.

NAREAU

Spider gods – father and son. **NAREAU** senior retired after initial creation leaving Nareau junior to carry on the good work with the assistance of an octopus called Na-Kika and an eel, whose slippery name escapes us for the moment. It was a brilliant combination. No humans have ever come near to matching their constructive brilliance. Only gods can add the final touches and make sunsets. Somewhere down the line there is also Te-Ikawai, descended from the spider dynasty. Nobody seems to know much about him. There are too many world wide webs for mere mortals to check.

OLIFAT

Prankster god, son of Lugeilan, he is an eternal pest who won't grow up. He uses lightning flashes to slide down to Earth, and rides back upwards on columns of smoke, which usually means he has to set fire to something to get home. He plagues other gods by upsetting cooking pots and distracting them with stupid tomfoolery – then tries to rape their daughters. When things get too hot in Heaven, it's out the back window and whizz – back to Earth in a flash. On Earth he fits sharks with teeth, and fixes stings onto scorpions. He encourages ants and termites to gnaw through roof beams causing houses to collapse. He is always setting fire to thatch, and if things get too hot it's back up to Heaven with the smoke. There is never a dull moment with him around and many humans would rather die than have to put up with him. So they do.

NAURA

AREOP

The spider goddess at the beginning of creation. In the great darkness of the void she found a clam shell. What a clam shell was doing in the void before creation is an as-yet-unexplained mystery. The clam shell was open, and inside was a tiny snail. **AREOP** was unable to resist having a peek inside, but wham! the shell snapped shut. The snail was now trapped inside. Areop suggested that the snail might be able to prise the clam open at the hinge, so the snail went to have a look, leaving a phosphorescent trail behind it. A little white wormy thing was revealed in the light. 'Hello, my name is Rigi,' it said. Meanwhile the snail, puffing and straining, was trying to open the shell. 'Hey, what's going on in there?' cried Areop, somewhat confused.

Rigi gave her a running commentary, but the snail's push-ups were not working. 'Let me have a go,' said Rigi, and set to work fortified with strength spells and encouraging shouts from Areop. He heaved so hard his sweat poured into pools, spread into lakes and finally became the sea. But how the seas and lakes appeared before the Earth was created has yet to be explained. This clam is bigger than you can imagine.

Eventually the Big Clunk came and the clam popped open. The lower portion was the Earth, covered in Rigi's sweaty sea, and the top half became the sky. The exhausted snail turned into the moon, and poor old Rigi, who did not survive the ordeal, was turned into the Milky Way. We're not sure what happened to Areop after that. We just hope she's not tempted to poke her spidery nose into the Great Clam again or the sky will come slamming down on top of us.

PAPUA NEW GUINEA
DARVI

Top god of the Demas, a race of half-spirit, half-human beings with a penchant for tinkering. The Demas invented all sorts of things and life was idyllic until they discovered fire. Of course, they just had to play with it until it got out of control and even the mountains caught alight. **DARVI** sent rain, but it wasn't working properly due to technical glitches. But he managed to grab a great chunk of land and heave it into the sea, along with a load of scorched animals. This is why crabs are red and herons have red legs. Indeed anything with red markings dates back to those scorching days. The chunk of Earth is now the island of New Guinea, and the Demas are a lot more careful.

HANA & NI

HANA and **NI** were brother and sister. Hana had thingies but Ni didn't, but she used to use a tree for pole dancing. One day Hana hid a sharp stone in the tree bark which caused an interesting wound in a naughty place. This unexpectedly led to sexual misbehaviour. The resulting offspring were left to their own devices as Hana was taken into care by the authorities to become the Moon and Ni had to set off to rise again as the Sun.

HONOYETA

A real snake in the grass. He had two wives, but when he set off to supposedly go and earn a crust in the morning, he nipped out of his snakeskin and became a handsome hunk who seduced other women with his devilish charm. When his wives became aware of his cheating ways they burned his snakeskin, so he could not return to the bonus of snaky writhings and had to remain human forever. He then invented death for humans so he could shake off old girlfriends, because after all he was a demon, and it was his business to be up to no good. What he does for sex now we cannot say.

POLYNESIA
FAUMEA

Mother goddess of fertility. Apparently she lived on an island – or possibly was the island – and secreted eels about her person in a way which only a lover or a dedicated customs officer could have detected. These eels were deadly, but **TANGAROA**, not willing to risk his anatomy, managed to lure them out. A marriage proposal followed shortly thereafter.

MAUI

A pest of a god. He would nick his brothers' fish off their lines with his own hook and they wouldn't take him fishing any more. Mum (Queen Taranga) was not pleased and sent him off to his dad Makea, king of the Underworld. Mum had never liked her son much since the day he was born looking like a jellyfish and she had thrown him into the sea. He was rescued by a god called Tama, who hung him up to dry. When he'd assumed a more child-like shape and grown into a scamp of a boy he was sent off back to mum. She had so many children by now she couldn't quite remember which one he was and couldn't remember his name so called him **MAUI**. We have no idea what this means, probably something like 'Oi You' or 'Thingy'.

His dad seemed quite pleased to see him however, and gave him a magic fishhook called Manai-Ka-Lani which meant he could catch his own fish. He tried to go fishing with his brothers again but they threw him out of the canoe. He kept pestering, and one day they relented and he had some big catches, but when he pulled them up they became islands. He also showed off and hooked the sun to make it move more slowly.

After this of course he became an unbearable smart-arse, discovered playing with fire and showing off at every opportunity in the best trickster tradition. He eventually came to a very tricky end. Finding the goddess Hinenuitepo asleep, he became very curious because she was a big lady. We are talking colossal here. Maui thought it would be fun to walk through her body – starting from an entrance not normally accessible. Now Hinenuitepo was not sleeping in a very ladylike position (although missionaries have since put it to good use). At the crucial moment, a flock of birds twittered in shock at the unusual spectacle and she woke up with a start. Her legs clapped together and Splunch! No more Maui.

TANE

God of light. He lets light into the world every day by lifting up a corner of the dark sky. He's also responsible for forests and trees, and invented the tasty Tui bird. **TANE** seems to work overtime under the name Tane-Mahuta. He's also associated in some obscure way with the Hawaiian **KANE**, and son of Polynesian creator god **RANGI**.

RAPANUI PEOPLE OF EASTER ISLAND

MAKE-MAKE

Top god of the Rapanui people of Easter Island. The all-powerful creator and benefactor, he was the only god they cared about, apart from a little Aku-Aku ancestor worship. The **MOAI** statues littering the island may once have been dedicated to him, but nothing is certain as it all went horribly wrong and now no-one remembers a thing. There was a terrible civil war in which the Moai were cast down, and a new cult sprang up which introduced **TANGATA-MANU**, the bird-man. **MAKE-MAKE** must have been pretty cross, as the fortunes of the Rapanui subsequently went from bad to worse.

MOAI

The mysterious statue figures of Easter Island. One of the most evocative images in the entire world, the **MOAI** are ancient brooding figures carved from great slabs of volcanic rock. More than a thousand Moai can be found scattered over the island, most of them standing with their backs to the sea. Hundreds more lie half-completed in a volcanic quarry, mysteriously abandoned after a tribal war.

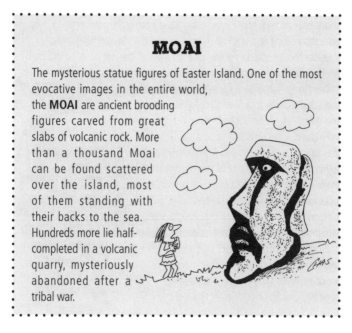

Opinion is divided regarding their purpose; some people believe they represent tribal leaders or ancient ancestors – and some people don't. The subject has been ripe with rampant speculation, and Easter Island attracts cranks like you wouldn't believe. The mystery is enhanced by the fact that most of the Moai weigh a truly ridiculous amount of tons. How did the primitive Rapanui islanders shift those colossal statues across the landscape without the benefit of computers and cell phones? Many theories have been proposed, including ingenious block-and-tackle engineering and extraterrestrial intervention by space aliens. But we prefer the simple solution, as explained by the native islanders: 'They just got up and walked by themselves.'

TANGATA-MANU

A thousand years ago, the Rapanui people were quite content to worship their ancestors, pay homage to **MAKE-MAKE** and build rather a lot of huge **MOAI** statues. But due to greed and a complete lack of ecological savvy, the flourishing forests were destroyed, the land was over-farmed, and Easter Island became a pretty tough place to live. There were two factions at the time, the Fat Ones and the Thin Ones. No-one knows for sure, but it seems that the Fat Ones owned all the juicy bits of land while the Thin Ones toiled and scratched. Result: revolution.

The Thin Ones rose up, slaughtered their rivals, threw down the Moai, and adopted a brand new deity. The cult of **TANGATA-MANU** was born and statue-building was abandoned overnight, leaving a graveyard of unfinished Moai to puzzle future archeologists. Tangata-Manu the Bird-Man was supposed to be Make-Make's Earthly ambassador, but he didn't object to a bit of devout fun. Thus began the Great Easter Island Egg Hunt, a yearly sporting event in which daring lads would scramble over cliffs and rocks in search of the first egg of the season. This was quite a dangerous mission, and whoever found and returned the egg safely was showered with praise and crowned bird-man of the Year.

Tangata-Manu himself is somewhat elusive. There are many carvings of him bending over an egg and looking at it in a rather perplexed manner. We don't know what to make of it either.

TAHITI
ORO

A battle god and son of Hina and **TA-AROA**. If you see him pick up his spear you know there is trouble ahead for someone – hopefully not you. He has three daughters who annoy and incite him, as they too revel in trouble-making. You can tell by their names what they are like: Toi-Mata 'Axe Eye', Ai-Tupuai 'Head Eater' and Mahu-Fatu-Rau 'Escape from a Hundred Stones'. His son Hoa-Tapu 'Faithful Friend' seems to have a more favourable disposition, but no – he is a war god. In the Cook Islands **ORO** had a different personality as a son of **TANGAROA** and ancester of the Rarotongan people.

TA-AROA

Creator god and father of **ORO**. He made the entire Universe using a clever piece of creative cookery. You will need two eggs, with yourself inside the second egg. On hatching you will need to boil your flesh into soil, stew your bones into mountains, roll your intestines into eels, steam your internal organs into clouds and squeeze your blood into birds. Now for the feathers (yes, you will have feathers). These are to be used for flower arrangements. Then, this being an economical recipe, you use leftover bits of shell for stars and things. If anything goes wrong you will still have an egg you made earlier and can do a simple omelette. This is a **TA-AROA** specialty and has never appeared in any cookery book.

TONGA
EITUMATUPUA

God of the sky. He came down from Heaven one day by shinning down a tree – not a very dignified entrance for a sky god, but it takes all sorts. While spending time on the Earth he had a fling with Ilaheva, a mortal lady. This impressed the neighbours no end and gave the resultant son, Ahoeitu. But while on a Heavenly visit to see his dad, Ahoeitu was ambushed by his jealous half-brothers. They were so jealous that they ate him. **EITUMATUPUA** was very cross indeed when he found out and the culprits were punished by being forced to regurgitate and then watch as Ahoeitu was lovingly reassembled by his doting father. Furthermore they were grounded, or in this case Heavened, and never allowed to visit Earth again. And they could only fret and fume from afar when Ahoeitu was made king of Tonga.

SISIMATAILAA

God of goodies. On his engagement his mama told him he was the son of a god and if he asked nicely she was sure his dad would be good for a wedding pressie. So he went up the hill to the appointed godspot and lo and behold, his dad beamed magnanimously and said: 'Good on you son. Here have two pressies. This one has all the dosh you will need but this one must not be opened until I say so.'

The marriage went well, but on the honeymoon boat it was already nag, nag, nag from the bride. 'Come on – open it now – we are married. It's half mine anyway. Well, just a peep won't hurt.' But it did. The package, unlike **PANDORA**'s box, contained only goodies, but goodies in such overflowing abundance soon there was no room on the boat. Soon there was no boat as it was sinking under the weight of the new cargo. Soon there were no newly weds because they went down with the boat. When the gods say 'don't open the box', they really mean it.

THE GODS OF CLASSICAL ROME

What the Romans did for us was to encourage godliness on a grand scale. You were spoilt for choice. The beliefs of subjugated peoples, far from being destroyed, were actively encouraged – and in many cases absorbed. The Romans just couldn't have enough gods. In fact, sometimes they invented ones for special occasions. Most of the Latin words still in use today seem to have a god connected to them. Discipline = Disciplina, Fauna = Faunus, and Fortune = **FORTUNA**. Just add an 'a' or an 'us' to the end of a Latin word and see what god you get. This is very good for creating pet names. How about our favourite, Bellyflufficus?

With romantic Romans, the more gods the merrier; and some could be very merry indeed. They gave the Greek pantheon a major makeover. The top deities were built up into the *Planet Suite*: Mars, Venus, Jupiter, etc.

In Tuscany, sandwiched between Greek and Roman civilisations, the Etruscans or Etrurians seem to have lived life to the full if their frescoes and artifacts are anything to go by – which is pretty much all we do have as Etruscan remains a dead language. Etruscan gods haven't fared much better although hints of them survived in many Roman deities.

ABUNDANTIA

Goddess of good luck, prosperity and success. What a lot she's got, a veritable cornucopia of goodies. She is the goddess of abundance, after all. Her image was used on Roman coins under her brand names of Annona or Felicitas.

BACCHUS

The Roman god of wine and orgies. Oh, you know about him already do you? This drunken rake used to be called Liber, but changed his name to avoid arrest for indecent behaviour. Known as

DIONYSUS among the Greek free-drinkers, he was constantly surrounded by nubile orgasmic ladies who called themselves Bacchae – although the Greeks called them Maenads and the newspapers called them something else entirely.

BELLONA

Goddess of war. A helmeted Sabine who drives the chariot of **MARS**. She also drives a mean spear in the thick of battle. In fact, she's a bloodthirsty warrior who loves to rampage on the battlefield. Rumours abound that under the helmet she may be the sister or wife of Mars. No-one seems very sure. Under the Greeks she was known as Enyo and was just as vicious.

CALVA

Goddess of bald women. This is not as bizarre as it sounds. Apparently many women suffered from hair loss in times of siege – due to sacrificing their precious strands to make bowstrings. May she never flip her wig.

CARNA

Goddess of door hinges. She's one strange nymph who submitted to sexual advances from **JANUS** in return for power over door hinges. She seems keen on the well-being of mortals, especially small children, and is particularly fond of being offered bacon and beans. What does she do to earn her breakfast? She keeps Striges out. These are nasty bogey women with clawed feet who try and get in at night to suck the blood of children.

CLOACINA

Goddess of the sewers, not to mention drains, gutters and sewage treatment facilities. Once an Etruscan goddess of marital bliss, she was, for reasons which remain obscure, placed in charge of the grand Roman uber-drainage system, the Cloaca Maxima. This was clearly a very important office for obvious reasons and it was in everyone's best interest to think of her as fair and benevolent, particularly when strange bubblings, burblings and knockings were heard – as they are even in the best plumbing systems. In such cases, it was deemed wise to offer libations. **CLOACINA** may have been at the bottom, but she's always capable of resurfacing. Why not engage her services for trouble-free plumbing?

CUPID

The god of love. Lovey, dovey, romance in the air. Isn't he sweet? **CUPID** is one of the most popular gods of all time, and rightly so. He's the Greek **EROS** gone Roman, hence the journey to Londinium where he resides on a plinth at Piccadilly Circus.

DIANA

Women's lib goddess. Sexy Roman re-hash of the Greek **ARTEMIS**. Still very popular.

DISCORDIA

Goddess of chaos, argument and discord. Yes, she's the Roman **ERIS**.

FAMA

Celebrity goddess of fame and infamy, the Roman version of Greek Pheme. She has her own trumpet, so we don't need to blow it for her. **FAMA** is famous for her many eyes and mouths which act like flashing paparazzi cameras and gabbling gossip-mongering podcasts. Her abode has a zillion windows on the world which she stares at like television screens. She has her finger on the pulse of society and has a hotline to all newspapers, radio stations and media moguls.

According to Ovid in his *Metamorphosis*, her celebrity cohorts include Susurri (gossip), Credulitas (error), Laetitia (happiness) and Timores (terror).

FEBRUUS

Why is February called February? It's named after **FEBRUUS**, the Roman god of purification. He lives in the Underworld – which probably needs purifying rather a lot, judging by the reports we've heard.

He originally belonged to the Sabine people of the Apennines. The Etruscans were also very keen on him, but he was borrowed by the conquering Romans who were looking for a god to help with the spring-cleaning. To get on his good side they held an annual festival called Februalia in his honour. This was so popular they named the second month after it. Februus, after starting the Lost Souls Cleaning Agency, was later promoted to king of the Underworld and changed his name to **PLUTO**, but no-one got around to changing the name of the month. Which is just as well as Plutoary sounds a bit weird.

FORTUNA

Goddess of chance and good luck. You'll be lucky! She wears a blindfold to make sure she's completely random and impartial. Her symbol is the Wheel of Fortune. Give it a spin and see if you win.

When the Romans were looking for a good luck goddess, they took a chance on the Greek Tyche, whose function was to bring random good luck. With a fresh supply of dice and a new name, the revamped **FORTUNA** became extremely popular among the Roman betting community.

Her name actually means 'Lot Distributor' – because at her temple there was lots on offer. Card games, fruit machines, roulette … And between games, visitors would draw the lots and priests would use them to interpret the future. So, despite what you might have heard, gambling is really quite respectable. It was good enough for Caesar in his palace, wasn't it?

As in ancient times, Fortuna is still very popular in the big city, where she has temples, casinos and the *Wheel of Fortuna* television game show. The Horn of Plenty could be yours! Unlimited cornucopias to be won! Place your bets and take a chance now! Just make sure the odds and the gods are on your side.

FRAUD

The goddess of fraud, deception and betrayal. You may see a nice smiling face swimming gently in the waters of the Coctys and think all is well. But what is this? A serpent's tail! A scorpion's sting! And if you look closely she has another face – for **FRAUD** is the two-faced goddess.

HERCULES

Roman reboot of **HERACLES** the Greek hero. The son of **JUPITER**, he started off a mere mortal with a big club and ended up a demi-god with his own seat at the Heavenly feast. With a near-identical life history to his Greek counterpart, only the names have been changed and a few details Romanified. Our entry under the Greek Heracles will give you the real version.

JANUS

Two-faced god of doors and corridors, **JANUS** lurks in doorways and may also be the god of janitors. He has two Roman noses and, looking in opposite directions, he symbolises the process of change and helps to turn the old into the new improved version. His biggest job is getting us from one year to the next, which is why Janus has a whole month named after him.

JUPITER

Supreme top god. Like most of the really big Roman gods, **JUPITER** started out as a primeval nature deity. A sky god, he was in charge of the fundamental forces of nature and ruled the weather with an iron grip and a big stick.

When Greek culture began to influence Roman thought, Jupiter took on the attributes of Greek god **ZEUS** – with added Latin. With his forceful personality, he became king of the gods and the special protector of Rome. His wife was Juno replacing the Greek **HERA**. The Romans were always keen to get the gods on their side and Jupiter was definitely a force to be reckoned with – especially with his thunderbolt-hurling propensities. They awarded him many flattering titles and put him in charge of their entire legal and political system.

Worshipped as Optimus Maximus, the all-powerful good guy, Jupiter kept order and brought prosperity to the people. As Jupiter Victor he led the Roman army to victory in wars and conquests time and time again. In fact, he was probably the Roman Empire's greatest asset after plumbing. Of course it all went terribly wrong in the end and the empire fell. Perhaps Jupiter was offended by the deification of human emperors, particularly the later ones who were a bit patchy. Or maybe the new-fangled Christianity craze was the final insult. Either way, Jupiter withdrew his support and sloped off, leaving the Romans to fend for themselves. Where is he now? Enjoying a well-earned grouchy retirement? Still hurling thunderbolts? Communing with the eagles? All sightings gratefully received. You can't miss him, he has a godly beard, holds a thunderbolt and is stark naked.

LARA

Goddess of gabble who never stopped talking. She was known as the Babbler – until **JUPITER** cut her tongue out in an effort to stop her interrupting. It didn't entirely work as she still makes very weird bubbling noises.

LUNA

Roman interpretation of Greek Moon goddess **SELENE**. **LUNA** may be responsible for lunacy. Have you ever wondered when the moon is full what it may be full of? And who empties it before it bursts.

MARS

God of war and unquenchable energy. Also has chocolate bars named after him. When the Romans revamped the Greek gods to fit in with their planet suite, **ARES** was upgraded to **MARS**. The bully boy was given a beard to impart greater dignity and his image was endowed with a more user-friendly identity.

He now became the father of Romulus and Remus via a vestal virgin named Rhea-Silvia. This led to a most important historical act – the founding of Rome. So if it wasn't for Mars the god of war, there would be no Roman Empire, no Roman Catholics, or Roman gods. All that Roman culture did not go to his head. He was still a lusty god of war; just a little more gregarious and willing to patronise farmers and horticulture. You can't beat a bit of cultivation after a good battle. Mustn't let all that bone meal go to waste.

MEN

God of intelligence, knowledge and mind-boggling. There is a club called Mensa, which you can only join if you can pass their IQ tests and go cross-eyed over crosswords and puzzles.

The name is taken from the Latin tag 'Mens Sana in Corpore Sano', which of course any Mensa member will tell you means 'A Healthy Mind in a Healthy Body'. It just so happens that the Latin word Mensa means 'table' according to our translations. Do they think around tables? Here is a little test for you. If **MEN** himself is depicted with a Thysis in his right hand and a pine cone in his left hand, which foot is resting on the head of a bull? Send your answers to Mensa or treat yourself to a new anorak.

MERCURY

Messenger god of commerce and the Roman revamp of **HERMES**. Has own planet, metal industry and name-leasing business.

MINERVA

She is more than just a brand name replacement for the Greek goddess **ATHENA**. In fact, she was around under the Etruscans who knew her as Menrva. Amazingly intelligent, she is credited with many creative ideas such as the invention of numbers (patent still pending) – and also musical instruments and medicine. She was especially beloved by Roman doctors for her medical knowledge, hence her nickname Minerva-Medica.

MITHRAS

Secret society god of discipline and courage. Males only. Born of the cosmic egg into a life of hardship, he was originally **MITHRA**, a Persian god of hard knocks. He was introduced to Rome by masochistic soldiers. Initiates into his mystery cult have to survive being stripped, bound, blindfolded and subjected to violence before being branded. Being a bit of a bully boy, he also likes bulls to be sacrificed. Lucky old **MITHRAS** must be thriving as this kind of thing seems to be on the increase.

MORS

The god of sleep. Nodded off whilst taking over from the Greek **MORPHEUS**. He has a sister called Mortia for extra lie-ins.

NEPTUNE

God of the ocean. Think trident, beard, and seawater. He is as familiar to us all as fish and chips – or seafood pasta if you are Roman. Usually seen striking a Greek **POSEIDON** pose. His unwilling wife is Salacia, forced to marry him after some unwelcome prompting with a trident.

ORCUS

An awesome Underworld god, **ORCUS** doesn't hang around waiting until your time is up; he will come and fetch you kicking and struggling if he has received instructions from the boss. You may have a right to appeal. It depends if your lawyer is where he belongs.

PALES

Goddess of sheep, shepherds and sexy frolicking. She started as a male god but had a sex change and in her frocks protected flocks and favoured fecundity. She has her own festival, the Palilia, on 21 April, which involves the Vestal Virgins and sacred cocktails with secret recipes. She also has her very own hill called the Palatine.

PARCAE

This is the Roman 'Tria Fata' or Three Fates package. They're very similar to the Greek **FATES**. Spinning life away are Nono who starts things off with birth, Decima who deals with marriage and Morta who arranges your visit to the mortician.

PAX

Goddess of peace. She is armed with an olive branch and a horn of plenty. She has a festival on 30 January, which is always ignored by world leaders.

PHOEBUS

You can't fool us – it's still **APOLLO**.

PICUS

The woodpecker seer and father of Faunus. Son of **SATURNUS**, he became a king of Latium and was known for delivering oracles with the aid of a woodpecker. The Greek enchantress Circe fancied him, but he spurned her advances so she changed him into a woodpecker. This made the peasants like him even more and he became an agricultural deity. He is particularly good at forecasting rain. His wife Canens was not happy about it and sang sad songs of soul-searing intensity as she sought him. Was he green or lesser spotted? She never found out as she faded away just before winning an award as the divinity of song. As to his fatherhood of **PAN** reboot Faunus, we can only presume that this event happened before his woodpecker transformation.

PLUTO

God of the Underworld and judge of the dead. The son of **SATURNUS**, he rules the gloomy roost with his part-time wife **PROSERPINA**. If you want to know more, consult his entry under the Greek **HADES**. 'Dis' is also annuder name for dat ole **PLUTO**. Nowadays he's always in the picture and never misses a chance to get himself painted. Raphael, Carrache,

Giordine, Walt Disney. Take your pick. Note: We are happy to confirm that Pluto is a god. Not a planet.

PROSERPINA

Underworld goddess of winter. She is the Roman version of **PERSEPHONE** and married to **PLUTO**. She lives in the dark dingy depressing depths of his Underworld realm for half a year – quite frankly a day would be too much.

SATURNUS

Ancient agricultural god of sowing seeds, later promoted to deity in charge of carnivals and free festivals. He originally started out as a primeval deity in charge of crops. But as Greek culture spread its influence over Roman thought, **SATURNUS** slowly began to take on the attributes of Greek titan **CRONUS**. He just couldn't help it.

One of these attributes was the nasty habit of eating his own children. Saturnus – presumably having read up on the Greek myths – was terrified that his kids would overthrow him. He therefore began to devour them, although not without some reluctance and guilt. Needless to say, one child was hidden from the gaping maw of his dad and survived. Little **JUPITER** did indeed become the master of the Universe instead of his father. But Saturnus was not overthrown; he was given a pardon in appreciation for his tireless work running the world and organising the crops in the idyllic golden age before the Greeks came along to mess it all up.

Being Roman, it was any excuse for a festival and his Saturnalia carnival came to dominate the calendar. This festival celebrated the winter solstice and all the normal rules of life were turned upside-down for a week. Bosses and slaves changed places, rudeness and lewdness were encouraged, and much fun was had by everybody. It's nice to be able to report a happy ending. And the

fun still goes on; as all pagans know, the climax of Saturnalian feasting and pleasure is 25 December. Never mind Santa Claus – it's Saturnus who should be the god of office Christmas parties. His wife is Ors, who is goddess of wealth and welfare.

SIBYL OF CUMAE

The oracle, a goddess of prophecies. There were several Sibyls on the Greek side of things and many prospered under the Romans too. **SIBYL OF CUMAE** underwent an inspired revival under the Romans after almost fading away under the Greeks. She grew in stature and was restored to former glory at the age of 700. She wrote nine books of prophecies and tried to sell them to Tarquin, the pre-republican king of Rome. He refused to meet her price, so she burnt three, offering the remainder at the original price. Again he refused so she burnt three more. Finally realising she was not bluffing, he paid the full price for the last three and she went away cackling.

Nobody understood a word of the surviving books, and we suspect the king had merely bought three volumes of indexes, footnotes and corrections for the first six. We know how he must have felt: trying to complete a set of secondhand books is fraught with peril and disappointment. However, the remaining books of prophecy did manage to cause rumour and intrigue in the Roman Empire for quite a while. Legends sprang up asserting that such-and-such a Caesar was predicted to die – and there was generally someone around willing to oblige. Sybil herself wisely vanished without trace.

SPES

The goddess of hope and speculation. As the Greek Elpis, she clung to the side of **PANDORA**'s box – and clung on long enough to be taken on board by the Romans. Sometimes hope is all we have, so cling on to the cling-on goddess.

STURCULINUS

To put it politely he is the god of fertiliser. We have stated before that the Romans had gods for everything – and this is the god of manure. His grand Latin name may bring to mind some succulent stir fry, but to avoid any such confusion the name used behind his back was 'Poopy'. We kid you not. Romans were keen on crops ripening and this rather smelly god was the epitome of 'Ripeness is All.'

VENUS

Goddess of love, the Roman version of **APHRODITE**. She had her own day. It's only a quirk of fate that we don't look forward to Venusday every week. Picture the scene: the ancient Roman forum of Greek gods up for grabs. Two purple-robed godpickers sift through the files…

Priest 1: Wow! Who is this cutie?

Priest 2: Aphrodite.

Priest 1: What kinda name is that for a classy lady like this? And so sexy with it! She's going to be a biggy. A sex symbol for all time. Why don't we call her Marilinus Monroeum?

Priest 2: Nah. She's bigger than a star – in all the right places. She belongs in the Planet Suite. What planets we got left?

Priest 1: Well, that old slob **ARES** is now the good guy **MARS** … **HERMES** got redelivered as **MERCURY** … We made **ZEUS** into **JUPITER** – he forgave **CRONUS** and gave him the new identity of **SATURNUS** … Hmm, all we got left is this steamy planet called Venus.

Priest 2: Venus! That's it! It's got that sexy sound – it rolls off the tongue. Get the scribes to work! 'New Sensational **VENUS** – voluptuous and desirable.' Boy, have we got something here! She's gonna run for ever and ever.

And that's how the Greek goddess of love became the first and only female planet.

VESTA

The hearth goddess with the Vestal Virgins. She had a festival called Vestalia on 7 June. Ceremonies were conducted by extra-special Vestal Virgins who had taken vows of chastity lasting thirty-nine years. (And after thirty-nine years we suspect they were not inclined to bother.) Greek equivalent: Hestia.

VOLUPTAS

Goddess of pleasure and bliss. Being the daughter of **CUPID** and Greek **PSYCHE**, you'll understand the kind of pleasure and bliss we're talking about. She keeps a strangely low profile for a goddess with such promise. If **VENUS** is booked up or you feel like an alternative this is the one. The personification of pleasure in all forms.

VULCAN

Famous fire and heavy metal god. He started out as Sethlans, the Etruscan god of volcanoes, lava and scorched Earth. Then with the Roman revamp of Greek gods he assumed the mantle of **HEPHAESTUS** the lame blacksmith. Such forgery.

THE SLAVIC AND BALTIC GODS

A strange range of gods ruling from Poland to the Baltic, the Czech Republic and Slovakia to the Ukraine. From simple do-it-yourself gods of digging a hole in the ground to ones with three silver heads and a golden veil in a temple full of wealth, they cover a lot of ground. The very word 'deity' may actually be of Baltic origin, deriving from the god **DIEVAS**, who has to be the all-time definitive deity. If you pore over ancient maps and peer into history books you will find Lithuania has always done its own thing.

The last country in Europe to accept Christianity, Lithuania managed to keep its own language, not get pole-axed by the Poles, or be pushed out by Prussia. It retained its own customs and identity even as a republic of Russia. The boundaries once spread from the Baltic to the Black Sea, including the Ukraine and large chunks of western Russia. So now you know.

ALBASTA

Siberian goddess of evil. She has a big head and massive breasts; although we cannot say if it's her physical deformities that cause her waywardness. The sharp talons and her propensity for strangling pregnant women do seem to be connected.

BOGATYRI

A band of Russian superheroes who took on demons and monsters. Their number included **MIKULA**, although how he got there who knows, and Ilya-Muromets who, although mortal, had superhuman strength bestowed upon him by a dying knight. He once flew into a rage and vandalised all the churches in Kiev. This didn't stop him from being sainted. Who would dare? As superheroes they had various special powers and bucketfuls of heroic pluck. Possibly also X-ray vision.

Like a somewhat down-to-Earth version of the knights of the Round Table, they were a motley collection of rustic folk who were elevated to hero rank and starred in many celebrated dragon-busting tales. They were squeezed out by the Christians and now only the legends remain. You can read all about it in *Why There Are No More Bogatyri in Holy Russia* – if you are into ancient Russian poetry and can find a copy.

BABA-YAGA

Slavic goddess of death. She's a horror thriller killer diller. She lives in a house built of human bones, complete with bone fence with inset skulls whose eye sockets light up in the dark. And it's a mobile home – it runs around supported on gigantic chicken legs. If this doesn't make you chicken out, her own eyes turn humans to stone, and her mighty mouth has knives for teeth. She can pole herself around in a giant pestle and mortar which she also uses to grind up and unpetrify her victims. Coming soon to a forest near you.

BANNIK

The Baltic bathroom bogeyman. He hides in the steam and is seldom seen. If you feel a soft touch things bode well – but a scratch from a claw could mean a scalding, a drowning – or a trapped cat. Always leave some soap and hot water, for cleanliness in this case is very much next to godliness.

DAZHBOG

Son of **SVAROG** the Latvian Sun god. He has very flashy sky transport with gold, silver and diamond horses. His disposition is sunny and when the Christians became over-zealous and toppled his famous statue into a river, he didn't take much notice. After all, the sun still shines.

DOMOVIK

Domestic guard god for your dwelling or domain in Russia. He lives under your doorstep or behind the stove and acts as a watchman, smoke alarm etc. His partner is Kikimora who will henpeck you as she appears in the form of a giant hen. Don't upset them or they could burn your house down. And always leave a snack in the fridge.

DIEVAS

Lithuaniann top creator god. He is the source of all good things, including peace, friendship, flowers and cute little birdies. He also created humans – accidentally – from the little flecks of dirt that fell while washing his face. His brother **VELNIAS** is not nearly so clever, and tends to stomp around being evil instead.

GABIJA

The great Lithuanian fire goddess. For women only. She must be carefully tended to. Only pure water must be used if a hearth fire needs to be banked. The flame is sacred and must only be allowed to go out at the time of Rasa, when new sacred fire must be obtained from the sacred source and transported by human chain or possibly a relay race for the rekindling ceremony.

GILTINE

Death goddess and sister of Lithuanian Laima, she comes dressed in white to do the final snuffing. She has a very nasty tongue because she collects poison from graveyards and if she licks your face you can kiss tomorrow goodbye.

LINKSMINE

Lithuanian goddess of good cheer. Let's link arms and 'mine's a beer.' Very popular for banquets and festive occasions.

MATI-SYRA-ZEMLYA

Earth Mother goddess. Her name means 'Moist Mother Earth'. Once gods have triple-barrel names and come from this part of the world they tend to veer towards the bizarre. **MATI-SYRA-ZEMLYA** manifests as a hole in the ground. Dig your own. Speak into it. If you are going on a journey, kiss it. She is very partial to bread, wine and beer.

Drop and pour it down. Don't be stingy. And if you plough a furrow round your house at night you will be plague-free.

MILDA

Lithuanian love goddess with Lady Godiva tendencies. She likes to ride naked in her dove-drawn chariot, causing hearts to flutter. One glimpse at her delightful vision as it wafts down the street and you're mere seconds away from love, romance, smooches and all the other stuff you've been waiting for.

MIKULA

Somebody must have poured something other than beer into Moist Mother Earth to produce such a fine strapping lad. He had a plough no-one could lift and could gallop faster than any living being, probably without using a horse. He joined the **BOGATYRI** as a superhero and despite the Christians trying to belittle him, he is remembered in a big way.

MOKOS

Very fussy goddess of wool spinning. She makes house calls during Lent disguised as an old woman. Your winter woollies production had better be up to scratch. On the other hand she has been known to help the hard-pressed with sheep shearing. Knit her something nice. Crochet a goddess today.

MOKOSH

Goddess of sperm. It's a messy job but someone has to control these things. **MOKOSH** is a potent Earth Mother who is very very fertile. In other words, she's always damp and easily soiled. So be careful where you spit as it could have unforeseen consequences.

NAGYBOLDOGASSZONY

This is a big powerful happy Magyar mother goddess. She is so big and so powerful that there are seven of her. She is a great protectress and her milk is holy. The Christians used one of her, Boldogasszony, as a makeover for the Virgin Mary. We have yet to learn the other names, but she may also go under a collective as the Asszony. It's important that you get the spellings right or she won't listen. I hope we've got this right or we shall expect a rap over the knuckles from Ingrid.

PERKUNAS

This is the Big P god. The major all-encompassing top thunder god of all Slavic countries. He is the one in charge. He wields an axe in a similar way to **THOR**, and it always returns when he throws it at demons. He is the king of the skies even if his chariot is drawn by a goat. It is the Billy Goats Gruff of goats, monumental and magnificent.

PERUN

Russian thunder god. Very popular in the Stone Age when young girls danced themselves to death to honour him. Was it clog dancing? Could be the origin of the phrase 'popping your clogs'. He's also known as **PERKUNAS** and all the other variations so you get a good run for your money.

PRIPARCHIS & KREMARA

Gods for the protection of pigs. **PRIPARCHIS** looks after weaning and **KREMARA** coddles the porker until slaughter time. Then you pour beer into the fire to invoke a blessing.

RADIGAST

Baltic god of sound advice and thought. He's easily recognisable – he carries a two-headed axe, has a bull's head on his chest and wears a flying swan on his head. We can only hope he's doing it for a bet.

RAGUTIS

One of our great value package deals. This is a Lithuanian holy brewery with three gods in charge. **RAGUTIS** is the god of beer, Ragutiene is the goddess of beer. And Raugupatis is the all-important god of fermentation.

SAULE

It's sunshine all the way with 'Sow-lay', the radiant and much respected Latvian goddess. She dresses in gold, which sets off her golden hair and golden crown and chariot, which is pulled by twin white horses (one doesn't want to overdo the gold) with golden manes. She is the mother of the planets – all daughters of hers. There was an unfortunate marriage to Meness, the Moon god, who committed indiscretions with his daughter Ausrine (**VENUS**). He was given a good thumping by either or both **SAULE** and **DIEVAS** and thrown out into the night. His face bears the scars to this very day.

Saule now devotes all her considerable energies to being as good as gold, and if she appears to slow down a bit in the winter, it is because she has lots of feast days and festivals to organise.

SEMARGL

God of barley. He may once have been two gods, Sem and Argl, but they got together over a friendly gargle and became inseparable drinking companions.

SVAROG

God of fire and welding. He's of profound importance in the scheme of Slavic smythology. He handed his powers on to his two sons Svarogich and **SVENTOVIT**. When you look into the flames of a fire and faces appear, it will be one of these allowing you to catch prophetic glimpses into godly affairs.

It is no use looking into a gas fire or expecting to learn anything from a central heating radiator. The flames must be live.

SVENTOVIT

Baltic godfather of fruitfulness and fertility. He has four necks and four faces, possibly even four bodies. His high priests are commanded to hold their breath when cleaning his temple, but that's hardly surprising as he keeps his horse there. His statues have drinking horns (replenishable) and have four faces facing north, east, south and west.

TRIGLAV

God of prophecy and soothsaying. He has three silver heads but keeps his eyes and mouths covered by a golden veil. This adds to his air of mystery and ensures he doesn't have to look at or speak to the pilgrims who flock to his golden statue in his temple at Szczecin. He is also known as Mr Ten Per Cent, which is what he charges for his soothsaying and prophecies. But strangely enough his black horse does all the work, going through some gymkhana-like event and trotting out the answers folk want to hear. You can't charge ten per cent for bad news can you?

VELES

God of sheep and the Underworld. Now there's a strange combination. He started his career as a mix-and-match warrior and shepherd god. Did he fight sheep? Lead lambs to the slaughter? No, he protected flocks – and was liable to get quite assertive about it. As time went on, people began to depict him with the horns of a ram. This seemed to sum up his demeanour quite nicely. Meanwhile, it seems his down-to-Earth nature had made him the ideal candidate for Underworld management.

VELNIAS

God of evil and brother of creator god **DIEVAS**. An Underworld god from Lithuania that needs warding off, he is not too bright, and is not even sure what his real name is, but he knows his job is to be Mr Nasty. So if you see him coming you shout '**PERKUNAS** is behind you!' and hide behind a tree when he turns to look. It fools him every time.

ZOSIM

God of bees and mead and bawdy songs. That sounds like a good thing. Don't worry about the bees – mead is made from honey.

THE GODS OF SOUTH AMERICA

South American mythology covers a vast and diverse area. We have already extracted the Inca civilisation from the top end as it has its own section. This leaves scattered tribes in Chile, Peru, Bolivia and Colombia where the El Dorado rumours started. Then we plunge through Brazil, down the Amazon and Xingu Rivers, until we reach the coast. We've skipped the Caribbean which has its own section and managed to avoid Borneo and other Indonesian bits.

ACAWAI OF ORINOCO
MAKUNAIMA

Creator of a huge multi-purpose tree to provide food for all. Sadly, someone had the bright idea of chopping it down so the goodies could be distributed more easily. But for some reason the tree stump was full of water – complete with merrily swimming fish. This would have been very pleasant except the water was trickling out. Soon it grew to a torrent and threatened to cover the entire Earth. It was left to…

SIGU

…to sort things out. When a great gush of water from the Sacred Life Tree threatened to cover the Earth, **SIGU** knew just what to do. First he made a magic basket to stop the flow. When that was accidentally knocked over by a curious monkey, he went for Plan B instead. This involved locking up all the animals in a huge cave and sealing it with wax. Then he shinned up a very tall tree to await developments. The flood waters covered the Earth for a long time … Sigu was very bored up in his tree. Every so often he'd drop a nut. Whenever it went 'plop' he sighed. Then one day it went 'thud'; the waters had subsided and it was now time to release the animals and start mopping-up operations.

ARAWAK OF GUIANA
AIOMUN-KONDI

Creator god. He tried to make a model world, but his activated beings evolved repugnant behaviour of their own devising. He was so disgusted he burnt his experiment and started again. Earth Mk II was not much better. Debauchery and depravity prevailed. So he wiped them out with a flood. He had lost interest by now anyway and went off to have a go at something else: deep-sea fishing, sky diving or flower arranging. Who knows?

KULIMINA

Creator goddess and long-suffering wife of creator god **KURURUMANY**. She created the first females after attempting to copy the human figures her husband had made. But important bits kept dropping off and hitherto unimportant bits expanded into a variety of rather pleasing feminine shapes. Between them they managed to create a small population that could breed by themselves. **KULIMINA** was very happy with her efforts, but her husband was furious. He had set his heart on all-male bonding images of himself with no nagging females or nappies to change.

Thwarted, he left off bothering with people and spent the rest of his time making creepy crawlies, savage animals and poisonous things that could cause death.

GUINECHEN

He's the only god trying to keep the world in order against the evil forces of demon king Guecufu and Pillan the volcano. It's a full-time job and it's all he has time for. According to those in the know, both adversaries are equally matched, and the never-ending battle of Good vs Evil is actually what keeps the Universe ticking over. Should either side ever win, the whole fabric of the cosmos would come crashing down like a badly fixed curtain.

CALINA PEOPLE
AMANA

Creator goddess. She started off riding on the crest of a wave which was the Milky Way and is full of sea creatures. She rides on a turtle and has a mermaid tail. She created the Sun for a bit of warmth but did not realise it was going to be so hot that it burnt the moon. So she constantly has to sink the sun in the ocean to prevent it from scorching and drying up the Earth. She then had to create two sons:

TAMULA & TAMUSI

TAMULA makes sure the night is dark by covering the sun with huge black covers and **TAMUSI** keeps the sun in check during the day, slicing bits off when it gets too hot. It keeps global warming in check. Sliced-off sun rays are cast into the sky where they splutter out as comets and shooting stars.

CHIBCHA OF COLUMBIA
BOCHICA

Top god of morals and laws. He turned up from nowhere. An old man with a beard, a golden staff and amazing creative teaching abilities. **BOCHICA** wandered far and wide teaching the natives right from wrong. His code of conduct was somewhat severe and a lot of wild parties came to an untimely end.

For some reason he was persuaded to marry, but his wife Chia was not at all nice. She took every opportunity to screw up all her husband's plans. She caused floods and much suffering for humans – and rumour suggests she may even have been Huitaca, the goddess of wanton behaviour. Bochica had not invented divorce yet, so he just turned his wife into the moon – or possibly an owl, or both. Then he got on with cleaving and clefting mountains to restore the water levels.

Bochica was Mr Good Guy god for many years. His regime of conformity, obedience and do-as-you-are-told culture brought stability and civilised behaviour to the region, even if it was boring. He celebrated by sipping from a small bottle of mineral water.

After creating all the laws needed by a decent civilisation, he handed control over to tribal chiefs. Even then he spent another 2,000 years on Earth as an ascetic, keeping a gentle eye on things before taking a well-earned Heavenly retirement. Now he rarely appears except in dire emergency situations. Mostly you'll find him sitting on goddess Chuchaviva's rainbow with his feet up, watching the Earth like a television programme. As one of his favourites we expect they sit side by side.

CHIBCHACHUM

Whilst top god **BOCHICA** was doing good and getting all the acclaim, **CHIBCHACHUM** was trying to deal with the contrary side of human nature. No-one seemed to take any notice of anything he said, so in a fit of pique he sent a flood. The Chibcha people fled to the mountains and were only saved when Bochica himself intervened. He came on a rainbow and hurled his staff at nearby Mount Teguendama, making a cleft for the waters to flow away. The result of his restructuring can be seen today in the form of the magnificent Tequendama waterfall which descends into Lake Guatavita.

Chibchachum was given a very heavy punishment. He was forced to descend into the Underworld to replace the wooden pillars that hold up the Earth. Now he bears the weight of the world on his shoulders. He still tries to rock the boat with earthquakes now and then.

HUITACA

Delightfully feminine, she loved to indulge herself with drinking, dancing and making merry. When she came to town, it was always party time. She was *very* popular. The ultra-righteous top god **BOCHICA** was horrified at her antics and accused her of wanton behaviour unbecoming a goddess. His slurs stuck fast and the bad press damaged her reputation terribly. In fact, to this day she's often considered a goddess of evil. As punishment for simply having a good time, **HUITACA** was turned into an owl. But that doesn't stop her from grooving the night away, and long may she continue. It's not often you see a drunken owl. It just shows the power of the press that she is now often identified (or else easily confused) with Bochica's wife Chia – who really was evil. In that version of events, her husband Nemterequeteba acts as a Bochica clone. But who gives a hoot?